Energy, Foresight, and Strategy

Thomas J. Sargent, Editor

S. Rao Aiyagari
Zvi Eckstein
Martin S. Eichenbaum
Dennis Epple
Lars Peter Hansen
Raymond G. Riezman
William Roberds

RESOURCES FOR THE FUTURE/WASHINGTON, D.C.

Published by Resources for the Future, Inc.
1616 P Street, N.W., Washington, D.C. 20036.

Resources for the Future books are distributed worldwide by
The Johns Hopkins University Press.

Library of Congress Cataloging in Publication Data
Main entry under title:

Energy, foresight, and strategy.

  Bibliography: p.
  Includes index.
  Contents: Energy, foresight, and strategy/
Thomas J. Sargent—Embargoes and supply shocks in
a market with a dominant seller/S. Rao Aiyagari and
Raymond G. Riezman—Oil supply disruptions and the
optimal tariff in a dynamic stochastic equilibrium
model/Zvi Eckstein and Martin S. Eichenbaum—[etc.]
  1. Energy policy—Addresses, essays, lectures.
2. Petroleum industry and trade—Government policy—
Addresses, essays, lectures. I. Sargent, Thomas J.
II. Aiyagari, S. Rao. III. Resources for the Future.
HD9502.A2E54393 1985 333.79 84-42691
ISBN 0-915707-10-1 (pbk.)

This book was prepared in RFF's Center for Energy Policy Research, Joel Darmstadter, director. It was edited by Charlene Semer and designed by Elsa B. Williams. The index was prepared by Florence Robinson.

Contents

Foreword

Energy price shocks have punctuated the last decade. While there is agreement that their affects have been large, estimates vary, and the mechanisms by which these effects move through the economy remain largely undefined. The fact that the shocks have occurred has altered the structure of the economy and the expectations of participants, but again, the ramifications of those changes are uncertain. A real world experiment is hence under way in which the energy-economy regime has been shifted in significant ways. This experiment offers an opportunity to learn more about how economies behave under normal circumstances and to gain insights that will contribute to wise policy actions when new shocks, from energy or any other source, occur in the future.

This volume reports on efforts to explore oil-related phenomena using dynamic economic theory. The research was motivated by a desire to understand better how oil markets and economies behave under stress, but the topics examined include basic processes operating in normal times as well. The central theme is that private actors in oil markets take actions by others and future developments, some of which are unknowable, into account in predictable and orderly ways.

Resources for the Future invited Professor Thomas J. Sargent to bring together a group of researchers to investigate topics in energy policy from this perspective as a component of the overall energy and national security program undertaken jointly by the Brookings Institution and RFF. This program was sponsored by the Department of Energy's Office of Policy, Planning, and Analysis. Nicolai Timenes, Jr., Lucian Pugliaresi, Jerry Blankenship, and Stephen Minihan of the department participated in structuring this program and administering the contract. This volume is based on reports submitted previously to the Department of Energy under contract DE-AC01-80PE70267.

The purpose of this research program is not to provide specific policy guidance. Instead, the goal is to provide background studies, analyses, and theoretical underpinnings helpful to the analysts who will devise and evaluate alternative mechanisms to reduce the size and frequency of oil shocks and to limit their impact on the economy. This volume fulfills this aim by advancing the state of knowledge in the dynamic economics framework and enriching our understanding of the problem of oil shocks and of their potential amelioration.

September 1984   Milton Russell, Former Director
                                        Center for Energy Policy Research
                                        at Resources for the Future, Inc.

Acknowledgments

The authors of chapter 2 would like to thank Thomas Sargent and other members of the Energy and National Security Program Project sponsored by Resources for the Future for helpful comments on an earlier draft.

The authors of chapters 3 and 4 would like to thank Jon Eaton, Robert Hodrick, W. David Montgomery, Thomas Sargent, and Charles Whiteman for helpful conversations and suggestions on an earlier draft of this paper. In addition, we are grateful to Ian Bain, Thomas Sargent, and Michael Toman for helpful comments and suggestions on an earlier draft of chapter 4. Elizabeth Davis verified the chapter. Responsibility for opinions, errors, and omissions rests with the authors alone and not with the sponsoring agency or Resources for the Future.

Early results from the model developed in chapter 6 were presented at Carnegie-Mellon University, the Massachusetts Institute of Technology, Tulane University, the Stanford Energy Modeling Forum, the Conference on Exploration for Energy Resources at New York University, and the Department of Energy Symposium on Oil and Gas Supply Modeling. Dennis Epple wishes to thank participants in these forums, particularly Gordon Kaufman, Robert S. Pindyck, and James Sweeney for their comments and suggestions. Thanks for helpful comments and suggestions are also due Douglas Bohi, Thomas Sargent, and the anonymous reviewers of this volume. The formulation of the model in section II is the result of joint research with Lars Hansen, and the derivation of the decision rules in that section is due to Lars Hansen. He also contributed many valuable suggestions to the development in the remainder of the paper. The able research assistance of Jong Park and John Zaehringer is gratefully acknowledged. This work was funded in part by NSF Grant DAR 79-24-787 and DOE Grant DE-AC02-79ET60003.

Energy, Foresight, and Strategy

1
Energy, Foresight, and Strategy

Thomas J. Sargent

This book contains five essays that use dynamic economic theory to study the processes by which energy sources are discovered, developed, priced, supplied, and stored. Dynamic economic theory is required for analyzing these processes because of the intertemporal nature of the economic problems that confront both the owners of energy sources and the customers they serve. Owners of energy sources face decisions about how rapidly to extract and sell their resources. Because energy sources are typically both durable and exhaustible, owners have strong incentives to care about the likely future time paths of the prices of their sources of energy and competing sources, as well as about the paths of cost factors such as tax rates.

Users of energy face decisions about designing plants that potentially can use different amounts and sources of energy. Because these plants are durable, users of energy care about the future prices both of energy and of complementary and substitute inputs and about the availabilities of alternative energy sources. Thus, participants on all sides of energy markets have strong incentives to exercise foresight about relevant aspects of the physical environment and about the future actions of other participants on all sides of such markets.

Thomas J. Sargent is Professor of Economics, University of Minnesota-Minneapolis and Adviser to the Research Department, Federal Reserve Bank of Minneapolis.

RATIONAL EXPECTATIONS THEORY

Successful analysis of the interaction of a collection of agents in such environments requires two things. First, it requires tools that permit analyzing individual agent's choices of intertemporal strategies, which are constrained both by the physical technologies and by the intertemporal strategies chosen by other market participants, both private and governmental. Second, it requires an equilibrium concept suitable for studying the dynamic interaction of a collection of agents. Such a concept must insure that agents' choices of intertemporal strategies are mutually consistent with the physical constraints and with their perceptions of each other's strategies. The essays in this book are united in using models that posit agents who solve stochastic optimal-control problems and that use an equilibrium concept in which agents accurately perceive those constraints that the physical environment and the strategies of other agents impose. Such dynamic theories are usually referred to as "rational expectations" theories.

The ostensible subject matter of the five essays in this book mostly concerns aspects of energy economics, but the essays use and develop methods of analysis that are applicable in many other fields. Many of the phenomena and problems that occur in energy markets closely resemble those that arise in other contexts. Any system of purposeful agents acting in a dynamic environment has essential features in common with energy markets.

A few general concepts help clarify the structure of these dynamic multiagent systems. The state of a system at date t consists of a list of variables that completely characterize the position of the system at date t. We let $x(t)$ denote the state at t and regard $x(t)$ as a vector. We imagine that the model describes n agents, each of whom faces choices that potentially influence the future position or state of the system. In particular, we imagine that the ith agent has the power to choose a control, or vector of controls, $u(t, i)$ at date t. The evolution of the state is supposed to be governed by the transition equations or "laws of motion"

$$x(t+1) = f[x(t), u(t,1), u(t,2), \ldots, u(t,n), e(t+1)] \qquad (1.1)$$

where $e(t + 1)$ is a random vector that is distributed independently and identically through time according to the cumulative distribution function $\text{Prob}[e(t + 1) < E] = F(E)$. The random vector $e(t + 1)$ is included as an argument of (1.1) to capture the idea that the process by which future states evolve out of past states and controls is partly shrouded in uncertainty.

Next we require a statement of the purposes that guide the n agents in their choices of controls $u(t, i)$. We shall suppose that agent i generally cares about the future paths of the state of, and all of the controls in, the system in a way that can be summarized by the function

$$E_t \sum_{s=t}^{\infty} R_s^i [x(s), u(s,1), \ldots, u(s,n)] \tag{1.2}$$

where E_t is the expectation operator conditional on the ith agent's information at time t. We call (1.2) the objective function of agent i.

In order to complete the specification of the structure of this system, we must describe the form of strategy or "strategy space" over which the ith agent is imagined to search for a maximizer of (1.2). Also necessary is a description of each agent's views about all other agents' strategy spaces and objective functions (1.2) in order that any of their maximization problems be well posed. Because strategy spaces can be specified in a variety of ways, we shall adopt a notation intended to accommodate a variety of possible alternative specifications. We suppose that agent i uses a strategy of the form

$$u(t, i) = h_i [I_i(t)] \tag{1.3}$$

where $I_i(t)$ is the information at t that agent i possesses and upon which the agent's decisions are contingent. We also assume that all other agents know agent i's objective function (1.2) and strategy space (1.3). We make this assumption for i extending across all n agents.

The system will not yet have been completely specified until we describe the structure of "dominance" across agents. Equations (1.1), (1.2), and (1.3) imply that the evolution of the state, and hence the value of agent i's objective, depend on the strategy (1.3) chosen by agent j, where j extends over the remaining $n-1$ agents. This means that, in general, agent i's optimal choice of strategy will depend on what the remaining $n-1$ agents choose as their strategies, and vice versa. Thus all the strategy choices are interdependent. This interdependence can be imagined to be structured in a variety of ways, each of them internally consistent, depending precisely on how the various agents are supposed to believe that agent i's choice of strategy influences their strategy choices.

Several distinct ways of modeling the structure of dominance are common. In a "Nash equilibrium," each agent i is assumed to know the strategies of the remaining $n-1$ agents but to regard them as fixed with respect to its own choice of strategy. In a "rational expectations competitive equilibrium," each agent i is imagined to take as given and beyond its influence the aggregate state variables that determine the evolution of market prices. (Usually the rational expectations competitive equilibrium is a limiting version of a Nash equilibrium when the number of agents n becomes large.) In a "dominant player" or "Stackelberg" equilibrium, one of the agents is imagined to take into account the influence that its choice of strategy has on the strategies some or all of the other agents choose, while the remaining agents are imagined to behave in a Nash or competitive way.

Given a structure of dominance and a specification of strategy spaces, an equilibrium is a collection of all n agents' strategies (1.3) that maximize their objective functions (1.2) subject to the laws of motion of the system (1.1) and also subject to their perceptions of other agents' strategies and the structure of dominance. In general, for each specification of a structure of strategy spaces (1.3) for the n agents, a distinct structure of dominance gives rise to a distinct equilibrium. Simply describing an equilibrium as a Nash equilibrium is incomplete unless supplemented with a description of strategy spaces. An example of this fact can be found in the chapter by Epple, Hansen, and Roberds. The Nash equilibrium they calculate using Euler equation methods assumes a different strategy space and results in a different dynamic equilibrium for the industry than does a Nash equilibrium defined in the space of feedback decision rules computed by "stacking" a system of matrix Ricatti difference equations. (For a discussion of this latter kind of Nash equilibrium, see Hansen and Sargent, 1984.)

Evidently, with a given description of the physical environment, the structure of strategy spaces and the structure of dominance across agents can be set up in a variety of alternative ways to produce distinct concepts of equilibrium. Descriptions of the physical environment (1.1), the objectives of the n agents (1.2), the strategy spaces (1.3), and the structure of dominance define what is known as a dynamic game, or differential game.

This brief excursion into the realm of differential games has been abstract, with no names attached to any of the variables in $x(t)$ or $u(t, i)$ and no identities assigned to the n agents playing the game. When x and u are defined appropriately, energy problems fit nicely into this framework. Imagine a system in which the state vector $x(t)$ includes (possibly noisy) measures of the stocks of energy sources possessed by their owners at t, together with measures of stocks of physical capital, energy sources, and employment of labor by users of energy at t. The $u(t, i)$s might include exploration and extraction rates chosen by owners of energy sources, together with users' rates of consumption and of addition to stockpiles of energy sources, as well as rates of accumulation of physical capital and employment, and also domestic tax rates and tariffs chosen by one or more governments. In such a setting, the n agents might be identified with the owners of energy, their customers, and possibly one or more governments. These categories of agents could be further subdivided in various ways, as is done, for example, in setups with a dominant supplier supplemented by a competitive fringe of suppliers (see the chapter by Aiyagari and Riezman). The analyses in this book all adopt definitions of states, controls, and agents that are chosen to illuminate some aspect of the economics of energy.

The preceding description has been vague about the forms of the functions f, R, and h in (1.1), (1.2), and (1.3), as well as about such matters as the existence, uniqueness, and computation of equilibria of differential games. Without restricting these functions, little or nothing can be said about these matters. Most of the models in this collection can be represented in a form in which R_s is quadratic, while f and h_i are linear. These assumptions are adopted for purposes of tractability because for this set of assumptions (or under a closely related set of log-linear, Cobb-Douglas assumptions), the most is known about existence, uniqueness, and computation of equilibria of differential games. Even for such linear-quadratic dynamic games, much remains to be learned. The chapter by Epple, Hansen, and Roberds develops new methods for studying the existence, character, and computation of equilibria of such games. Eckstein and Eichenbaum (chapters 3 and 4) require new results about the existence and uniqueness for vector stochastic expectational difference equations in order to characterize the equilibrium of their optimal-tariff model. (The results they need are closely related to the Epple, Hansen, and Roberds work on factoring nonsymmetric matrix characteristic polynomials.) These new theoretical results and applications, although initially inspired by the energy examples treated in this book, will also be useful in other contexts.

SOME ENERGY APPLICATIONS

All the models in this book are based on differential games. Aiyagari and Riezman (chapter 2) study two kinds of dynamic games that owners of energy sources might play with their customers. The authors first undertake to analyze embargoes as a recurrent intermittent strategy that suppliers of energy consider using. Thinking about this problem in a differential game context directs the authors to study the effects that a strategy of occasionally imposing embargoes will have on the demand behavior of oil customers. Aiyagari and Riezman adopt a particular probabilistic structure for the form of the embargo, which amounts to choosing a strategy space that permits a randomized strategy. They analyze how energy customers, behaving as Nash players, use decision rules with parameters that are functions of the parameters characterizing the randomized embargo strategy of the supplier. The supplier is then imagined to behave as a dominant player with respect to customers. The authors characterize the conditions under which the economic interests of such a dominant supplier will be served by imposing a randomized embargo strategy within the particular strategy space they consider. Roughly speaking, only for high discount rate economies does their analysis predict that such behavior is in the interests of the supplier.

Two features of this analysis are noteworthy. First, adopting a differential game framework immediately directs Aiyagari and Riezman not to take demand curves as structural, or invariant, with respect to variations in the supplier's choice of embargo strategy. Second, Aiyagari and Riezman's analysis directs our attention to the question of how embargoes and other supply disruptions are to be conceived and modeled. Are they to be imagined as uncontrollable random shocks chosen by nature or as the result of a purposeful, albeit perhaps randomized, choice by suppliers?

Inspired by this second point, Aiyagari and Riezman go on to analyze another setup in which supply disruptions emanate from uncontrollable random shocks to the supplies of a competitive fringe of suppliers. The dominant seller takes the supply curve of the competitive fringe as given and chooses how to respond to these supply shocks to maximize its own expected present value. The dominant seller behaves as a dominant player with respect to the customers in the market and takes into account how its strategy influences the decision rule of energy users, who are imagined to behave in a Nash-like fashion.

Chapter 3, by Eckstein and Eichenbaum, is an analysis of dynamic strategic issues surrounding the demand for and holding of inventories of sources of energy by a country that imports all of its energy sources. Eckstein and Eichenbaum set up a closed stochastic dynamic competitive equilibrium model of a single country that draws down stockpiles of energy in order to produce consumption goods. As a whole, the country is a large demander of energy in the sense that its aggregate energy imports influence the world price via an upward-sloping world supply price of energy. The authors take this supply curve as given (compare and contrast this with the spirit of the Aiyagari-Riezman analysis) and proceed to study the optimality of the rational expectations competitive equilibrium for the home country.

Eckstein and Eichenbaum find that the rational expectations competitive equilibrium fails to maximize the expected present value of home country consumer surplus net of home country social costs of production. The reason is that competitive players neglect the market power that, taken as a whole, the country possesses in the energy market. The authors construct an intervention strategy by the home government that corrects this failure of the competitive equilibrium. This intervention amounts to a dynamic optimum-tariff strategy supplemented by a rebate program. In choosing this tariff strategy, the home government is imagined to behave as a dominant player with respect to home country private agents, while home country firms and households behave competitively. By selecting the strategy space for the government in a rich enough way, in particular by permitting the tariff to depend both on countrywide and on individual firm energy import levels, the government is able to design an optimal tariff that is time consistent. Had they restricted their strategy spaces more, Eckstein and Eichenbaum's optimal tariff would have exhibited the time inconsistency described and analyzed by Kydland and Prescott (1977). Eckstein and Eichenbaum indicate how to calculate equilibria and optimal-tariff and rebate strategies for some dynamically rich specifications of the assumed supply curve of energy that confronts the home country.

This analysis directs our attention to a couple of points. First, Eckstein and Eichenbaum's economy is one in which, in the presence of a horizontal supply curve for imported energy, private firms in the competitive rational expectations equilibrium use strategies for private storage of energy that maximize social welfare in the home country. This is true in spite of the facts that adjustment costs make adjusting to supply shocks and other random events expensive and give rise to cyclical behavior in response to shocks. As in other versions of such Lucas-Prescott models (Lucas and Prescott, 1971), the rational expectations equilibrium has the property that the economy adjusts to these shocks in the socially optimal way. This analysis is relevant as a benchmark against which to judge proposals for government intervention into the energy storage business, and it establishes a presumption against such intervention unless the government has access to a storage technology that private agents do not. Eckstein and Eichenbaum do show that government intervention is appropriate where the country possesses market power against which no threat of retaliation exists. Even in this case, however, a national petroleum reserve is not the optimal intervention.

Second, a point very much in the spirit of Aiyagari and Riezman and one that should be emphasized is that the success of the Eckstein-Eichenbaum optimal tariff depends on the assumption that the foreign suppliers of energy will not launch some strategic retaliation. The authors assume that the home country takes the parameters of the "price of energy process" as given. Deviations from this assumption will affect the details of the optimal tariff but are unlikely to salvage optimality for the rational expectations competitive equilibrium.

Eckstein and Eichenbaum's second model (chapter 4) can be regarded as an exercise in dynamic disequilibrium theory. Under a regime in which prices are being stabilized by the actions of an authority that issues sales or production quotas to firms, firms face different dynamic constraints, or laws of motion (1.1), than they would in the absence of such regulation. This implies that the firms' supply schedules as a function of observables (that is, their decision rule h_i) will be different than it would be without such regulation. Eckstein and Eichenbaum illustrate how time series data generated over a period in which a market was regulated by authorities with the aim of stabilizing the output price could still be used to create estimates useful for predicting supply responses after the market is completely deregulated. At first glance, this might seem a magical feat, because the force of the regulation during the sample period is imagined to stabilize the price so completely that price is eliminated as a variable capable of helping to predict supply. Indeed, if an econometric analysis were directed at estimating only the parameters of the producers' supply curves, this feat would be impossible. What enables Eckstein and Eichenbaum to accomplish it is that they go after deeper prey—the parameters of firm's objective functions and constraints. (See Sargent, 1981, for an argument that this is often a good idea.) By using the extensive cross-equation restrictions implied by rational expectations, the authors in principle can identify the parameters of firms' objectives and constraints during the sample period. This permits them to re-solve firms' optimization problems under the new constraints that firms would face after deregulation and so to predict firms' supply behavior under such a new regime.

Eckstein and Eichenbaum motivate their particular parameterizations of the regulatory strategies partly by a desire to reproduce some of the Granger-causality structure they found in vector autoregressions calculated on postwar U.S. data for energy prices and several measures of supply. Their models roughly reproduce the data's lack of Granger causality to and from prices. According to their interpretation of the data, this evidence does not necessarily imply low supply responses after deregulation.

Epple, Hansen, and Roberds (chapter 5) study a variety of games that might be played by two producers who are exploiting an exhaustible resource. This is a study in dynamic, stochastic duopoly theory. One novel feature of their setup is that they specify cost parameters in a fashion that preserves a linear-quadratic setup while also capturing the notion that the resource is exhaustible. They accomplish this by specifying that marginal costs of extraction rise linearly with the cumulated amount of the resource extracted. This feature of the cost structure is what injects the only endogenous dynamic elements into their structure.

(In effect, it is a shrewd definition of one of the state variables as cumulated extraction, which permits a representation of the notion of exhaustibility while remaining within the domain of linear models. Such shrewdness is often required if the full potential of linear models for modeling dynamic systems is to be realized.)

Other novel features in chapter 5 involve the construction of new methods of solving dominant player differential games. Epple, Hansen, and Roberds use classical, or Euler equation, methods to formulate and solve these games; this involves substantive assumptions because such a choice of formulation partly affects the strategy space that is convenient to specify.

Two of Epple, Hansen, and Roberds' dominant player equilibria are particularly noteworthy. In the first (their game E), the dominant player maximizes its expected present value knowing the response pattern of the other player, who behaves as a competitive player and whose decisions are represented partly as a function of all present and future decisions of the dominant player. Epple, Hansen, and Roberds formulate the dominant player's problem as maximizing its expected present value subject to a sequence of constraints posed by the competitive player's decisions and expressed as a function of current and future decisions of the dominant player. The authors cast this optimization problem as a Lagrangian problem, attaching a sequence of stochastic Lagrange multipliers to the sequence of constraints formed by the competitive player's decisions as a function of the dominant player's decisions. They solve the game by finding stochastic processes for the pair of decisions (extraction rates) for the two players and for the Lagrange multiplier that attaches to the constraints. These stochastic processes solve an Euler equation, so the equilibrium can be computed using standard methods. The time inconsistency of the dominant player's optimal strategy surfaces in the feature that its decisions optimally feed back on the stochastic Lagrange multiplier. The Lagrange multiplier partly reflects the value that the dominant player attaches to the effects of its decisions at date s (the starting date for the process) on the actions of the competitive player at dates before date s. The solution is time inconsistent in the sense that if the dominant player's problem is re-solved at some later date s', the appropriate maneuver would be to set the Lagrange multiplier pertaining to dates preceding the new initial date s' equal to zero. Thus the dominant player would want to ignore the influence of its decision at s' on the decisions of the competitive player for dates earlier than s'. The temptation on the part of the dominant player to reinitialize these Lagrange multipliers as time unfolds captures in a revealing way the nature of time inconsistency. The source of the time inconsistency is that the dominant player cares about the influence of its future actions on preceding actions of the other player. Technically, this prevents the dominant player's problem from being a recursive one, so we cannot expect its solution to be time consistent. (See Lucas and Sargent, 1981, for a related discussion.)

Epple, Hansen, and Roberds analyze a second game, game f, in which the dominant player is imagined to construe its choices in a more restricted fashion. This lowers its expected present value but also eliminates time inconsistency in the solution. In particular, the dominant player at date t is imagined to consider the effects of its actions at t on the other player's actions at date t and later but to neglect the effects of its actions on the other player at dates preceding t. The dominant player is modeled as though it were actually a sequence of decision makers, such as governments or administrations, each with similar intertemporal objective functions but with no authority to bind its successors. As can be seen from the constrained optimization problem that the authors pose and solve, this structure eliminates the source of time inconsistency. The authors show how to compute the equilibrium of such a game by using classical methods. Accomplishing this task requires nontrivial modifications of methods for factoring matrix characteristic polynomials like those that appear in Euler equations, because for the authors' problem, the matrix characteristic polynomial is nonsymmetric.

In addition to developing these methods for solving games, Epple, Hansen, and Roberds apply them for the purpose of comparing different equilibria for their model of an exhaustible resource. They obtain a variety of interesting results about how extraction rates compare across different market structures for versions of their model. They also briefly indicate how equilibria of the games they study can be estimated using econometric techniques that have been developed to estimate linear rational expectations models.

Epple (chapter 6) uses a specification of the cost structure along the lines of the preceding chapter to construct a model that he actually applies empirically. One of the virtues of the linear-quadratic setups used throughout this book is that they are tractable enough to be applied empirically, as Epple has done. Epple has thought carefully about specifying costs, technologies, and stochastic processes driving output prices in ways that are consistent with his understanding of the industry and with evidence from the data. At the same time, these specifications are expressible in the context of a linear-quadratic model. Such an endeavor requires compromises; the question is whether they are successful ones. Partly because of the way output prices seemed to behave during the sample period, Epple models the industry as a single agent facing an exogenous output price process. Thus, Epple's model is, in effect, the solution of a single agent playing a "game against nature." Readers of the preceding chapters will recognize how Epple's model and estimation procedures could have been modified to incorporate either a Lucas-Prescott rational expectations competitive equilibrium or some other multiagent equilibrium notion, had the data on output prices indicated that the model should also account for feedback from other variables in the model to prices.

AREAS FOR FUTURE RESEARCH

A theme that recurs repeatedly, if only implicitly, throughout this volume is that differential games and rational expectations are unfinished subjects. All of the applications in this book are intended as useful steps forward, but they are not the last word. Indeed, the strategic considerations of which the theoretical framework continually reminds us indicate criticisms of the work in this volume, on its own grounds, on a number of points. In particular, each of the analyses in this book cuts off the chain of strategic reactions and interactions at some point, as for example when Eckstein and Eichenbaum compute an optimal tariff under the assumption of no retaliation. It is usually possible to argue, sometimes convincingly, that the chain of strategic interactions has been prematurely truncated. A virtue of the style of analysis used here is that such questions naturally arise, even if the demands of obtaining tractable models have forced us to make compromises.

The language and concepts used and developed in this book are useful for understanding a variety of issues involving the interpretation of observations and the framing of policy questions. To take one example of enormous influence during the last decade, recall Lucas' "critique" of econometric policy evaluation procedures (Lucas, 1976), which was that by treating private agents' decision rules h_i as structural, or invariant with respect to the government's choice of its decision rules, systematically nonoptimal behavior was being attributed to private agents. Lucas called for building dynamic theories and a dynamic econometrics that would assume that private agents would vary their choices of strategy optimally with respect to the strategies chosen by the government.

The studies in this volume are part of the effort to use and create methods that answer Lucas' call. Much of the early work that attempted to meet Lucas's call, including some of my own (Sargent, 1981), in effect reversed the asymmetry that Lucas criticized, at least insofar as estimating time series models is concerned. This work typically posited arbitrary, although sometimes quite general, stochastic processes for government instruments, such as the money supply, while assuming that private agents solved stochastic dynamic control problems. Estimation aimed at recovering the free parameters of private agents' objective functions and the parameters of the laws of motion posited for government policy and other driving variables. This setup is precisely the reverse of the older literature, such as Friedlander (1973), that aimed to estimate the parameters of the government authorities' objective functions, taking as given the decision rules of private agents. A hope was that estimation of the parameters of private agents' objective functions would make possible prediction of how their decision rules would change as a function of the government policy strategy. The operating characteristics of the system could then be optimized by choosing the optimal policy rule for the government, that is, by solving a differential game with the government as a dominant player. Usually, however, this literature carries the assumption that the historical data were not necessarily generated by the solution of the game with the government acting as a dominant player or even as a purposeful intelligent agent.

The most powerful challenge to the relevance of the Lucas critique for interpreting data and making normative statements about policy has come from Christopher Sims (1980, 1983). A major part of Sims' challenge, at least as I understand it, can be stated using the framework of Epple, Hansen, and Roberds. In effect, Sims has criticized the asymmetry that is involved in estimating and interpreting time series with a model in which private agents solve dynamic optimal-control problems but the government uses arbitrarily specified and possibly readily improved upon stochastic processes for its instruments. Sims has argued that a more appropriate assumption for the time series observations would be that government policy has been approximately optimal, relative to his conception of the game. Sims has argued against regarding observations on policy decisions as reflecting a conscious choice of regime, as in Epple, Hansen, and Roberds' game E. Instead, Sims proposed interpreting government policy as emerging from a game like game F, in which an administration does not pretend to be able to commit future administrations to a policy but only to expect that future administrations will have a similar objective function. One's position on these matters will influence how one formulates and interprets models of the observable time series and also the urgency and seriousness with which one views normative analyses of government policy regime changes. My own interpretation of Sims' position is that analyses of changes in a government policy regime (or strategy) are of limited interest, because such regimes rarely if ever change; a good positive reason for them not to change is that they are themselves endogenous and are determined as the outcome of a dynamic game like Epple, Hansen, and Roberds' game F.

A critic of Sims' view might note that the sequence of administrations under such a game F actually attains a lower value of the dominant player's objective function than is achieved by the time-inconsistent but optimal plan under game E. Because the outcome of game F can be improved upon from the dominant player's viewpoint, which in many games is a social welfare function, consideration of social institutions or mechanisms that move the system closer to attaining an outcome like that of game E is appropriate. This amounts to analyzing and comparing "regimes" in the manner recommended by Lucas, Prescott, and others.

These conflicting conceptions of policy have only begun to be clearly articulated by the economics profession, and the differences are far from resolved. The methods and language used in this volume create a fruitful framework for understanding these and other frontier issues in the dynamic theory of economic policy.

REFERENCES

Friedlander, A. F. 1973. "Macro Policy Goals in the Postwar Period: A Study in Revealed Preference," *Quarterly Journal of Economics* vol. 87, pp. 25–43.

Hansen, Lars P., and Thomas J. Sargent. 1984. "Filtering, Control, and Rational Expectations." Manuscript (publication pending).

Kydland, Finn E., and Edward C. Prescott. 1977. "Rules Rather than Discretion: The Inconsistency of Optimal Plans," *Journal of Political Economy* vol. 85, no. 3, pp. 473–491.

Lucas, Robert E., Jr. 1976. "Econometric Policy Evaluation: A Critique," in K. Brunner and A. Meltzer, eds., *The Phillips Curve and Labor Markets*, Carnegie-Rochester Conference on Public Policy 1 (Amsterdam, North-Holland).

_____, and Edward C. Prescott. 1971. "Investment Under Uncertainty," *Econometrica* vol. 39, no. 5, pp. 659–681.

_____, and Thomas J. Sargent. 1981. "Introduction," in Robert E. Lucas and Thomas J. Sargent, eds., *Rational Expectations and Econometric Practice* (Minneapolis, Minn., University of Minnesota Press).

Sargent, Thomas J. 1981. "Interpreting Economic Time Series," *Journal of Political Economy* vol. 89, no. 2, pp. 213–248.

Sims, Christopher A. 1980. "Macroeconomics and Reality," *Econometrica*, vol. 48, no. 1, pp. 1–48.

_____. 1983. "Policy Analysis with Econometric Models," in William Brainard and George Perry, eds., *Brookings Papers on Economic Activity* vol. 1, pp. 107–152.

2

Embargoes and Supply Shocks in a Market With a Dominant Seller

S. Rao Aiyagari and Raymond G. Riezman

This chapter uses dynamic game theory and rational expectations to analyze the nature and effects of supply shocks in oil markets. Research in applying rational expectations methodology in dynamic macroeconomics has emphasized the importance of going beyond postulating demand and supply curves to analyzing the agents' optimization problems (see, for example, Sargent, 1982). Traditional macroeconomics has often proceeded by drawing demand and supply curves for various sectors of the macroeconomy with dynamic elements introduced by including lagged variables. Dynamic elements have been viewed as arising from adjustment costs, lags in decision making, and most importantly from expectations of agents regarding future values of variables. Agents are assumed to form their expectation by using various schemes based on past observations. Analysts applied these models empirically by regarding the parameters of these dynamic demand and supply curves as "structural" (in the sense of being invariant to alternative policy rules of government or, in the present context, OPEC) and using the estimated parameter values for analyzing the effects of different policies. Implicit in this

S. Rao Aiyagari is Assistant Professor of Economics, University of Wisconsin, Madison. Raymond G. Riezman is Associate Professor of Economics, University of Iowa.

procedure is the assumption that the parameters in the expectation formation schemes of agents are also "structural."

Rational expectations research in macroeconomics interprets the various dynamic demand and supply curves of traditional macroeconomics as the decision rules of optimizing economic agents in a dynamic environment. Given this view, inevitably the principle of optimization carries over to the formation of expectations; that is, agents form expectations of future values of variables in an optimal way by taking correct account of the evolution of these variables and do not make systematic errors in prediction. In particular, because different government policy rules have different effects on the future evolution of the variables an agent might be interested in predicting, parameters in agents' expectation formation schemes cannot be viewed as policy invariant. Consequently, agents' dynamic decision rules will change with changes in the policy environment. Hence the procedure of positing demand and supply curves and expectation formation schemes and conducting policy analysis by treating the parameters in these schemes as policy invariant is incorrect.

Another of the important developments to have come out of rational expectations research has been the distinction between policy rules and policy actions. A policy rule is a description of how the government chooses a policy action at each date in response to the economic circumstances of that date. The insight of rational expectations has been that a policy rule must be specified in order to analyze its effects and only policy rules can be compared. Asking about the effects of an isolated policy action or comparing different policy actions is meaningless without specifying the underlying policy rules that generate those actions. The principal reason for this shift in emphasis from policy actions to policy rules is that without an understanding of the policy rule the dynamic optimization problem of agents (in particular, the problem of optimal prediction) is not completely specified.

Thus rational expectations research goes beyond agents' decision rules and focuses on their optimization problems (including optimal forecasting); it then isolates the parameters of agents' objective functions and technology, which may legitimately be viewed as policy invariant, in order to interpret time series observations and analyze different policies. In this way, the analysis can take account of the changes in agents' decision rules that will occur when the policy regime changes.

This chapter explores the implications of these general principles to such oil market issues as (1) the effects of "supply shocks" in the oil market on production, consumption, and inventory behavior in the importing countries, and (2) the strategic behavior of importing countries vis-à-vis the oil exporting countries, which may conveniently be viewed as a monopoly with or without a fringe of competitive producers.

The importance of strategic issues was brought home perhaps most vividly by the Arab oil embargo. Another round of shortages followed later during the Iranian crisis. All of this led to considerable discussion of various counter strategies—holding strategic reserves; decontrolling oil and natural gas to spur exploration and production; conserving energy, possibly through taxes; investing in research to develop alternative energy sources; a new policy toward exploration; and other measures. All of these proposals were designed to lessen the impact on the U.S. economy of similar events (actual or threatened) in the future.

In a dynamic environment with rational expectations, the behavior of producers and consumers in the importing countries depends on their views regarding the nature of supply shocks and the price and production strategies of the exporting countries. Both the reason for supply disruptions and their likely frequency will influence the behavior of agents in the importing country. Thus analyzing the impact of a supply shock requires analysis of agents' expectations with regard to similar events in the future. In a like fashion, if supply shocks occur because of external factors rather than deliberate policy, the dominant seller may or may not choose to adjust production to smooth out the resulting price fluctuations. The behavior of agents in the importing country will clearly depend on their expectations of future prices, which in turn depend on the pricing and production policy the seller is pursuing.

The next step is to recognize that the dominant seller in the oil market can hardly be expected to ignore the effects of its policies on demand behavior in the importing countries. The seller's strategy regarding the imposition and the frequency of supply shocks must take into account that greater exploration, use of less energy-intensive technologies, or development of substitutes or other responses may gradually curtail demand. Even if such shocks are politically motivated, their frequency will depend on the economic costs vis-a-vis the (possibly political) benefits. The seller also would likely take into account the effect of its pricing and production strategies on buyers' demand behavior.

The strategic issues may be even more complicated than this description suggests. For instance, a discussion of whether the government of the importing country should pursue a policy of imposing tariffs, acquiring strategic reserves, and developing alternative energy sources should take into account the effects of such policies on private behavior and, more importantly, on the exporting countries' behavior. The exporting countries would be likely to take into account policies that may have the net effect of curtailing demand for their exports. Thus game theoretic issues in a dynamic context can be of considerable importance in analyzing oil markets.

Tolley and Wilman (1977) consider optimal policies in the face of some probability that an embargo will be imposed. This probability may also be regarded as the fraction of any given length of time the importing country expects to spend under an embargo. Tolley and Wilman's analysis is conducted mostly with the aid of short- and long-run demand curves (adjustment costs and/or habit formation could lead to this difference). They ignore the possibility, however, that these demand curves may depend on the exporter's policy—in this case, the probability of an embargo. Consumers (or producers who use the commodity as an input) would be likely to take the probability of facing an embargo into account, which ought to be reflected in their demand behavior.

For instance, consider the case in which the seller has not imposed an embargo in the current period, but some probability exists that it will in the future. Intuitively, current demand ought to be higher the greater the probability of an embargo in the future. This feature, that demand curves depend systematically on the probability of embargo via expectations, appears to be missing in Tolley and Wilman's analysis.

Another aspect of the embargo issue is whether the exporter ever profits from imposing purely economic embargoes. If demand during nonembargo periods is higher than usual because buyers expect an embargo in the future, an embargo policy would seem to enhance demand for the exporter and be profitable. In order for the threat of embargoes to be believable, however, embargoes would have to be imposed with some frequency, and sales during an embargo period would be considerably less than normal. Hence average profits for the exporter would depend on average sales (taking embargo and nonembargo sales together, weighted by the respective probabilities), which may or may not be higher than normal demand under a policy of no embargoes. If the exporter never profits from imposing frequent embargoes, then the threat of embargoes as a purely *economic* strategy becomes less believable. The economic effects of such a policy (even if motivated by noneconomic reasons) on exploration, production, consumption, and inventory accumulation in the importing country are still of interest, however (see Aiyagari and Riezman, 1982a, 1982b).

Another view of supply disruptions is that exogenous factors, such as political disturbances or natural disasters, may interrupt exports by some suppliers. In such a situation, the dominant exporters can adopt either of two policies. One would be to increase production in the unaffected countries and try to smooth out the large price fluctuations that would otherwise occur. The other would be not to increase production and to let such shocks be fully reflected in price fluctuations. These different policies will have different implications for demand behavior and hence for the revenues of the exporting countries because of their differing effects on expectations of agents regarding the time paths of prices in the future. Consequently, the dominant exporters would choose their response to such exogenous shocks in terms of their pricing and production policies, taking into account the influence of their policies on behavior in the buying countries.

Another aspect of oil pricing and production that has attracted attention (see, for example, Ulph and Ulph, 1981) is that the oil-exporting countries have large amounts of capital invested in the economies of the importing countries. Because capital and energy are both inputs into the production process, an energy exporter's pricing policy affects the rate of return to capital and hence the exporter's investment income. Thus the exporting country might want to consider not only the influence on demand but also the influence on the rate of return to capital in choosing a price policy. In this connection, the question of whether capital and energy are complements or substitutes becomes relevant, because the effect of the price of energy on the rate of return to capital will depend on the substitutability of these inputs.

Dynamic rational expectations models can be analytically quite complicated, and the issue of what is the appropriate equilibrium concept is somewhat open. In the terminology of game theory, our description of the strategic issues corresponds to the notion of dominant player games. The importing country is viewed as a Nash/Cournot player; it takes the policy of the exporting country as given and chooses its own optimal policy (which consists of production, consumption, inventory accumulation, and possibly other decisions at each date during the entire planning horizon). The exporting country is viewed as the dominant player; it chooses an optimal policy (which could consist of embargo or no embargo, price, and production decisions at each date during the planning horizon), taking into account the effects of its policy choice on the behavior of the importing country. In such a case, the decisions of the importing country at any time depend not only on the current decisions of the dominant player but also on its expectations of the dominant player's future policy. Consequently, the dominant player would have to take into account the fact that both its current decisions and its future policy (correctly anticipated by the other player) will affect the current behavior of the importing country and hence the current payoff (export revenues) of the dominant player.

The issue of the appropriate equilibrium concept arises precisely because of this dependence of current payoffs on future actions. Bellman's principle of optimality for dynamic programs does not apply in such cases.[1] We use the open-loop equilibrium concept, in which the dominant player is viewed as announcing in advance the entire sequence of its actions during the whole planning horizon in advance. The dominant player will choose the most favorable sequence, taking into account its effects on the nondominant player. Such behavior may be dynamically inconsistent, however, because the dominant player may have an incentive to depart from its initially announced action for some future date, once that date arrives. Other solution concepts, such as closed-loop or feedback, may be used, but they too have some unsatisfactory features.[2]

I. EMBARGO STRATEGIES

The methodology described can be applied in the context of simple but explicit models to some important energy issues: the economic rationale on the part of a monopolist to use an embargo strategy; the economic effects on the buying country of such a strategy; optimal pricing and production strategies for the dominant seller when the supply by a fringe of small competitive suppliers is interrupted by exogenous shocks, taking into account effects on the dominant seller's rate of return to capital. The models presented are abstractions designed to bring out the main points, omitting certain potentially relevant considerations in the interest of analytical tractability. Important among these are the exhaustibility of oil and exploration and domestic production of oil in the importing country. Epple, Hansen, and Roberds in chapter 5 show that exhaustibility can be taken into account by a suitable modification of cost functions. Allowing domestic production and exploration would simply modify the demand functions of buyers.

We start with a static setup and view an embargo strategy as a stochastic rationing scheme. The buyer has an endowment of w_y units of a commodity y and wishes to consume good y as well as another good x, which the seller produces using y as the only input. The seller behaves as a monopolist and sets the price P (of x in terms of y), as well as the following rationing scheme. The buyer has to place an order for good x. Then, with probability π, the seller imposes a partial embargo and fills only a fraction λ of the order; with probability $(1 - \pi)$, the order is completely supplied; $\lambda = 0$ corresponds to a probability π of a total embargo.

---

[1] This principle may be stated as, "An optimal policy has the property that, whatever the initial state and decision, the remaining decisions must constitute an optimal policy starting from the state resulting from the first decision." Bellman (1957).

[2] For a discussion of these issues in greater depth, see Kydland (1975) and Kydland and Prescott (1977).

The buyer chooses an order x taking this rationing scheme into account by maximizing expected utility.

$$\pi u(\lambda x, w_y - P\lambda x) + (1 - \pi)u(x, w_y - Px) \qquad (1.1)$$

Here, both x and y are consumer goods entering a utility function $u(.,.)$. If x were treated as an input into production and the buyer as a firm maximizing expected profits, (1.1) would become

$$\pi[f(\lambda x) - P\lambda x] + (1 - \pi)[f(x) - \overset{\cdot}{P}x] \qquad (1.2)$$

and $f(\cdot)$ would be thought of as a production function. If $u(x, w_y - Px) \equiv f(x) + (w_y - Px)$ and $w_y = 0$, (1.1) is the same as (1.2).

For either interpretation, the optimal order for x is a function,

$$x = \bar{x}(P, \pi, \lambda) \qquad (1.3)$$

Under general assumptions, $\bar{x}(.,.,.)$ is decreasing in P and λ and increasing in π. Thus a high probability that an embargo will occur or that a small fraction of the order will be filled will cause the buyer to increase the order. Consequently, the seller's revenues will be higher than normal in a nonembargo state. The expected profits of the seller depend on expected sales, however, which will be λx with probability π and x with probability $(1 - \pi)$. Expected profits are

$$\pi(P - c)\lambda\bar{x}(P, \pi, \lambda) + (1 - \pi)(P - c)\bar{x}(P, \pi, \lambda) \qquad (1.4)$$

where c is the constant unit cost of production of x. The optimal strategy for the seller is to set $\pi = 0$ (or $\lambda = 1$) and choose P to be the usual monopoly price. Thus the seller has nothing to gain by confronting the buyer with an embargo strategy. The basic reason is that while the order size $\bar{x}(P, \pi, \lambda)$ is increasing in π (and decreasing in λ), expected sales $\pi\lambda\bar{x}(P, \pi, \lambda) + (1 - \pi)\bar{x}(P, \pi, \lambda)$ are decreasing in π and increasing in λ. Thus, although the seller could enhance the order size by using an embargo strategy, expected profits will necessarily go down.[3]

The question of whether it pays a monopolist to use quantity constraints in addition to price has been investigated in the literature (see, for example, Honkapohja, 1980, and Maskin and Polemarchakis, 1980). Under standard conditions (of which the above is an example), the answer is no. Uncertainty with regard to the buyer's demand function,

---

[3] The algebra is relatively simple and has been omitted. See Aiyagari and Riezman (1982a) for a full account.

however, coupled with the prohibitive cost of choosing a different price for each state of demand or the inability of a monopolist seller confronted by several buyers to price discriminate, could make quantity rationing profitable. With these exceptions, in a static context quantity rationing is not profitable for a seller that can control price.

In an intertemporal context, however, the role of stocks, adjustment costs, and expectations of the possibility of future embargoes can be taken into account to (1) see if the monopolist-seller could increase revenues by imposing embargoes, and (2) analyze the effects of such actions (assuming they are taken for other than purely economic reasons) on the buying country. If the probability of an embargo does affect demand, Tolley and Wilman's analysis is not entirely accurate.

For this purpose, consider a simple two-period model. The buying country imports a single storable commodity, which is used as an input into the production of a single nonstorable consumption good. The periods are indexed by t, which takes values 1 and 2, and

M_t = imports in period t

x_t = amount of the input used in production in period t

$y_t = f(x_t, x_{t-1})$ = production function for the consumption good y. (Note that the production function is written with current as well as last period's inputs as arguments in order to capture the role of adjustment costs in changing input levels from one period to the next.)

s_t = stocks of the input in the importing country held from t to $t+1$

p_t = price of x in terms of y in period t set by the exporter of x and taken as given by the buyer

The seller also has in effect an embargo threat described by π. In period 2, with probability π imports will be denied completely, whereas with probability $(1 - \pi)$ imports will be fully supplied. We assume no embargo is in effect in period 1. The buyer's problem is formulated as one of maximizing expected discounted profits, taking storage costs and the terminal value of stocks into account. The objective function of the buyer is given by

$$E_1\left\{ \sum_{t=1}^{2} \beta^{t-1}\left[f(x_t, x_{t-1}) - p_t z_t M_t - h(s_t)\right] + \beta g(s_2)\right\}$$

subject to

$$s_0, x_0, p_1, p_2, \pi \text{ given}, s_t = s_{t-1} + z_t M_t - x_t \qquad t = 1, 2$$

In this problem, $z_1 = 1$ and z_2 is a random variable with the distribution

$$z_2 = \begin{cases} 0 & \text{with probability } \pi \\ 1 & \text{with probability } (1 - \pi) \end{cases}$$

$E_1(\cdot)$ is the expectation at date $t = 1$. The realization of the random variable z_2 describes whether an embargo is in effect in period 2. $g(s_2)$ is meant to capture the terminal value of stocks at the end of period 2, whereas $h(s_t)$ represents storage costs. $\beta(0 < \beta < 1)$ is the discount rate for the buyer.

The seller is assumed to maximize his expected discounted revenues, which are given by

$$p_1 M_1 + \delta E_1(p_2 z_2 M_2)$$

where δ is the seller's discount rate.

The model shows that embargo threats are not profitable for the seller, given full flexibility in choosing prices. The algebra is relegated to appendix A, but the basic reason is as follows. The embargo threat described is equivalent to the alternative policy of charging a random second-period price (denoted by $\tilde{p}_2$).

$$\tilde{p}_2 = \begin{cases} p_2' & \text{with probability } \pi \\ p_2 & \text{with probability } (1 - \pi) \end{cases}$$

p_2' is a price that is just high enough so that the buyer would just choose $M_2 = 0$ when confronted with that price. It may alternatively be thought of as the shadow price attached to the embargo constraint; that is, it is the marginal value to the buyer of being allowed to import an extra unit starting from a situation of zero imports. The seller will never gain (at least in a linear-quadratic framework) by randomizing over second-period prices, because the seller's discounted revenue is a concave function of $\tilde{p}_2$ and hence a mean-preserving spread in the distribution of $\tilde{p}_2$ will always reduce expected discounted revenues. Consequently, even though an embargo threat enhances current demand, the seller cannot benefit by adopting it.

Tolley and Wilman (1977) consider the buyer's choice of optimal policies (say, a tariff) when faced with an exogenous probability of an embargo. Their analysis uses short- and long-run import demand functions, and they show how the optimal policy depends on the probability of an embargo. They, however, ignore the effects of changes in the embargo probability on the demand functions themselves.

In appendix A, we analyze the effects on the buying country of changes in the probability of an embargo. We show that an increase in the future probability of an embargo increases current imports, reduces current input use, and increases end-of-period stocks. Analyses of optimal policy responses by the buying country that ignore these effects may not be entirely accurate.

II. PRICE POLICY UNDER EXOGENOUS SUPPLY SHOCKS

We now consider the alternative interpretation of supply shocks as arising from exogenous shocks to supply in some of the exporting countries. The supply side consists of a dominant seller and competitive fringe framework, and a single (representative) competitive buyer constitutes the demand side. The dominant seller chooses the price policy, taking its effects on the competitive fringe and the buyer into account. The fringe suppliers take the price policy of the dominant seller as given and choose their supply, which is subject to some exogenous shocks. Similarly, the buyer decides on demand, taking the price policy as given. The issue in this context is whether, and if so under what conditions, the dominant seller has an incentive to adjust production to compensate for exogenous supply shocks and thereby smooth out their potential effects on price.

If the dominant seller adopts a constant-price policy, it would make up any shortages in the fringe supply or would cut back production when fringe supply is high. Alternatively, the dominant seller could keep production constant and let the price adjust to clear markets. Obviously, any policy in between these two extremes is possible as well. The question is how much the dominant seller will let price adjust when a shock changes the fringe supply.

As a preliminary step, in Aiyagari and Riezman (1982c), we considered an essentially static setup in which with probability π the fringe producers supply exports according to their supply curve, given the price, and with probability $(1 - \pi)$, their exports are reduced to a fraction λ of the amount corresponding to their supply curve. We considered only two (admittedly extreme) policies on the part of the dominant seller. One is the guaranteed price policy, in which the seller maintains a constant price (whether or not fringe supply is reduced) by adjusting the seller's own production appropriately. The second policy is the no-guarantee policy, in which the dominant seller does not adjust production but lets the shock to fringe supply be reflected in a higher price. We did not explicitly consider the buyer's optimizing behavior but simply postulated that demand under the no-guarantee policy was some fraction of the demand under the guarantee policy (because the greater price uncertainty under the no-guarantee policy may adversely affect demand). Which of the two policies is superior for the dominant seller depends on the extent to which greater price uncertainty causes a reduction in demand.

We now consider a model in which the seller could adopt any price policy between the two extremes and buyers explicitly optimize. The model is a simple, two-person, dynamic, dominant player game with rational expectations. The buyer is assumed to maximize expected discounted profits given by:

$$E_0\left\{ \sum_{t=0}^{\infty} \beta^t \left[f(x_t) - (1+\tau)P_t x_t - \frac{d}{2}(x_t - x_{t-1})^2 \right] \right\} \qquad (2.1)$$

x_t is the amount of the imported good used as an input into production. $f(x_t) = ax_t - (b/2)x_t^2$ is the production function. P_t is the price of the input x_t (in terms of output); $d(x_t - x_{t-1})^2/2$ equals the costs of adjustment. τ is the tariff on imports of x_t imposed by the government of the importing country.[4] $E_0(\cdot)$ is the expectation conditional on information available at $t = 0$, and β is the buyer's discount rate. The buyer takes the stochastic process for $\{P_t\}$ as given in choosing a (dynamic) demand decision rule. The supply curve from the competitive fringe is assumed given by $f_0 + f_1 P_t + \theta_t$, where θ_t is the supply shock assumed to be i.i.d. with zero mean.

The dominant seller is assumed to choose a price policy that will maximize expected discounted profits, given by the following expression:

$$E_0\left\{ \sum_{t=0}^{\infty} \sigma^t (P_t - c)\left[x_t - (f_0 + f_1 P_t + \theta_t) \right] \right\} \qquad (2.2)$$

subject to the constraint given by the buyer's decision rule. c is the constant unit cost of production for x_t, and $[x_t - (f_0 + f_1 P_t + \theta_t)]$ is the net demand facing the dominant seller. $0 < \sigma < 1$ is the discount rate for the dominant seller.

A detailed analysis of this dynamic game is given in appendix B. The solution to the buyer's optimization problem is the quasi-decision rule,[5]

$$x_t = A + \lambda x_{t-1} + B \sum_{j=0}^{\infty} \mu^j E_t(P_{t+j}) \qquad (2.3)$$

---

[4] It is assumed that the buyer country is small. In addition, the tariff revenue generated is assumed to have a negligible effect on the demand for the good the buying country produces.

[5] See, for example, Sargent (1979), ch. 14.

where A, λ, B, and μ depend on the parameters in the buyer's objective function $(a, b, d, \tau,$ and $\beta)$. $A = \lambda a / d(1 - \lambda\beta)$, $B = -\lambda(1 + \tau)/d$ and $\mu = \lambda\beta$. (Equation (2.3) corresponds to (B.1) in appendix B.) As is apparent, the buyer's expectations of the entire future path of prices enter in (2.3). These expectations are formed on the assumption that prices evolve as follows:

$$P_t = \alpha_0 + \alpha_1 P_{t-1} + \alpha_2 \theta_t + \alpha_3 \theta_{t-1} \tag{2.4}$$

We will later find values for the parameters $(\alpha_0, \alpha_1, \alpha_2, \alpha_3)$ such that buyer's expectations are rational, that is, based on the dominant seller's optimal price policy. Using (2.3) and (2.4), the buyer's decision rule may be formulated as

$$x_t = \left[A + \frac{B\mu\alpha_0}{(1-\mu)(1-\mu\alpha_1)} \right] + \lambda x_{t-1} + \frac{B}{(1-\mu\alpha_1)}(P_t + \mu\alpha_3\theta_t) \tag{2.5}$$

We can now substitute for P_t from (2.5) in terms of (x_t, x_{t-1}, θ_t) into the dominant seller's objective function and express the seller's profits in terms of (x_t, x_{t-1}, θ_t). Because θ_t is assumed to be i.i.d. with zero mean, the solution to the dominant seller's optimization problem is

$$x_t = A' + \lambda' x_{t-1} + B'\theta_t \tag{2.6}$$

where A', λ' and B' are constants defined in equation (B.9) of appendix B. Operating on both sides of (2.5) by $(1 - \lambda' L)$, where L is the lag operator, and using (2.6),

$$A' + B'\theta_t = (1 - \lambda') \left[A + \frac{B\mu\alpha_0}{(1-\mu)(1-\mu\alpha_1)} \right] + \lambda \left(A' + B'\theta_{t-1} \right)$$

$$+ \frac{B}{(1-\mu\alpha_1)} \left[P_t - \lambda' P_{t-1} + \mu\alpha_3 \left(\theta_t - \lambda'\theta_{t-1} \right) \right] \tag{2.7}$$

which may be rewritten as

$$P_t = \alpha_0' + \alpha_1' P_{t-1} + \alpha_2' \theta_t + \alpha_3' \theta_{t-1} \tag{2.8}$$

See equation (B.11) in appendix B for the definition of coefficients α_0', α_1', α_2', and α_3'. We can now equate the coefficients in (2.4) and (2.8) and solve for the unknown coefficients $(\alpha_0, \alpha_1, \alpha_2, \alpha_3)$. Once this is done, we can substitute for x_t from (2.6) into (2.5) and express the dominant seller's optimal price policy as

$$P_t = g_0 + g_1 x_{t-1} + g_2 \theta_t \tag{2.9}$$

The coefficients in this price policy will depend on the structural parameters in the buyer's objective function (a, b, d, β), those in the dominant seller's objective function (σ, c), the parameters describing fringe supply (f_0, f_1), and the policy parameter τ. For the details, see equation (B.19) in appendix B. We are, in particular, interested in the dependence of P_t on θ_t under the optimal price policy, that is, in the coefficient g_2. Knowing its dependence on the various structural parameters and the policy parameter τ makes possible a description of the conditions under which price will be more or less sensitive to the supply shock θ_t.

The coefficient g_2 turns out to be a very complicated function of the structural parameters, and general analytical results are difficult to achieve. In view of this, we have computed an example to see how $\partial P_t/\partial \theta_t = g_2$ changes when the structural parameters change. The results from the example are summarized in the table below. (Details are in appendix B.)

Parameter	$\dfrac{\partial P_t}{\partial \theta_t} = g_2$
$\beta \uparrow$	Very little effect
$\sigma \uparrow$	Very little effect
$b \uparrow$	$-g_2 \uparrow$
$d \uparrow$	$-g_2 \uparrow$
$f_1 \uparrow$	$-g_2 \downarrow$
$\tau \uparrow$	$-g_2 \downarrow$

For the example computed, the discount rates, β and σ, had very little effect on the responsiveness of price g_2. A higher value for b increases the effect of the supply shock on price because a higher b implies a more inelastic long-run demand; hence the seller finds "passing on" the supply shock in the form of a higher price easier. A higher d works the same way, because a high d means high adjustment cost and a more inelastic short-run demand.

An increase in f_1, implies a more elastic fringe supply. Passing on supply shocks becomes more difficult for the dominant seller, so g_2 falls. A higher tariff works the same way, because it essentially makes the buyer's long-run demand more elastic.

This analysis takes proper account of the buyer's dynamic optimization problem and shows how the buyer's decision rule depends on the expected future path of prices, which in turn will depend on the dominant seller's price policy. The dominant seller takes into consideration the fact that different price policies will lead to different decision rules for the buyer and chooses an optimal price policy accordingly. Thus parameters in the buyer's and dominant seller's decision rules depend on the structural parameters in both of their objective functions. This method also shows the proper way to conduct policy experiments, here represented by changing values of the tariff τ. These changes affect the buyer's decision rule and hence the dominant seller's optimal price policy, which consequently affects the sensitivity of price to the supply shock.

Another issue, considered in Aiyagari and Riezman (1982d), is the optimal price policy for the dominant seller in the face of shocks to fringe supply when the dominant seller has capital invested in the importing country and takes the effect of its price policy on its investment income (via the effect on rate of return to capital) into account. As can be seen from the previous example, even for simple specifications such dynamic games tend to become analytically quite complicated. We therefore did not undertake a detailed analysis of the buyer's decision problem but postulated demand functions with intuitively reasonable properties and then analyzed the dominant seller's optimal price policy given the objective of maximizing expected discounted profits. Again, our interest was on how, under the optimal price policy, price would change in response to the competitive fringe's supply shock. In three situations, the dominant seller would adjust price less and production more in response to a supply shock. The greater the price sensitivities of net income (output less payments for imports less interest payments on capital held by the dominant seller), imports, and the rate of return to capital in the buying country, the smaller is the effect of a supply shock on the price set by the dominant seller; that is, the seller will adjust production more and price less under those conditions. The three price sensitivities appear to be intimately connected to the question of complementarity/substitutability in production between the imported energy input on the one hand and capital and labor on the other. These price sensitivities may be expected to be high if the imported input is highly substitutable for capital and labor and low in the contrary case.

III. CONCLUSION

Use of the rational expectations methodology directs one to go beyond demand and supply curves to an analysis of agents' objective functions and technological constraints. Even when relatively simple examples are analyzed, insistence upon optimizing behavior and rational expectations makes for a complicated analysis, but it also offers compensating benefits. The example used to analyze whether an embargo strategy is useful for a monopolist (in a dynamic context with stocks and adjustment costs) shows how the buyer's dynamic demands for imports, stocks, and input use depend, via expectations, on the parameters of the embargo strategy (the sequence of prices and the probability of an embargo). It also shows that when proper account is taken of this dependence an embargo strategy is not useful for the monopolist on purely economic grounds. Such a strategy may be pursued for noneconomic motives, however, in which case the model is useful for analyzing the effects of such threats of supply interruptions on the buyer.

An example of the dominant player's optimal price policy in the face of exogenous supply shocks among fringe competitors was analyzed in the context of a dynamic dominant player game. The buyer's dynamic decision rule was obtained by optimization based on rational expectations in the presence of adjustment costs. The advantage of this approach is that the effect of the supply shock on price can be described by relatively few structural parameters that have an easy economic interpretation. These parameters relate to the buyer's and seller's discount rates, an adjustment cost parameter for the buyer, supply elasticity for the competitive fringe, and long-run demand elasticity for the buyer. Such an analysis also indicates how the dominant player's optimal price policy can be expected to change with a change in any of these parameters. The usefulness of this approach was exemplified by considering the effect of a tariff on imports imposed by the buying country. This analysis also suggests the pitfalls of using existing time series data to project the likely effects of the imposition of a new and different level of the tariff. Accurate prediction of the effect of a change in tariff rates on imports requires explicitly taking into account the effect the tariff has on the price policy of the dominant seller.

We also briefly discussed the optimal price policy of the dominant seller for the case in which the dominant seller has some capital invested in the buying country and must consider how price changes will affect the rate of return to capital. The price sensitivity of the rate of return to capital emerges as another factor that may cause the dominant seller to smooth out the price path in response to supply shocks.

Much of our analysis has been conducted in the context of simple examples that exclude potentially relevant circumstances. Principal among these issues are the exhaustibility and the domestic exploration and production of oil. The analysis could be modified to take account of these circumstances by using the Epple, Hansen, and Roberds approach (see chapter 5) and by modifying the net demand function of buying countries. The present analysis should provide useful insights for future research along similar lines designed to overcome some of the limitations.

APPENDIX A

The buyer's optimization problem is to maximize

$$E_1\left\{\sum_{t=1}^{2}\beta^{t-1}\left[f(x_t, x_{t-1}) - p_t z_t M_t - h(s_t)\right] + \beta g(s_2)\right\}$$

subject to

$$s_t = s_{t-1} + z_t M_t - x_t \qquad t = 1, 2$$

$$p_1, p_2, s_0, x_0 \text{ given}$$

$$z_1 = 1$$

$$z_2 = \begin{cases} 0 \text{ with probability } \pi \\ 1 \text{ with probability } (1 - \pi) \end{cases}$$

At the beginning of period 2, if $z_2 = 1$, the buyer maximizes the following over x_2, M_2, s_2:

$$f(x_2, x_1) - p_2 M_2 - h(s_2) + g(s_2) \qquad (A.1)$$

subject to

$$s_2 = s_1 + M_2 - x_2$$

This maximization yields the first order conditions,

$$\left.\begin{aligned} &f_1\left(x_2^{NE}, x_1\right) - p_2 = 0 \\ &-p_2 - h'\left(s_2^{NE}\right) + g'\left(s_2^{NE}\right) = 0 \\ &M_2^{NE} = s_2^{NE} + x_2^{NE} - s_1 \end{aligned}\right\} \qquad (A.2)$$

where the superscript NE indicates no embargo and the superscript E embargo. By substituting the solutions of (A.2) back into (A.1), the expression (A.1) may be written as a function of s_1 and x_1,

$$V^1(s_1, x_1) = f\left(x_2^{NE}, x_1\right) - p_2 M_2^{NE} - h\left(s_2^{NE}\right) + g\left(s_2^{NE}\right) \qquad (A.3)$$

and it may be verified that

$$\frac{\partial V^1}{\partial s_1} = p_2, \quad \frac{\partial V^1}{\partial x_1} = f_2\left(x_2^{NE}, x_1\right) \tag{A.4}$$

Following a similar procedure, if there is an embargo in period 2, the maximization problem for the buyer yields the first-order conditions,

$$\left. \begin{aligned} &f_1\left(x_2^E, x_1\right) + h'\left(s_2^E\right) - g'\left(s_2^E\right) = 0 \\ &s_2^E = s_1 - x_2^N \end{aligned} \right\} \tag{A.5}$$

The maximum value of the buyer's second-period objective function when an embargo is in effect may be written as

$$V^0(s_1, x_1) = f\left(x_2^E, x_1\right) - h\left(s_2^E\right) + g\left(s_2^E\right) \tag{A.6}$$

and it may be verified that

$$\left. \begin{aligned} &\frac{\partial V^0}{\partial s_1} = -h'\left(s_2^E\right) + g'\left(s_2^E\right) \\ \\ &\frac{\partial V^0}{\partial x_1} = f_2\left(x_2^E, x_1\right) \end{aligned} \right\} \tag{A.7}$$

Now, coming to period 1, the buyer maximizes

$$f(x_1, x_0) - p_1 M_1 - h(s_1) + \beta\left[\pi V^0(s_1, x_1) + (1 - \pi)V^1(s_1, x_1)\right]$$

subject to:

$$s_1 = s_0 + M_1 - x_1$$

This problem yields the first-order conditions,

$$\left. \begin{aligned} &f_1(x_1, x_0) - p_1 + \beta\left[\pi\frac{\partial V^0}{\partial x_1} + (1 - \pi)\frac{\partial V^1}{\partial x_1}\right] = 0 \\ \\ &-p_1 - h'(s_1) + \beta\left[\pi\frac{\partial V^0}{\partial s_1} + (1 - \pi)\frac{\partial V^1}{\partial s_1}\right] = 0 \\ \\ &s_1 = s_0 + M_1 - x_1 \end{aligned} \right\} \tag{A.8}$$

We now show that such an embargo policy is equivalent to charging a random second-period price (denoted $\tilde{p}_2$) with the following distribution:

$$\tilde{p}_2 = \begin{cases} p_2' \text{ with probability } \pi \\ p_2 \text{ with probability } (1-\pi) \end{cases}$$

and

$$p_2' = -h'\left(s_2^E\right) + g'\left(s_2^E\right) \qquad (A.9)$$

Facing this price in the second period, the buyer maximizes

$$f(x_2, x_1) - p_2' M_2 - h(s_2) + g(s_2)$$

subject to

$$s_2 = s_1 + M_2 - x_2$$

which yields the first order conditions,

$$f_1(x_2, x_1) - p_2' = 0$$
$$-p_2' - h'(s_2) + g'(s_2) = 0$$
$$s_2 = s_1 + M_2 - x_2$$

Equations (A.5) and (A.9) show that $M_2 = 0$, $s_2 = s_2^E$, $x_2 = x_2^E$ solve the above three equations. Hence the maximum value of the buyer's objective function in period 2 when facing the price p_2' is identical to that given in (A.6). Therefore the buyer's optimization problem in period 1 faced with such a random price is the same as before, and the solutions are as described by (A.8); the seller's expected discounted revenues are also exactly the same. Thus an embargo policy is equivalent to charging a random price in the second period.

We now show that such a strategy is not profitable for the seller, at least in a linear-quadratic framework. Let $\tilde{p}_2$ denote the (random) second-period price. By analogy with (A.2), (A.3), and (A.4), in period 2 when $\tilde{p}_2$ is realized

$$\left.\begin{array}{l} f_1(x_2, x_1) - \tilde{p}_2 = 0 \\[6pt] -\tilde{p}_2 - h'(s_2) + g'(s_2) = 0 \\[6pt] M_2 = s_2 + x_2 - s_1 \end{array}\right\} \qquad (A.10)$$

$$V(s_1, x_1, \tilde{p}_2) = f(x_2, x_1) - \tilde{p}_2 M_2 - h(s_2) + g(s_2)$$

and

$$\frac{\partial V}{\partial s_1} = \tilde{p}_2, \quad \frac{\partial V}{\partial x_1} = f_2(x_2, x_1)$$

(A.11)

In period 1, the optimization problem is to maximize

$$f(x_1, x_0) - p_1 M_1 - h(s_1) + \beta E V(s_1, x_1, \tilde{p}_2)$$

subject to

$$s_1 = s_0 + M_1 - x_1$$

In view of (A.11), the first-order conditions for this problem can be written as

$$f_1(x_1, x_0) - p_1 + \beta \cdot E\left[f_2(x_2, x_1)\right] = 0$$

$$-p_1 - h'(s_1) + \beta E(\tilde{p}_2) = 0$$

$$s_1 = s_0 + M_1 - x_1$$

(A.12)

The seller's expected discounted revenues $E(R)$ are

$$
\begin{aligned}
E(R) &= p_1 M_1 + \delta E(\tilde{p}_2 M_2) = p_1(s_1 + x_1 - s_0) \\
&\quad + \delta E\left[\tilde{p}_2(s_2 + x_2 - s_1)\right] \\
&= -s_1\left[\delta E(\tilde{p}_2) - p_1\right] + \delta E(\tilde{p}_2 s_2) \\
&\quad - p_1 s_0 + p_1 x_1 + \delta E(\tilde{p}_2 x_2)
\end{aligned}
$$

(A.13)

We now consider the following quadratic specification:

$$f(x_2, x_1) = a x_2 - \frac{b}{2} x_2^2 - \frac{d}{2}(x_2 - x_1)^2$$

$$h(s_2) = \frac{h_1}{2} s_2^2$$

$$g(s_2) = g_0 s_2 - \frac{g_1}{2} s_2^2$$

(A.14)

which has the solutions,

$$s_2 = \frac{g_0 - \tilde{p}_2}{h_1 + g_1} \tag{A.15}$$

$$x_2 = \frac{a + dx_1 - \tilde{p}_2}{b + d} \tag{A.16}$$

$$x_1 = \frac{a + dx_0 - p_1 + \dfrac{\beta d}{(b+d)}\left[a - E(\tilde{p}_2)\right]}{b + d + \dfrac{\beta bd}{(b+d)}} \tag{A.17}$$

$$s_1 = \frac{\left[\beta E(\tilde{p}_2) - p_1\right]}{h_1} \tag{A.18}$$

$$M_2 = s_2 + x_2 - s_1 \tag{A.19}$$

$$M_1 = s_1 + x_1 - s_0 \tag{A.20}$$

The above solutions may be substituted in (A.13) to evaluate $E(R)$. Doing so reveals that $E(R)$ is a function of p_1, $E(\tilde{p}_2)$ and $E(\tilde{p}_2)^2$ and that terms in $E(\tilde{p}_2^2)$ occur with negative sign; that is, for fixed p_1 and $E(\tilde{p}_2)$, $E(R)$ is decreasing in $E(\tilde{p}_2^2)$. This immediately implies that a mean-preserving spread in the distribution of $\tilde{p}_2$ must lead to a reduction in the seller's expected discounted revenues.

We now consider the embargo scheme described previously in order to consider the effects of a change in π (the probability of an embargo) on the buying country. As noted before, this is equivalent to the random pricing scheme,

$$\tilde{p}_2 = \begin{cases} p_2' & \text{with probability } \pi \\ p_2 & \text{with probability } (1 - \pi) \end{cases}$$

and p_2' is such that at that price $M_2 = s_2 + x_2 - s_1 = 0$. From (A.15) and (A.16) it follows that p_2' solves

$$\frac{g_0 - p_2'}{h_1 + g_1} + \frac{a + dx_1 - p_2'}{b + d} - s_1 = 0$$

Hence,

$$p_2' = \frac{g_0(b+d) + (a + dx_1)(h_1 + g_1) - s_1(b+d)(h_1 + g_1)}{b + d + h_1 + g_1} \tag{A.21}$$

Further,

$$E(\tilde{p}_2) = \pi p_2' + (1 - \pi) p_2 \tag{A.22}$$

We can now use (A.17), (A.18), (A.20), (A.21), and (A.22) to solve for s_1, x_1, and M_1 as functions of π. In order to determine how these variables change with respect to π, we may differentiate (A.17) and (A.18) with respect to π and use (A.21) and (A.22). To simplify the expressions, let

$$\gamma_0 = \frac{\beta d}{(b+d)\left[b+d+\dfrac{\beta bd}{(b+d)}\right]}$$

$$\gamma_1 = \frac{d(h_1 + g_1)}{(b+d+h_1+g_1)}$$

$$\gamma_2 = \frac{(b+d)(h_1+g_1)}{(b+d+h_1+g_1)}$$

We then have

$$\frac{\partial x_1}{\partial \pi} = -\gamma_0 \frac{\partial}{\partial \pi} E(\tilde{p}_2)$$

$$= -\gamma_0 \left(p_2' + \pi \frac{\partial p_2'}{\partial \pi} - p_2 \right)$$

$$= -\gamma_0 (p_2' - p_2) - \pi \gamma_0 \left(\gamma_1 \frac{\partial x_1}{\partial \pi} - \gamma_2 \frac{\partial s_1}{\partial \pi} \right) \tag{A.23}$$

Similarly,

$$\frac{\partial s_1}{\partial \pi} = \frac{\beta}{h_1} \frac{\partial}{\partial \pi} [E(\tilde{p}_2)] = \frac{\beta}{h_1} \left(p_2' + \pi \frac{\partial p_2'}{\partial \pi} - p_2 \right)$$

$$= \frac{\beta}{h_1} (p_2' - p_2) + \frac{\beta \pi}{h_1} \left(\gamma_1 \frac{\partial x_1}{\partial \pi} - \gamma_2 \frac{\partial s_1}{\partial \pi} \right) \tag{A.24}$$

Obviously,

$$\frac{h_1}{\beta} \frac{\partial s_1}{\partial \pi} + \frac{1}{\gamma_0} \frac{\partial x_1}{\partial \pi} = 0 \tag{A.25}$$

which indicates that s_1 and x_1 move in opposite directions when π

changes. Further, from (A.20),

$$\frac{\partial M_1}{\partial \pi} = \frac{\partial s_1}{\partial \pi} + \frac{\partial x_1}{\partial \pi} = \frac{\partial s_1}{\partial \pi}\left(1 - \gamma_0 \frac{h_1}{\beta}\right) \tag{A.26}$$

Now, $p_2' > p_2$ because p_2' is the price such that second-period imports are zero. Using this and (A.25), we find from (A.23) and (A.24) that

$$\frac{\partial s_1}{\partial \pi} > 0, \qquad \frac{\partial x_1}{\partial \pi} < 0$$

Further, because it is reasonable to assume that current imports M_1 are increasing with respect to second-period price, we have [from (A.17), (A.18), and (A.20)]

$$1 > \gamma_0 \frac{h_1}{\beta}$$

Hence, from (A.26) we obtain

$$\frac{\partial M_1}{\partial \pi} > 0$$

APPENDIX B

The buyer's optimization problem is to maximize

$$E_0\left\{ \sum_{t=0}^{\infty} \beta^t \left[ax_t - \frac{b}{2}x_t^2 - (1+\tau)P_t x_t - \frac{d}{2}(x_t - x_{t-1})^2 \right] \right\}$$

The solution to this is quite standard (see ch. 14, Sargent, 1979) and yields the quasi-decision rule,

$$x_t = \frac{\lambda a}{d(1 - \lambda\beta)} + \lambda x_{t-1} - \frac{\lambda(1+\tau)}{d} \sum_{j=0}^{\infty} (\lambda\beta)^j E_t(P_{t+j}) \tag{B.1}$$

where $0 < \lambda < 1$ is a root of the quadratic equation in Z,

$$Z^2 - \left(1 + \frac{1}{\beta} + \frac{b}{\beta d}\right)Z + \frac{1}{\beta} = 0 \tag{B.2}$$

The buyer assumes that (P_t) evolves according to

$$P_t = \alpha_0 + \alpha_1 P_{t-1} + \alpha_2 \theta_t + \alpha_3 \theta_{t-1} \tag{B.3}$$

Using (B.3), (B.1) can be solved to obtain the buyer's decision rule in the form,

$$x_t = \frac{\lambda a}{d(1 - \lambda\beta)} + \lambda x_{t-1} - \frac{\lambda(1 + \tau)}{d(1 - \lambda\beta\alpha_1)} \left[\frac{\alpha_0 \lambda\beta}{(1 - \lambda\beta)} + P_t + \lambda\beta\alpha_3\theta_t \right] \tag{B.4}$$

which may be rewritten as

$$P_t = A + \delta(\lambda x_{t-1} - x_t) - \lambda\beta\alpha_3\theta_t \tag{B.5}$$

$$A = \frac{1}{(1 - \lambda\beta)} \left[\frac{a(1 - \lambda\beta\alpha_1)}{(1 + \tau)} - \alpha_0\lambda\beta \right] \tag{B.6}$$

$$\delta = \frac{d(1 - \lambda\beta\alpha_1)}{\lambda(1 + \tau)} \tag{B.7}$$

The dominant seller now maximizes his objective function

$$E_0 \left\{ \sum_{t=0}^{\infty} \sigma^t (P_t - c) [x_t - (f_0 + f_1 P_t + \theta_t)] \right\} \tag{B.8}$$

subject to (B.5). Substituting for P_t from (B.5) into (B.8), we have Maximize

$$E_0 \left\{ \sum_{t=0}^{\infty} \sigma^t [(A - c) + \delta\lambda x_{t-1} - \delta x_t - \lambda\beta\alpha_3\theta_t] \right.$$
$$\left. \cdot [(1 + f_1\delta)x_t - f_1\lambda\delta x_{t-1} + (f_1\lambda\beta\alpha_3 - 1)\theta_t - (f_0 + f_1 A)] \right\}$$

The stochastic Euler equation for this problem is

$$-2\delta(1 + f_1\delta + \sigma f_1\lambda^2\delta)x_t + \delta\lambda(1 + 2f_1\delta)x_{t-1}$$
$$-\theta_t(\lambda\beta\alpha_3 - \delta + 2f_1\delta\lambda\beta\alpha_3)$$
$$+\sigma E_t [(2f_1\lambda\beta\alpha_3 - 1)\theta_{t+1} + \delta\lambda(1 + 2f_1\delta)x_{t+1}] + B = 0$$

where B is a constant. Since θ_t was assumed to be i.i.d. with zero mean, the solution to the above is straightforward and is given by

$$x_t = B' + \mu x_{t-1} - \frac{\mu \theta_t}{\delta \lambda (1 + 2f_1 \delta)} \left[\lambda \beta \alpha_3 (1 + 2f_1 \delta) - \delta \right] \tag{B.9}$$

where $0 < \mu < 1$ is the root of the quadratic equation in Z,

$$Z^2 - \frac{2(1 + f_1 \delta + \sigma \lambda^2 f_1 \delta)}{\sigma \lambda (1 + 2f_1 \delta)} Z + \frac{1}{\sigma} = 0 \tag{B.10}$$

and B' is a constant.

Operating on both sides of (B.5) by $(1 - \mu L)$ where L is the lag operator and using (B.9), we obtain

$$P_t - \mu P_{t-1} = (1 - \mu) A + \delta \lambda \left\{ B' - \frac{\mu \theta_{t-1}}{\delta \lambda (1 + 2f_1 \delta)} \left[\lambda \beta \alpha_3 (1 + 2f_1 \delta) - \delta \right] \right\}$$

$$- \delta \left\{ B' - \frac{\mu \theta_t}{\delta \lambda (1 + 2f_1 \delta)} \left[\lambda \beta \alpha_3 (1 + 2f_1 \delta) - \delta \right] \right\}$$

$$- \lambda \beta \alpha_3 (\theta_t - \mu \theta_{t-1})$$

which may be rewritten as

$$P_t = (1 - \mu) A - \delta (1 - \lambda) B' - \theta_t \left[(\lambda - \mu) \beta \alpha_3 + \frac{\mu \delta}{\lambda (1 + 2f_1 \delta)} \right]$$

$$+ \theta_{t-1} \frac{\mu \delta}{(1 + 2f_1 \delta)} + \mu P_{t-1} \tag{B.11}$$

Equating the coefficients of P_{t-1}, θ_t, and θ_{t-1} in (B.3) and (B.11), we have

$$\alpha_1 = \mu \tag{B.12}$$

$$\alpha_2 = - \left[(\lambda - \mu) \beta \alpha_3 + \frac{\mu \delta}{\lambda (1 + 2f_1 \delta)} \right] \tag{B.13}$$

$$\alpha_3 = \frac{\mu \delta}{(1 + 2f_1 \delta)} \tag{B.14}$$

A solution for α_1 is found by substituting for δ from (B.7) into (B.10) and using (B.12). This shows that $0 < \alpha_1 < 1$ is the root of the following cubic equation in Z:

$$\lambda\left[1 + \frac{2f_1 d}{\lambda(1+\tau)}\right] - 2Z\left[1 + \frac{\lambda f_1 d\beta}{(1+\tau)} + \frac{(1+\sigma\lambda^2)f_1 d}{\lambda(1+\tau)}\right]$$

$$+ Z^2\left[\sigma\lambda + \frac{2f_1 d\sigma}{(1+\tau)} + \frac{2(1+\sigma\lambda^2)f_1 d\beta}{(1+\tau)}\right]$$

$$- Z^3\frac{2\lambda f_1 d\beta c}{(1+\tau)} = 0 \tag{B.15}$$

(B.7) and (B.12) through (B.14) become

$$\delta = \frac{d(1 - \lambda\beta\alpha_1)}{\lambda(1+\tau)} \tag{B.16}$$

$$\alpha_3 = \frac{\alpha_1\delta}{(1 + 2f_1\delta)} \tag{B.17}$$

$$\alpha_2 = -\alpha_3\left[\frac{1}{\lambda} + \beta(\lambda - \alpha_1)\right] \tag{B.18}$$

Thus (B.15) solves for α_1, (B.16) for δ, (B.17) for α_3, and (B.18) for α_2. We can now write the dominant seller's optimal price policy in terms of the state variables (x_{t-1}, θ_t) at t by substituting for x_t from (B.9) into (B.5). Noting that $\mu = \alpha_1$, this yields

$$P_t = (\text{Constant}) + \delta(\lambda - \alpha_1)x_{t-1} + \alpha_2\theta_t \tag{B.19}$$

Because $0 < \lambda < 1$ and $0 < \sigma < 1$, it may be verified that the cubic expression in (B.15) is positive for $Z = 0$ and negative for $Z = \lambda$. Hence a root $0 < \alpha_1 < \lambda$ exists for (B.15). Therefore δ and α_3 are positive, while from (B.18) α_2 is negative. From (B.19), this implies that price responds negatively to the supply shock θ_t, which is as it should be because a higher θ_t implies an increase in fringe supply and hence a lower net demand facing the dominant seller.

As can be seen from (B.4) and (B.19), the buyer's and dominant seller's decision rules depend on all of the structural parameters in the model: those in buyer's objective function (a, b, d, β), those in seller's objective function (α, c), those in competitive fringe's supply curve (f_0, f_1), and the policy parameter τ. Further, the dependence of price on the supply shock θ_t represented by the coefficient α_2 is a very complicated function of these structural parameters. It is difficult analytically to see how α_2 responds to changes in any of these parameters.

In view of this, we have computed some numerical examples to show the effects on α_2 of each of the structural parameters. It can be seen from the equations determining α_2 that the parameters a, c, and f_0 have no effect on it. Hence we only look at the effects of b, d, β, σ, f_1, and τ. We started with the following "basic" parameter values:

$$\beta = 0.95, \ \sigma = 0.95, \ \tau = 0.15, \ b = 10.0, \ d = 10.0, \text{ and } f_1 = 10.0$$

We then changed the parameters one at a time while keeping the values of all other parameters at the original values. These results are shown below.

Parameter Values	$-\alpha_2$
Basic	.04976
$\beta = 0.93$	.04977
$\beta = 0.97$	.04977
$\sigma = 0.93$	.04976
$\sigma = 0.97$	.04976
$\tau = 0.10$	.04976
$\tau = 0.20$	.04974
$b = 5.0$	.04967
$b = 15.0$	.04981
$d = 5.0$	.04969
$d = 15.0$	.04980
$f_1 = 5.0$	.09904
$f_1 = 15.0$	.03322

These effects were calculated as responses to small changes in parameter values in the neighborhood of the original values, which were picked arbitrarily. It is clear that a high f_1 leads to a smaller α_2 (in absolute magnitude), that is, to a smaller effect of the supply shock θ on the price. This effect seems reasonable, because a high f_1 implies a more elastic supply curve for the fringe suppliers. A high value of the adjustment cost parameter d leads to a greater effect of θ on P. This is also to be expected, because a high d would imply a more inelastic short-run demand from the buyer, so the dominant seller can more readily pass on the supply shock in the form of a higher price. A high b also leads to a greater effect of the supply shock on price. A high value of b implies a more inelastic long-run demand from the buyer, because in the absence of adjustment costs, long-run demand can be obtained as

$$a - bx_t - (1 + \tau)P_t = 0 \tag{B.20}$$

or

$$x_t = \frac{1}{b}\left[a - (1 + \tau)P_t\right]$$

(B.20) is obtained by maximizing the buyer's objective function with respect to x_t in the absence of adjustment costs. Consequently, the effect of b on the effect of the supply shock on price is also reasonable.

The effect of the tariff τ is to reduce the response of price to the supply shock. This also happens because the buyer's long-run demand becomes more elastic as τ is higher. The dominant seller's discount rate σ and the buyer's discount rate β appear to have very negligible effects, at least in the range of values considered.

REFERENCES

Aiyagari, S. R., and R. Riezman. 1982a. "Quantity Rationing in Oil Markets: Static Results." Mimeo (Madison, Wis., University of Wisconsin, Department of Economics, May).

_____. 1982b. "Stochastic Rationing in Dynamic Economic Models," Mimeo (Madison, Wis., University of Wisconsin, Department of Economics, May).

_____. 1982c. "Supply Interruptions and Cartel Behavior." Mimeo (Madison, Wis., University of Wisconsin, Department of Economics, May).

_____. 1982d. "Supply Shocks and the Price Policy of a Dominant Seller," Mimeo (Madison, Wis., University of Wisconsin, Department of Economics, May).

Bellman, R. 1957. *Dynamic Programming* (Princeton, N.J., Princeton University Press).

Honkapohja, S. 1980. "A Note on Monopolistic Quantity Rationing," *Economics Letters* vol. 6, pp. 203–209.

Kydland, F. E. 1975. "Non-Cooperative and Dominant Player Solutions in Discrete Dynamic Games," *International Economic Review* (June).

_____, and E. C. Prescott. 1977. "Rules Rather Than Discretion: The Inconsistency of Optimal Plans," *Journal of Political Economy* vol. 85, pp. 473–493.

Maskin, E., and H. M. Polemarchakis. 1980. "Rational Quantity Rationing." Discussion paper no. 78 (New York, Columbia University, Department of Economics, August).

Sargent, Thomas J. 1979. *Macroeconomic Theory* (New York, Academic Press).

_____. 1982. "Beyond Demand and Supply Curves in Macroeconomics," *American Economic Review Papers and Proceedings* vol. 72, no. 2, pp. 382–389.

Tolley, G. S., and J. D. Wilman. 1977. "The Foreign Dependence Question," *Journal of Political Economy* vol. 85, no. 2, pp. 323–347.

Ulph, A. M., and D. T. Ulph. 1981. "International Monopoly-Monopsony Power Over Oil and Capital." Mimeo (Southampton, Eng., University of Southampton).

3

Oil Supply Disruptions and the Optimal Tariff in a Dynamic Stochastic Equilibrium Model

Zvi Eckstein and Martin S. Eichenbaum

The importance of petroleum as a source of energy to the United States and other industrialized economies is by now a matter of common knowledge. Partly in response to the Mideastern oil cutoffs since 1973, as well as the recognition of the U.S. economy's dependence on foreign sources of oil, many economists have advocated a variety of government policies aimed at mitigating the effects of disruptions in the international oil supply network. Examples of such proposals, which range from tariffs on imported oil to government-held strategic petroleum reserves, may be found in Nichols and Zeckhauser (1977), Nordhaus (1974), Teisberg (1981), Tolley and Wilman (1977), and Wright and Williams (1982), among others. In essence, all of these proposals revolve around the notion that the private sector of the economy is somehow incapable of dealing in a socially optimal way with shocks to the supply of oil.

The purpose of this chapter is to examine the welfare-enhancing role of government interventions in decentralized economies that are subject to uncertainty regarding the price of oil. In order to do so, we first construct

Zvi Eckstein is Assistant Professor of Economics, Yale University and Tel Aviv University. Martin S. Eichenbaum is Assistant Professor of Economics, Carnegie-Mellon University.

41

a stochastic general equilibrium model of an economy that imports energy. The economy consists of a finite number of infinite-lived consumers and firms. Consumers maximize the expected discounted utility derived from leisure and consumption, while producers maximize the expected present value of profits. Output of this economy consists of a single good, which may be used for consumption or capital. The production function of the good in question depends on three inputs, labor, capital, and energy, and is subject to costs of adjustment in capital. In order to emphasize the transmission of oil shocks into domestic labor and capital markets, we restrict uncertainty in this economy to the pricing of oil.

The nonintervention equilibrium is characterized for a fairly general parameterization of the stochastic process that governs the evolution of energy prices over time. For the model under consideration, the rational expectations competitive equilibrium is optimal if, and only if, at each time period the conditional elasticity of world energy prices with respect to domestic imports is equal to infinity. Put somewhat differently, there is no room for welfare-enhancing government interventions if, and only if, aggregate domestic imports have no effect on current and future world energy prices. Essentially, this finding follows from the fact that competitive agents view those aggregate domestic state variables that influence the distribution of energy prices as being beyond their ability to control or influence. As a result, the latent ability of the country as a whole to influence energy prices goes unexploited. A social planner, however, when determining optimal contingency plans, would take into account the country's ability to influence the equilibrium distribution of energy prices. Thus the standard nonoptimalities involved in static optimal tariff arguments can be viewed as a special case of the nonoptimalities in the present dynamic, stochastic environment.

Given the general nonoptimality of the competitive equilibrium, we proceed to analyze the set of interventions that support an optimal equilibrium. When only current aggregate imports affect energy prices, a dynamic optimal tariff that exploits the country's ability to influence both the first and second moments of the energy price process is sufficient to support an optimal equilibrium. When current energy prices depend on lagged as well as current imports, however, an optimal tariff must be combined with an import tax for which firm-specific tax rates are fixed functions of lagged import levels. Thus by searching over alternative sets of policy instruments, it is possible to support a decentralized equilibrium that reproduces the unique time-consistent optimal solution of the relevant Pareto problem. This approach is in contrast to the situation that typically emerges when optimal policy is conceived as corresponding to the best use that can be made of a set of prespecified policy instruments.

As Kydland and Prescott (1977) point out, these sorts of rules typically lead to time-inconsistent policies. Moreover, unless the instrument list happens to be specified correctly, these rules lead to equilibria that are, in general, Pareto-inferior to the equilibrium that emerges from the solution of the relevant social planning problem.

The procedures we have used lead to a time-consistent set of policies that succeed in reproducing the allocation that a social planner would choose to maximize the expected utility of the representative consumer, subject only to the physical constraints imposed by technology. Taken as a whole, then, our results indicate that the critical issues regarding optimality do not seem to depend so much on the uncertainty of oil prices per se but rather on the way the oil pricing process depends on aggregate domestic variables such as imports and inventories of energy.

The dependency of private agents' decision rules, and consequently the equilibrium of the system, is an important part of this analysis. Abstracting from this dependency would be equivalent to modeling policy as a "game against nature," an assumption that is fundamentally inconsistent with the notion that private agents are solving their optimization problems correctly. This is, in effect, our major criticism of much of the existing literature (for example, Nordhaus, 1974, and Teisberg, 1981), which begins analysis by postulating the existence of a static deterministic demand function for oil that is invariant with respect to both the stochastic process governing the evolution of oil prices and the various government intervention policies that are considered.

Put somewhat differently, we begin by assuming that the question of how agents will respond to arbitrary sequences of tariffs, energy prices, or strategic petroleum reserve targets is simply not well posed. To quote Sargent (1981), "... unless the researcher specifies precisely the perceived laws of motion for the forcing variables, he has not specified the constraints subject to which decision makers are thought to be acting." Because of this, we are forced to specify the policy rules and probability laws governing the evolution of these variables over time. Viewed in this way, our results indicate that the method of analysis is both applicable and tractable in the context of general equilibrium models of energy-related phenomena in which policy analysis is based on standard Pareto criteria.

The analysis also leads to a natural link between the theory and quantitative policy evaluation. In order to accomplish this latter objective, we confine ourselves to environments in which the equilibrium movements of aggregate quantities and prices, though highly nonlinear in the underlying structural parameters, take the form of time-invariant linear stochastic difference equations. This feature, along with the fact that the model maps the route from the fundamental parameters of the problem to the decision rules of agents and the resulting dynamic equilibrium process of market-determined variables, is extremely convenient from the point of view of estimation. Hence the model is capable, in principle, of quantitative as well as qualitative policy evaluation.

I. A DYNAMIC GENERAL EQUILIBRIUM MODEL WITH STOCHASTIC ENERGY PRICES

The basic economy that is modeled here produces a single consumption good by combining labor, domestically owned capital, and imported energy. A dynamic neoclassical general equilibrium model is used to evaluate the desirability of a class of government interventions that have been advocated in the literature. Embedded in the model are certain characteristics of technology that have been claimed to make the economy particularly vulnerable to shocks in the supply of energy. In particular, we assume that the technology available to firms is fixed and that capital and energy are perfect complements in production. We also assume that changing the stock of capital at the firm level entails adjustment costs but that no such costs attach to the hiring and firing of labor. As such, the model attempts to capture the fundamental environment implicit in the widely held view that, although the vulnerability of the economy to oil shocks may be alleviated in some ten or twenty years by concerted conservation measures and the development of alternative sources of energy and new production technologies, the options for reducing the harm induced by shocks to the supply of energy over some shorter time horizon are far more limited.

The model comprises the following elements:

$L(t)$ = hours of leisure of the representative consumer at time t
$Q(t)$ = consumption of the representative consumer at time t
$Y(t)$ = output of the representative firm at time t
$K(t)$ = capital stock of the representative firm at time t
B = discount factor, $0 < B < 1$
n = the number of firms in the economy, assumed constant over time; without loss of generality, we assume that $n = 1$
$1 - \delta$ = the rate of depreciation of a unit of capital per unit of time
$I(t)$ = inventories of energy resources held by the representative firm at the end of time period t
$P(t)$ = price of a unit of energy in terms of the consumption good at time period t

$S(t) =$ savings of the representative consumer during time period t

$N(t) =$ the number of hours the representative consumer works during time period t

$\bar{L} =$ total hours available to the representative consumer during time period t

$G(t) =$ units of energy the representative firm uses for production during time period t

$M(t) =$ units of energy the representative firm purchases during time period t

$W(t) =$ the real hourly wage rate during time period t

The representative consumer faces the problem of choosing $N(t)$ and $Q(t)$ to maximize the present value of expected utility. Because the critical issues in the literature seem to revolve around the dynamic behavior of firms, and given our desire to obtain explicit analytical solutions, the specification of consumer preferences is extremely simple. In particular, the utility derived from leisure and consumption is assumed to be time separable, quadratic in leisure, and linear in consumption. Given these assumptions, one may assume without loss of generality that no borrowing or lending occurs in this economy. Consumers receive dividends $\pi(t)$, however, at each time period t. As such, the real savings in this economy essentially occur at the firm level in the form of investment in real capital and inventories of energy.

The representative consumer chooses $N(t)$ and $Q(t)$ so as to maximize

$$E_0 \sum_{t=0}^{\infty} B^t \left[AQ(t) - RN(t) - \frac{V}{2} N^2(t) \right] \tag{1.1}$$

subject to

$$Q(t) = W(t)N(t) + \pi(t) \tag{1.2}$$

and

$$\bar{L} = L(t) + N(t)$$

The representative consumer is a price taker and therefore takes as given the stochastic processes $\{W(t)\}_{t=0}^{\infty}$ and $\{\pi(t)\}_{t=0}^{\infty}$. It is straightforward to establish that the solution to the consumer's problem is given by the following inverse labor supply function:

$$W(t) = \frac{R}{A} + \frac{V}{A}N(t) \tag{1.3}$$

The problem of the representative firm, which seeks to maximize the present value of its expected profits, is considerably more complicated.[1] We assume that output produced at time t may be used as capital during time period $(t + 1)$, so that the cost of a unit of capital is identically equal to one unit of the consumption good. In the absence of internal adjustment costs, output of the firm is given by

$$Y(t) = aN(t) - \frac{b}{2}N^2(t) + dN(t)K(t) + eK(t) - \frac{f}{2}K^2(t) \tag{1.4}$$

and output sold is equal to $Y(t) - [K(t + 1) - \delta K(t)]$. Energy use appears only implicitly here because capital and energy are used in fixed proportions, $K(t) = gG(t)$ for all t. Because investment decisions are made at time t, $K(t + 1)$ is determined at time t. But this, and the assumption that capital and energy are used in fixed proportions, imply that $G(t + 1)$ is also determined at time t. Hence $G(t)$ is given to the firm at time t. In addition, the firm is assumed to bear internal capital-adjustment costs of $(c/2)[K(t) - K(t - 1)]^2$. The cost term $(h/2)[rG(t) - I(t - 1)]^2$ is included to capture the notion that the firm incurs real costs from using energy during time period t in amounts that deviate from some proportion of beginning-of-period inventories.[2] More specifically, we assume that some optimum relationship exists between the two, $G(t)/I(t - 1) = 1/r$, so that the firm is penalized, in a symmetric way, when this relationship is not satisfied. Throughout, we assume that $0 \leq r \leq 1$ so that, abstracting from other considerations, firms would like beginning-of-period inventories to be equal to some fraction of time t energy use. One of the advantages of assuming such a technology is that it allows the model to capture, in an analytically tractable way, the view that inventories of energy are held for reasons, in addition to the

---

[1] A simpler model than the one employed in this chapter could generate many of our results regarding the optimality characteristics of decentralized equilibria. The motivation for the approach used here is to show that costs of adjustments and the presence of inventories per se do not give rise to a welfare-improving role for the government in the presence of stochastic disturbances to energy prices.

[2] For the sake of simplicity, adjustment costs are stated in terms of gross investment. It is straightforward to analyze the case in which the cost of capital adjustment term is written as $(c/2)[K(t) - \delta K(t - 1)]^2$.

speculative motive, related to the firm's expected future use of energy. (See Auerbach and Green, 1981, for a detailed discussion of firms' raw materials inventory behavior.)

The problem of the representative firm is to choose contingency plans for $N(t)$, $G(t)$, and $I(t)$ to maximize its expected present real value.

$$V_0 = E_0 \sum_{t=0}^{\infty} B^t \Big\{ aN(t) - \frac{b}{2} N^2(t) + dgN(t)G(t) + egG(t)$$

$$- \frac{fg^2}{2} G^2(t) - g[G(t+1) - \delta G(t)]$$

$$- \frac{cg^2}{2} [G(t) - G(t-1)]^2 - \frac{h}{2} [rG(t) - I(t-1)]^2$$

$$- P(t)[G(t) + I(t) - I(t-1)] - W(t)N(t) \Big\} \qquad (1.5)$$

where $I(-1)$, $G(0)$, $G(-1)$, as well as the stochastic processes governing the behavior over time of $W(t)$ and $P(t)$, are given to the firm. Notice that (1.5) uses the relationship $K(t) = gG(t)$ and the fact that the firm loses $K(t+1) - \delta K(t)$ units of the good through net investment. Finally, $W(t)N(t)$ represents the firm's labor costs at time t, while $P(t)[G(t) + I(t) - I(t-1)]$ represents the real costs of energy imports at time t. The operator E_t is defined by $E_t Z \equiv E[Z|\Omega(t)]$, where Z is a random variable, E is the linear least squares projection operator, and $\Omega(t)$ is the information set available to the firm at time t. We assume that $\Omega(t)$ includes at least $\{N(t), N(t-1), \ldots, I(t), I(t-1), \ldots, G(t+1), G(t), G(t-1), \ldots, W(t), W(t-1), \ldots, P(t), P(t-1), \ldots\}$. The firm maximizes (1.5) by choosing decision rules for $N(t)$, $G(t+1)$, and $I(t)$ from the set of decision rules that are functions of the elements of the information set $\Omega(t)$. Finally, we assume that the stochastic processes $\{W(t), P(t)\}$ are jointly covariance stationary. More specifically, the price process is assumed to be of the general form,

$$P(t) = F_0 + \sum_{J=1}^{q} F_J \overline{M}(t - J + 1) + J(t) = F_0 + F(L)\overline{M}(t) + J(t)$$

$$(1.6)$$

where $\overline{M}(t)$ represents the aggregate quantity of imports of energy by the country under consideration, $F(L)$ is a polynomial in the lag operator L of order q, and

$$J(t) = D(L)\epsilon(t) = \sum_{J=0}^{\infty} D_J \epsilon(t - J), \qquad \sum_{J=0}^{\infty} D_J^2 < \infty \qquad (1.7)$$

where $\varepsilon(t)$ is an independently and identically distributed white noise random variable. It is important to state at the outset that the price function (1.6) is ad hoc in the sense that it is not directly derived from a well-defined optimization problem. It does, however, embody in a specific functional form three sources of influences on energy prices. The constant term F_0 represents the deterministic components of energy prices that do not depend upon the actions of the domestic country. This term could easily be expanded to include nonstochastic polynomial functions of time without affecting the qualitative conclusions of the analysis. The term $D(L)\varepsilon(t)$ summarizes the random components of energy prices that do not emanate from and are not attributable to the actions of the domestic country. Thus $\varepsilon(t)$ is thought of as corresponding to the time t shock to energy prices in that $E_{t-1}\varepsilon(t)=0$.

The terms $F(L)\overline{M}(t)$ summarize the deterministic and potentially dynamic impact of the domestic country's imports upon $P(t)$. The small-country assumption thus corresponds to the hypothesis that $F(L)$ is equal to the zero operator, in which case domestic imports have no effect on current or future world energy prices. In that event, we could proceed under the assumption that $\varepsilon(t)$ is fundamental for $P(t)$; that is,

$$\varepsilon(t) = P(t) - E[P(t)|P(t-1), P(t-2),\ldots]$$
$$= P(t) - E[P(t)|\varepsilon(t-1), \varepsilon(t-2),\ldots]$$

The first-order necessary conditions for the maximization of (1.5) consist of a set of Euler equations and associated transversality conditions.[3] The Euler equations for the control variables of the firm are

$$a - bN(t) + dgG(t) - W(t) = 0 \tag{1.8}$$

$$B\varphi_1 E_t G(t+2) + \varphi_0 G(t+1) + \varphi_1 G(t) + dgE_t N(t+1) + hrI(t)$$
$$= E_t P(t+1) - g\left(e + \delta - \frac{1}{B}\right) \tag{1.9}$$

$$I(t) = r[G(t+1)] + \frac{1}{h}E_t\left[P(t+1) - \frac{P(t)}{B}\right] \quad \text{for all } t = 1, 2, \ldots, \tag{1.10}$$

where

$$\varphi_0 = -g^2\left[c(1+B) + \frac{hr^2}{g^2} + f\right]$$

$$\varphi_1 = cg^2$$

---

[3] See Hansen and Sargent (1981) for a discussion of solution procedures for models such as these.

Before proceeding to find the rational expectations competitive equilibrium for this economy, we focus on equations (1.8)–(1.10) in order to discuss the behavior of inventories, use of energy, and employment for arbitrary sets of expectations.

For equilibrium in the labor market, we require that the supply of labor be equal to the aggregate demand for labor, or from (1.3) and (1.8)

$$N(t) = \psi_1 + \psi_2 G(t) \tag{1.11}$$

where

$$\psi_1 = \frac{aA - R}{V + Ab}, \qquad \psi_2 = \frac{dgA}{V + Ab}$$

Substituting (1.11) into (1.9), we obtain

$$B\varphi_1 E_t G(t+2) + (\varphi_0 + dg\psi_2)G(t+1) + \varphi_1 G(t) + hrI(t)$$
$$= E_t P(t+1) - g\left(e + \delta - \frac{1}{B}\right) - dg\psi_1 \tag{1.9'}$$

Notice that for arbitrary sets of expectations, (1.10) implies that inventories of energy are an increasing function of expected energy use and therefore, ceteris paribus, expected output at time $(t+1)$. Similarly, inventories of energy are a decreasing function of $P(t)$, the opportunity cost of holding a unit of energy, as well as an increasing function of expected speculative gains, $BE_t P(t+1) - P(t)$. Thus,

$$\frac{\partial I(t)}{\partial G(t+1)} > 0, \qquad \frac{\partial I(t)}{\partial r} > 0$$

$$\frac{\partial I(t)}{\partial P(t)} < 0, \qquad \frac{\partial I(t)}{\partial E_t P(t+1)} > 0$$

While this model stresses the dynamics of the capital stock and oil consumption, it also gives rise to rich dynamics in the behavior of energy inventories. This follows from the fact that inventories depend, other things being equal, on consumption of oil at time $G(t+1)$, so that $I(t)$ inherits some of the dynamics in the movements of $G(t+1)$. Hence the firm holds inventories of energy in order to support future output, as well as to speculate on movements in the price of energy. This, of course, will have important consequences for both the representative firm's decision rule and the equilibrium law of motion of inventories of energy. To see this, notice that if no nonprice speculative motives for holding inventories exist, so that the parameter r is equal to zero, then (1.10) may be written as $I(t) = (1/h)E_t[P(t+1) - P(t)/B]$, which is equivalent with standard formulations in which speculators hold inventories at a level that equates holding costs to the difference between the current price of energy and the expected present value of next period's price. However, when r is not equal to zero, inventories at time t will not depend only upon $P(t)$ and $E_t P(t+1)$. Given costs of adjusting capital, the stock of capital and therefore energy use at time t depend upon the entire sequence of current and future expected prices. But unless r is equal to zero, firms would like to have a certain percentage of inventories of energy available for use. Hence, because capital and energy use depend upon the entire sequence of current and expected energy prices, so will energy inventories.

Having outlined the main features of the model, we now define a rational expectations equilibrium and derive the vector expectational difference equation whose solution corresponds to the rational expectations competitive equilibrium laws of motion for aggregate energy use and the stock of energy inventories. Before proceeding, we set the parameter q in equation (1.6) equal to 2. Thus we allow contemporaneous and lagged aggregate imports to affect current energy prices. Limiting the lagged effects to one period considerably simplifies our exposition while still allowing for nontrivial dynamics in the law of motion for prices. In section V, we return to the more general specification of (1.6) and indicate the nature of the equilibrium for arbitrary values of q.

Let the bar over a variable denote that it is industrywide. Then, using the fact that $\overline{M}(t) = \overline{G}(t) + \overline{I}(t) - \overline{I}(t-1)$, rewrite (1.6) as

$$P(t) = F_0 + F_1 [\overline{G}(t) + \overline{I}(t) - \overline{I}(t-1)]$$
$$+ F_2 [\overline{G}(t-1) + \overline{I}(t-1) - \overline{I}(t-2)] + J(t) \qquad (1.12)$$

As before, individual agents continue to view prices parametrically. In the context of (1.12), this implies that firms view the entire time sequence of aggregate energy use and inventories as beyond their ability to control or influence.

Recall that equations (1.9′) and (1.10) embody both the first-order conditions for maximizing the firm's expected present value and the equality between the demand for and supply of labor. To ensure that energy markets clear, we substitute (1.12) into (1.9′) and (1.10). Thus we obtain

$$B\varphi_1 E_t G(t+2) + (\varphi_0 + dg\psi_2) G(t+1) + \varphi_1 G(t) + hrI(t)$$
$$= E_t \{ F_0 + F_1 [\overline{G}(t+1) + \overline{I}(t+1) - \overline{I}(t)]$$
$$+ F_2 [\overline{G}(t) + \overline{I}(t) - \overline{I}(t-1)] + J(t+1) \} + c_g \qquad (1.13)$$

where $c_g = -Bg(e + \delta - 1/B) - Bdg\psi_1$, and

$$
\begin{aligned}
hBI(t) = \ & hrBG(t+1) \\
& + BE_t\{F_0 + F_1[\bar{G}(t+1) + \bar{I}(t+1) - \bar{I}(t)] \\
& + F_2[\bar{G}(t) + \bar{I}(t) - \bar{I}(t-1)] + J(t+1)\} \\
& - F_0 - F_1[\bar{G}(t) + \bar{I}(t) - \bar{I}(t-1)] \\
& - F_2[\bar{G}(t-1) + \bar{I}(t-1) - \bar{I}(t-2)] - J(t)
\end{aligned}
\tag{1.14}
$$

Equations (1.13) and (1.14) make clear that solving for the firm's optimal decision rules or the equilibrium will require attributing to firms well-specified views about how aggregate energy use and stocks of inventories evolve over time. In a rational expectations competitive equilibrium, agents' views regarding the law of motion of aggregate variables must be consistent with the actual equilibrium laws of motion of those variables. More specifically, assume that in equilibrium $\bar{I}(t)$ and $\bar{G}(t)$ follow the linear laws of motion,

$$
\bar{I}(t) = \bar{C}^1(L)\varepsilon(t) + C_{\bar{I}}
\tag{1.15}
$$

$$
\bar{G}(t) = \bar{C}^2(L)\varepsilon(t) + C_{\bar{G}}
\tag{1.16}
$$

and that firm-level inventories and energy use evolve over time in a way given by

$$
I(t) = C^1(L)\varepsilon(t) + C_I
\tag{1.17}
$$

$$
G(t) = C^2(L)\varepsilon(t) + C_G
\tag{1.18}
$$

Formally, we define a rational expectations competitive equilibrium as a quadruple of sequences,

$$
\{C_i^1\}_{i=0}^{\infty}, \quad \{C_i^2\}_{i=0}^{\infty}, \quad \{\bar{C}_i^1\}_{i=0}^{\infty}, \quad \text{and} \quad \{\bar{C}_i^2\}_{i=0}^{\infty}
$$

and four scalar constants, $C_{\bar{I}}$, $C_{\bar{G}}$, C_I, and C_G, such that (1) given $\{\bar{C}_i^1\}_{i=0}^{\infty}$, $\{\bar{C}_i^2\}_{i=0}^{\infty}$, $C_{\bar{I}}$, $C_{\bar{G}}$, and (1.6), the law of motion for the price of imports, $I(t) = C^1(L)\varepsilon(t) + C_I$ and $G(t) = C^2(L)\varepsilon(t) + C_G$, maximize the representative firm's expected present value subject to the constraint that labor and energy markets clear at each point in time; and (2) the firm's choice of $\{C_i^1\}_{i=0}^{\infty}$, $\{C_i^2\}_{i=0}^{\infty}$, C_I, and C_G imply the aggregate laws of motion $\bar{I}(t) = \bar{C}^1(L)\varepsilon(t) + C_{\bar{I}}$ and $G(t) = \bar{C}^2(L)\varepsilon(t) + C_{\bar{G}}$ for all realizations of the $\{\varepsilon(t)\}$ process. The assumption of a one-firm economy implies that

$$
\bar{C}_J^1 = C_J^1 \quad \text{for all } J \quad \text{and} \quad C_{\bar{I}} = C_I, \quad \text{or} \quad \bar{I}(t) = I(t) \quad \text{for all } t
\tag{1.19}
$$

as well as

$$\bar{C}_J^2 = C_J^2 \quad \text{for all } J \quad \text{and} \quad C_{\bar{G}} = C_G, \quad \text{or} \quad \bar{G}(t) = G(t) \quad \text{for all } t$$
(1.20)

To compute the rational expectations equilibrium for $\bar{I}(t)$ and $\bar{G}(t)$, we substitute (1.19) and (1.20) into (1.13) and (1.14). Collecting terms, we obtain the vector expectational difference equation for aggregate energy use and inventories whose solution corresponds to the rational expectations competitive equilibrium for this economy.

$$H_1 E_t z(t+1) + H_0 z(t) + H_{-1} z(t-1) + H_{-2} z(t-2) = X(t) \quad (1.21)$$

where

$$z'(t) = [I(t), G(t+1)]$$
$$X'(t) = [F_0(1-B) + J(t) - BE_t J(t+1), E_t J(t+1) + F_0 + c_g]$$

$$H_1 = \begin{bmatrix} BF_1 & 0 \\ -BF_1 & B^2\varphi_1 \end{bmatrix}$$

$$H_0 = \begin{bmatrix} -hB - F_1(1+B) + BF_2 & B(hr + F_1) \\ B[hr + (F_1 - F_2)] & B(\varphi_0 + dg\psi_2 - F_1) \end{bmatrix}$$

$$H_{-1} = \begin{bmatrix} F_1 - F_2(1+B) & BF_2 - F_1 \\ BF_2 & B(\varphi_1 - F_2) \end{bmatrix} \quad H_{-2} = \begin{bmatrix} F_2 & -F_2 \\ 0 & 0 \end{bmatrix}$$

For notational convenience, we write

$$X(t) = A(L)\varepsilon(t) \tag{1.22}$$

where

$$A(L) = \left[D(L)\left(1 - \frac{B}{L}\right) + \frac{BD_0}{L} + F_0(1-B), \quad \frac{D(L)}{L} - \frac{D_0}{L} + F_0 + c_g \right]'$$

Notice that with the exception of the transversality conditions associated with the firm's maximization problem, (1.21) embodies the necessary conditions for a rational expectations competitive equilibrium.[4] Hence a solution of (1.21), if it exists, corresponds to the equilibrium laws of motion of the economy and will be of the form,

$$z(t) = \hat{C}(L)\varepsilon(t) + \hat{C}_1 \tag{1.23}$$

---

[4] This expectational difference equation has the initial conditions that $z(-1)$ and $z(-2)$ are given a priori and the condition that

$$E \sum_{0t=0}^{\infty} B^t z(t)' z(t) < \infty.$$

where

$$\hat{C}(L) = [\hat{C}^1(L), \hat{C}^2(L)]$$
$$\hat{C}_1 = (\hat{C}_I, \hat{C}_G)$$

Notice that when $F_2 = 0$, then $H_1 = BH'_{-1}$. It is shown in section III that (1.21) then corresponds to a Euler equation for a well-defined optimum problem. Given this fact, lemma 1 of Hansen and Sargent (1981) can be used to prove that a unique solution to (1.21) always exists. When $F_2 \neq 0$, the results in Blanchard and Kahn (1980) establish necessary and sufficient conditions for the existence of a unique solution to (1.21). There is no guarantee, however, that these conditions will be met for arbitrary values of the model's parameters.

II. THE SOCIAL PLANNER PROBLEM AND OPTIMALITY

In considering the issue of the desirability of government intervention in our model economy, we conduct our analysis within the paradigm of neoclassical welfare theory. Thus, rather than adopting an ad hoc government criterion function, we consider the issue of optimality from an essentially Paretian point of view. In particular, we consider the problem of a social planner who maximizes the expected discounted utility of the representative consumer in this economy.

The social planning problem consists of choosing a stochastic process for employment, energy consumption, and the stock of energy inventories that maximizes the representative consumer's expected utility (1.1) subject to the technology of the economy, as well as the law of motion for the price of energy; that is, the planner maximizes

$$E_0 \sum_{t=0}^{\infty} B^t \left[AQ(t) - RN(t) - \frac{V}{2} N^2(t) \right] \tag{2.1}$$

subject to

$$Y(t) = \left[aN(t) - \frac{b}{2} N^2(t) + dN(t)K(t) + eK(t) - \frac{f}{2} K^2(t) \right] \tag{2.2}$$

$$K(t) = gG(t) \tag{2.3}$$

$$P(t) = F_0 + F_1[G(t) + I(t) - I(t-1)]$$
$$+ F_2[G(t-1) + I(t-1) - I(t-2)] + D(L)\varepsilon(t) \tag{2.4}$$

and the government's budget constraint, (2.5), which states that net consumption at time t, $Q(t)$, is equal to output minus net investments and the costs of adjusting capital, inventories, and energy. Given that trade is balanced, consumption at time t is therefore given by

$$Q(t) = \left\{ Y(t) - [K(t+1) - \delta K(t)] - \frac{c}{2}[K(t) - K(t-1)]^2 \right.$$
$$\left. - \frac{h}{2}[rG(t) - I(t-1)]^2 - P(t)[G(t) + I(t) - I(t-1)] \right\}$$

(2.5)

Substituting (2.2), (2.3), (2.4), and (2.5) into (2.1), the problem becomes to maximize

$$E_0 \sum_{t=0}^{\infty} B^t \left(A \left\{ aN(t) - \frac{b}{2}N^2(t) + dgG(t)N(t) + egG(t) - \frac{fg^2}{2}G^2(t) \right. \right.$$

$$-g[G(t+1) - \delta G(t)] - \frac{cg^2}{2}[G(t) - G(t-1)]^2$$

$$-\frac{h}{2}[rG(t) - I(t-1)] - F_1[G_t + I_t - I_{t-1}]^2$$

$$-F_2[G(t) + I(t) - I(t-1)][G(t-1) + I(t-1) - I(t-2)]$$

$$\left. -[G(t) + I(t) - I(t-1)][J(t) + F_0] \right\}$$

$$\left. -RN(t) - \frac{V}{2}N^2(t) \right)$$

(2.6)

subject to $I(-1)$, $G(0)$, and $G(-1)$ given. The first-order necessary conditions for this problem can be written as

$$N(t) = \psi_1 + \psi_2 G(t), \qquad \psi_1 = \frac{Aa - R}{V + Ab}, \qquad \psi_2 = \frac{dgA}{V + Ab}$$

(2.7)

$$dgE_tN(t+1) + B(cg^2 - F_2)E_tG(t+2)$$
$$- \left\{ g^2[B(1+c) + hr^2 + f] + 2F_1 \right\}G(t+1) + (cg^2 - F_2)G(t)$$
$$- BF_2E_tI(t+2) - (2F_1 - BF_2)E_tI(t+1)$$
$$+ (hr + 2F_1 - F_2)I(t) + F_2I(t-1) = D(L)E_tJ(t+1) + F_0 + cg$$

(2.8)

$$B^2F_2E_tG(t+2) + B(hr + 2F_1 - F_2) + (BF_2 - 2F_1)G(t) - F_2G(t-1)$$
$$+ B^2F_2E_tI(t+2) + B[2F_1 - F_2(1+B)]E_tI(t+1)$$
$$- [hB + 2(1+B)F_1 - 2BF_2)]I(t) + [2F_1 - (1+B)F_2]I(t-1)$$
$$+ F_2I(t-2) = J(t) - BE_tJ(t+1) + F_0(1-B)$$

(2.9)

as well as the relevant transversality conditions.

By substituting (2.7) into (2.8) and defining $z'(t) = [I(t), G(t+1)]$, the resulting system of first-order conditions may be written as

$$G_2 E_t z(t+2) + G_1 E_t z(t+1) + G_0 z(t) + G_{-1} z(t-1)$$
$$+ G_{-2} z(t-2) = X(t) \tag{2.10}$$

where

$$X'(t) = \left[F_0(1-B) + J(t) - BE_t J(t+1), \; E_t J(t+1) + F_0 + c_g \right]$$

$$G_2 = \begin{bmatrix} B^2 F_2 & 0 \\ -B^2 F_2 & 0 \end{bmatrix} \qquad G_{-2} = \frac{1}{B^2} G_2'$$

$$G_1 = \begin{bmatrix} B[2F_1 - F_2(1+B)] & B^2 F_2 \\ -B(2F_1 - BF_2) & B^2(cg^2 - F_2) \end{bmatrix} \qquad G_{-1} = \frac{1}{B} G_1'$$

$$G_0 = \begin{bmatrix} -[hB + 2(1+B)F_1 - 2BF_2] & B(hr + 2F_1 - F_2) \\ B(hr + 2F_1 - F_2) & B(\varphi_1 - 2F_1 + dg\psi_2) \end{bmatrix}$$

Hence solving (2.10) is equivalent to solving the social planning problem. Equation (2.10) is a system of Euler equations corresponding to a well-defined linear quadratic optimization problem. Thus one can use the results in Hansen and Sargent (1981) to establish that a unique solution to (2.10) always exists.

Given these results, we now consider the optimality of the competitive equilibrium. This is done by comparing the vector expectational difference equations (1.21) and (2.10) whose solutions correspond to the competitive equilibrium and socially optimal laws of motion for $z(t)$ respectively.

The characteristic polynomial corresponding to (1.21) is

$$H(Z) = H_1 Z^{-1} + H_0 + H_1 Z + H_{-2} Z^2 \tag{2.11}$$

where H_1 has full rank and the second row of H_{-2} contains all zeros. The characteristic polynomial corresponding to (2.10) is

$$G(Z) = G_2 Z^{-2} + G_1 Z^{-1} + G_0 + \left(\frac{G_1'}{B} \right) Z + \left(\frac{G_2'}{B^2} \right) Z^2 \tag{2.12}$$

where G_1 has full rank and the first column of G_2 contains all zeros. Notice that $G(Z)$ can be written as

$$G(Z) = H(Z) + [F_1 + BF_2 Z^{-1}] \begin{bmatrix} (BZ^{-1} - 1)(1-Z) & (B-Z) \\ -B(Z^{-1} - 1) & -B \end{bmatrix} \tag{2.13}$$

Consider the class of covariance stationary processes $X(t)$ given by (1.22). We say that the competitive equilibrium is Pareto optimal, if and only if, for an arbitrary stochastic process in that class, the competitive equilibrium laws of motion for $z(t)$ are identical to the laws of motion of $z(t)$ corresponding to the solution of the social planning problem. Comparing (1.21) and (2.10), we see that, in general, the competitive equilibrium will not be optimal. This result is formalized in the following proposition:

PROPOSITION I. *The rational expectations competitive equilibrium for the model under consideration is Pareto optimal if and only if $F_1 = F_2 = 0$.*

Proof

Let

$$E(Z) = \begin{bmatrix} -hB & Bhr \\ Bhr & B^2\varphi_1 Z^{-1} + B\bar{\varphi} + B\varphi_1 Z \end{bmatrix}$$

$$\bar{\varphi} = \varphi_0 + dg\psi_2$$

Then

$$H(Z) = E(Z) + (F_1 + F_2 Z)\begin{bmatrix} (BZ^{-1} - 1)(1 - Z) & (B - Z) \\ -B(Z^{-1} - 1) & -B \end{bmatrix}$$

and

$$G(Z) = E(Z) + \left(2F_1 + F_2 Z + BF_2 Z^{-1}\right)$$

$$\times \begin{bmatrix} (BZ^{-1} - 1)(1 - Z) & (B - Z) \\ -B(Z^{-1} - 1) & -B \end{bmatrix}$$

If $F_1 = F_2 = 0$, then $H(Z) = G(Z)$, so that equations (1.21) and (2.10) and their solutions are identically equal.

To establish the other portion of the proposition, we begin by assuming that $F_2 = 0$. Notice that $\det H(Z) = \det E(Z) + F_1\lambda(Z)$ and $\det G(Z) = \det E(Z) + 2F_1\lambda(Z)$, where $\lambda(Z) = hB^2 + B^2hr(Z^{-1} - 1) - Bhr(B - Z) + (B^2\varphi_1 Z^{-1} + B\bar{\varphi} + B\varphi_1 Z)(BZ^{-1} - 1)(1 - Z)$. It is sufficient to show that if $\bar{Z}$ is a root of $\det H(Z) = 0$, then it cannot be a root of $\det G(Z) = 0$. We proceed by contradiction. Suppose that $F_1 \neq 0$ and $\det H(\bar{Z}) = \det G(\bar{Z}) = 0$. Then it must be true that $\det E(\bar{Z}) = \lambda(\bar{Z}) = 0$.

This implies that $(B^2\varphi_1\overline{Z}^{-1} + B\overline{\varphi} + B\varphi_1\overline{Z}) = -Bhr^2$. Thus,

$$\lambda(\overline{Z}) = hB^2 + hB^2r(\overline{Z}^{-1} - 1) - hBr(B - \overline{Z})$$
$$- hBr^2(B\overline{Z}^{-1} - 1)(1 - \overline{Z}) = 0$$

which may be written as

$$-(1 - r)(B\overline{Z}^{-1} - 1)(1 - \overline{Z}) = -\frac{B}{r} - (1 - B)$$

Notice that $(BZ^{-1} - 1)(1 - Z)$ attains its minimum value of $-(1 - \sqrt{B})^2$ at $\overline{Z} = \sqrt{B}$. But $(1 - r)(1 - \sqrt{B})^2 < B/r + (1 - B)$ so that we have a contradiction because this implies that $-(1 - r)(BZ^{-1} - 1)(1 - Z) > (-B/r) - (1 - B)$ for all Z. Next consider the case of $F_2 \neq 0$. As before, it is sufficient to show that there exists a root $\overline{Z}$ of $\det H(Z) = 0$ that is not a root of $\det G(Z) = 0$. Suppose that there exists a $Z = \overline{Z}$ such that $\det H(\overline{Z}) = \det G(\overline{Z}) = 0$. This implies that $\det E(\overline{Z}) + (F_1 + F_2\overline{Z})\lambda(\overline{Z}) = 0$ and $\det E(\overline{Z}) + (2F_1 + F_2\overline{Z} + BF_2\overline{Z}^{-1})\lambda(\overline{Z}) = 0$. Thus it must be true that $(F_1 + F_2\overline{Z})\lambda(\overline{Z}) = (2F_1 + F_2\overline{Z} + BF_2\overline{Z}^{-1})\lambda(\overline{Z})$. This implies that

(i) $\quad \lambda(\overline{Z}) = 0$

or

(ii) $\quad \lambda(\overline{Z}) \neq 0 \quad$ and $\quad \overline{Z} = -\dfrac{BF_2}{F_1} \quad$ so that

$$(F_1 + F_2\overline{Z}) = (2F_1 + F_2\overline{Z} + BF_2\overline{Z}^{-1}) = \frac{(F_1^2 - BF_2^2)}{F_1}$$

Case (i) implies that $\det E(\overline{Z}) = \lambda(\overline{Z})$, which leads to a contradiction. Even if $\overline{Z} = BF_2/F_1$ this implies that at most one of the six roots of $\det G(Z) = 0$ and the five roots of $\det H(Z) = 0$ are the same. By appropriately restricting the parameters of the model it is possible to rule out even this case, although this is not necessary in terms of establishing the proposition. This result is very much in the spirit of the static optimal tariff literature. As in those discussions, the fundamental reason for the general nonoptimality of the competitive equilibrium is that competitive agents view the price process and therefore, aggregate imports, as being beyond their influence and or control. Because of this the latent ability of the country as a whole to influence the price process goes unexploited. On the other hand, the planner, while taking the price function as given, does exploit the country's ability to influence the first and second moments of the equilibrium distribution of energy prices.

This interpretation of the nonoptimality of the competitive equilibrium naturally leads to optimal tariff considerations. We now turn our attention to such issues in order to understand more fully the static and intertemporal inefficiencies associated with noninterventionist competitive equilibria, as well as to examine the nature of optimal policy in such environments.

III. OPTIMAL POLICY CONSIDERATIONS

By optimal policy, we mean a (possibly) state-dependent intervention on the part of the government such that the resulting rational expectations competitive equilibrium is identical to the unique solution of the social planning problem considered in section II. In this we differ from Kydland and Prescott (1977), who define a policy as being optimal relative to a given, arbitrary set of policy instruments. Defined in the latter way, optimal policy will, in general, be time inconsistent. In our analysis, however, we search over sets of instruments, so that the optimal policy reproduces, in a decentralized way, the unique time-consistent solution of the social planning problem.

In order to understand more fully the nature of the nonoptimality of the competitive equilibrium, we begin by considering the case in which only contemporaneous imports affect energy prices. Thus with $F_2 = 0$, the law of motion for energy prices is given by

$$P(t) = F_0 + F_1 \overline{M}(t) + D(L)\varepsilon(t)$$

Notice that in this case the rational expectations competitive equilibrium does solve a well-defined maximization problem. It is the incorrect one, however, from a social point of view. In particular, if in the social planning problem we replace

$$-F_1[G(t) + I(t) - I(t-1)]^2 \quad \text{by} \quad \frac{-F_1}{2}[G(t) + I(t) - I(t-1)]^2$$

the resulting Euler equation will be identical to (1.21), the vector expectational difference equation whose solution completely characterizes the competitive equilibrium for this economy. Thus, when $F_2 = 0$, the fundamental inefficiency associated with the competitive equilibrium is that private agents ignore the contemporaneous effect of their imports on current energy prices. In contrast, the planner realizes that the marginal cost of an additional unit of imports is greater than the existing price.

It is straightforward to show that the optimal policy under these circumstances consists of an optimal tariff and rebate system. Denote by $\hat{P}(t)$ the internal price of energy, and denote the international price by $P(t)$. Then imposing an internal price process of

$$\hat{P}(t) = 2P(t) - F_0 - J(t) = P(t) + F_1\overline{M}(t) \tag{3.1}$$

where

$$F_0 + J(t) = P(t) - F_1\overline{M}(t) \tag{3.2}$$

is rebated to firms, results in a socially optimal equilibrium. To prove this, simply substitute $\hat{P}(t)$ in place of $P(t)$ in our derivation of (1.21), the vector expectation difference equation whose solution yields the competitive equilibrium of section I. The resulting system will match up exactly with the Euler equation associated with the social planning problem. As such, the competitive equilibrium under a 100 percent ad valorem tariff and appropriate rebates will result in a Pareto optimal allocation.

Notice that the unconditional value of the rebates, $F_0 + J(t)$, will be equal to F_0, while the unconditional expected value of the internal price will be twice the value of the unconditional expected value of the world price of oil minus F_0. As (3.1) indicates, however, a simple 100 percent tariff will not support a Pareto optimal equilibrium. Put somewhat differently, under the optimal policy, $\hat{P}(t)$ deviates from $P(t)$ by a specific tariff that is proportional to imports, $F_1\overline{M}(t)$. Thus the government must distribute the proceeds from the tariff to consumers in an appropriate way. Moreover these rebates are state specific in that they depend on the current and lagged values of shocks to energy prices.

Now consider the case in which $F_2 \neq 0$, so that current imports have both a contemporaneous and an intertemporal effect on energy prices. This intertemporal impact of imports on prices accounts for the difference in the basic lag structures of equations (1.21) and (2.10). The absence of a term involving $E_t z(t + 2)$ in equation (1.21) reflects the fact that competitive firms ignore not only the effect of current imports on the current price of oil ($F_1 \neq 0$) but also the effect of these imports on future energy prices ($F_2 \neq 0$).

Recall that in the case where $F_2 = 0$, a tariff plus tax policy that depends only on aggregate-state variables is sufficient to support an optimal equilibrium. With $F_2 \neq 0$, however, we must expand the list of instruments to include a state-dependent, firm-specific import tax. More specifically, imagine that the government taxes imports at the firm-specific rate $\tau(t)$. $\tau(t)$ is set equal to $F_2 M(t - 1)$, where $M(t - 1)$ is the quantity of the firm's imports at time $t-1$. Thus the representative firm's time t taxes are given by

$$\tau(t)M(t) = F_2 M(t-1)M(t) \tag{3.3}$$

In addition, the government sets the domestic price process of oil equal to

$$\hat{P}(t) = 2P(t) - F_0 - J(t) - 2F_2\overline{M}(t-1) = F_0 + 2F_1\overline{M}(t) + J(t) \tag{3.4}$$

Notice that (3.4) can be interpreted as a 100 percent tariff combined with appropriate proportional rebates that depend on lagged aggregate imports and on current and lagged energy price shocks. Because $P(t)$ depends only on economywide variables, private agents continue to view it parametrically. Firms, however, regard the tax rate $\tau(t)$, as opposed to the tax schedule, as being controllable, because $\tau(t)$ depends on a firm-specific control variable, $M(t-1)$. Finally, regardless of whether F_2 is equal to zero, the government must impose lump-sum taxes of $F_1\overline{M}_t^2$ to insure that its budget constraint is met at each time period.

Given the above tax and tariff policy, the competitive equilibrium will reproduce the solution to the social planning problem. To see this, consider the problem of the representative firm.

Maximize

$$V_0 = E_0 \sum_{t=0}^{\infty} B^t \left\{ aN(t) - \frac{b}{2}N^2(t) + dgN(t)G(t) + egG(t) - f\frac{g^2}{2}G^2(t) \right.$$

$$- g[G(t+1) - \delta G(t)] - \frac{cg^2}{2}[G(t) - G(t-1)]^2$$

$$- \frac{h}{2}[rG(t) - I(t-1)]^2 - \hat{P}(t)[G(t) + I(t) - I(t-1)]$$

$$\left. - \tau(t)[G(t) + I(t) - I(t-1)] - W(t)N(t) \right\} \tag{3.5}$$

subject to (3.3), (3.4), $I(-1)$, $G(0)$, and $G(-1)$ given. The first-order necessary conditions for this problem consist of a set of Euler equations and associated transversality conditions. By equating the demand for and the supply of labor and substituting into the Euler equations for $I(t)$ and

$G(t + 1)$, we obtain

$$B(cg^2 - F_2)E_tG(t+2) + (\psi_0 + dg\psi_2)G(t+1) + (cg^2 - F_2)G(t)$$
$$- BF_2E_tI(t+2) + BF_2E_tI(t+1) + (hr - F_2)I(t) + F_2I(t-1)$$
$$= E_t\hat{P}(t+1) + Cg \tag{3.6}$$

$$B^2F_2E_tG(t+2) + B(hr - F_2)G(t+1) + BF_2G(t) - F_2G(t-1)$$
$$+ B^2F_2E_tI(t+2) - BF_2(1+B)E_tI(t+1) - (hB - 2BF_2)I(t)$$
$$- (1+B)F_2I(t-1) + F_2I(t-1) = \hat{P}(t) - BE_t\hat{P}(t+1) \tag{3.7}$$

As in section I, we require, in a rational expectations equilibrium with the number of firms normalized to one, that $\overline{M}(t) = M(t)$ for all t. Hence upon substitution of (3.3) into (3.6) and (3.7), we obtain the following vector expectational difference equation whose solution corresponds to the equilibrium laws of motion of $I(t)$ and $G(t + 1)$ under the policy regime under consideration:

$$R_2E_tz(t+2) + R_1E_tz(t+1) + R_0z(t)$$
$$+ R_{-1}z(t-1) + R_{-2}z(t-2) = X(t) \tag{3.8}$$

where

$$z(t)' = [I(t), G(t+1)]$$
$$X'(t) = [F_0(1 - B) + J(t) - BE_tJ(t+1), J(t+1) + F_0 + Cg]$$

$$R_2 = \begin{bmatrix} B^2F_2 & 0 \\ -B^2F_2 & 0 \end{bmatrix} \qquad R_{-2} = \frac{1}{B^2}R_2'$$

$$R_1 = \begin{bmatrix} B[2F_1 - F_2(1+B)] & B^2F_2 \\ -B[2F_1 - BF_2] & B^2[cg^2 - F_2] \end{bmatrix} \qquad R_{-1} = \frac{1}{B}R_1'$$

$$R_0 = \begin{bmatrix} -[hB + 2(1+B)F_1 - 2BF_2] & B[hr + 2F_1 - F_2] \\ B[hr + 2F_1 - F_2] & B[\varphi_0 - 2F_1 + dg\psi_2] \end{bmatrix}$$

Equation (3.8) is identically equal to equation (2.10), however. Thus the tariff and tax policy summarized by equations (3.3) and (3.4) succeeds in supporting an equilibrium allocation that is identical to that produced by the solution to the social planning problem.

In concluding this section, some comments are in order regarding the robustness of the optimal policies that have been derived. It is straight-

forward to verify that including costs of adjustment regarding leisure in
the utility function of the representative consumer, while considerably
enriching the dynamics of the system, would not influence the optimal
tariff rules. On the other hand, the optimal tariff and tax system is not
invariant to the number of lagged values of imports that enter the law of
motion of energy prices. To see this, notice that if prices had been
parameterized as obeying

$$P(t) = F_0 + \sum_{J=1}^{q} F_J \overline{M}(t - J + 1) + D(L)\varepsilon(t)$$

then the analogues to equation (1.21) would be vector expectational
difference equations of the general form

$$H_1 E_t z(t+1) + H_0 z(t) + H_{-1} z(t-1)$$
$$+ H_{-2} z(t-2) + \cdots + H_{-q} z(t-q) = X(t) \tag{3.9}$$

while the analogues to equation (2.10) would be of the form

$$\sum_{J=0}^{q} B^J G_J' E_t z(t+J) + \sum_{J=1}^{q} G_J z(t-q) = X(t) \tag{3.10}$$

It is immediately evident that the optimal tax and tariff will be functions
of q. It is also true, however, that the set of instruments required to
support an optimal equilibrium does not depend on the value of q, given
that $q \geq 1$.

Finally, it should be noted that we have abstracted from the possibility
of retaliatory tariffs on the part of oil-supplying countries. This is, in a
sense, not inconsistent with our specification of an ad hoc supply
function for oil. One way of modeling such tariffs would be to make the
supply function an explicit function of the tariffs imposed by oil-import-
ing countries. To the extent that this is true, our assumption that the
social planner may view the supply function of oil as invariant to the
planner's actions will be incorrect. A complete analysis of this possibility
is clearly beyond the scope of this chapter.

IV. CLOSED FORM SOLUTIONS

Closed form solutions for the above model are of interest for two
reasons. First, such solutions greatly facilitate econometric applications
of the model aimed at identifying the structural parameters of prefer-

ences and technology, as well as in testing the underlying assumptions of the theory. Secondly, such solutions greatly aid in the analysis of the comparative dynamics of the system, that is, comparing the equilibrium laws of motion for the various endogenous variables of the model, such as oil imports, energy prices, capital, and employment, corresponding to different specifications of the oil supply equation and to different values of the underlying structural parameters of taste and technology in the economy.

Several solution methods exist for obtaining closed form solutions for models of the kind developed in this chapter. Recall from section III that, in general, the rational expectations competitive equilibrium corresponds to the solution of the vector expectational difference equation,

$$H_1 E_t z(t+1) + H_0 z(t) + H_{-1} z(t-1) + \cdots + H_{-q} z(t-q) = X(t)$$

$$(4.1)$$

Similarly, the Pareto optimal laws of motion for $I(t)$ and $\overset{\backprime}{G}(t+1)$ are given by the solution to

$$\sum_{J=0}^{q} B^J G_J' E_t z(t+J) + \sum_{J=1}^{q} G_J z(t-J) = X(t) \qquad (4.2)$$

In both cases, energy prices are given by

$$P(t) = F_0 + \sum_{J=1}^{q} F_J \overline{M}(t-J+1) + D(L)\varepsilon(t) \qquad (4.3)$$

In order to discuss the solution to both (4.1) and (4.2) simultaneously, we consider the general vector expectational difference equation,

$$E_t \left[\sum_{J=0}^{n} K_J z(t+J) + \sum_{J=1}^{q} R_J z(t-J) \right] = X(t) \qquad (4.4)$$

where

$$n \geq 1, \qquad \sum_{J=0}^{n} K_J L^{-J} = K(L^{-1}), \quad \text{and} \quad \sum_{J=1}^{q} R_J L^J = R(L)$$

The reader may verify that $X(t)$ does not depend on q and is the same in both (4.1) and (4.2). To facilitate our exposition, we set all constants in the model to zero. Thus, the solutions discussed here should be thought of as deviations from steady-state values. Under this procedure, the linearly indeterministic covariance stationary stochastic process $X(t)$ is given by

$$X'(t) = [J(t) - BE_tJ(t+1), E_tJ(t+1)]$$

$$= \left[D_0\varepsilon(t) + \sum_{J=1}^{\infty} (D_{J+1} - D_J)\varepsilon(t-J), \sum_{J=1}^{\infty} D_J\varepsilon(t-J) \right]$$

For the sake of convenience, we rewrite the above expression for $X(t)$ as

$$X(t) = A(L)\varepsilon(t) \tag{4.5}$$

where

$$A(L) = \begin{bmatrix} D_0 + \sum_{J=1}^{\infty} (D_{J+1} - D_J)L^J \\ \sum_{J=1}^{\infty} D_J L^J \end{bmatrix}$$

A solution for equation (4.4) is a one-sided moving average representation for $z'(t) = [I(t), G(t+1)]$; that is,

$$z(t) = \sum_{J=0}^{\infty} C_J\varepsilon(t-J) \equiv C(L)\varepsilon(t) \tag{4.6}$$

which must hold for any realization of $\varepsilon(t)$ and where $z(t)$ is of mean exponential order less than $1/\sqrt{B}$. Equation (4.6) may also be written as

$$I(t) = C^1(L)\varepsilon(t)$$

and

$$G(t+1) = C^2(L)\varepsilon(t)$$

Then we can solve for real wages and employment as moving averages of the oil price shocks; that is,

$$N(t) = \frac{dgA}{V + Ab} C^2(L)\varepsilon(t-1)$$

and

$$W(t) = \frac{Vdg}{V + Ab} C^2(L)\varepsilon(t-1)$$

Observe that whether real wages and employment depend positively or negatively upon shocks to the price of energy depends solely upon the sign of d, which summarizes whether labor and capital (and therefore energy) are complements or substitutes in production.

The conditions for the existence and uniqueness of such a solution are given in Blanchard and Kahn (1980). Here, we assume that a unique solution exists.

Whiteman (1983) provides an algorithm for finding the sequences of matrices, $\{C_J\}_{J=0}^{\infty}$, for given values of $\{K_J\}_{J=0}^{\infty}$, $\{R_J\}_{J=1}^{q}$ and $\{A_J\}_{J=0}^{\infty}$.[5] The model considered in this chapter provides a mapping from the underlying structural parameters of the economy and the law of motion of energy prices. Thus the theory taken as a whole provides us with an explicit mapping from the specification of the forcing variables and the structural, policy-invariant parameters, to the market-determined laws of motion of the endogenous variables of the model in the form of (4.6). In the case in which $q = n$ (social planner problems and optimal competitive equilibria) or when $q = 1$, the methods proposed by Hansen and Sargent (1980) are equivalent.

To proceed with estimation of the model, we must introduce additional variables that are observable to economic agents but unobservable to the econometrician. Such a procedure is necessary in order to avoid the implication that exact relationships exist between the variables of the model that are observed by the econometrician. A general discussion of error terms in linear rational expectations models is contained in Hansen and Sargent (1980).

V. EXTENSIONS AND MARKET IMPERFECTIONS

In addition to suggesting a rationale for government intervention in the form of optimal dynamic tariffs, the results in section III imply that in the absence of various sorts of market imperfections, a government-run strategic petroleum reserve cannot be justified. Furthermore, the results of Lucas and Prescott (1971), as well as much of the existing literature on dynamic stochastic rational expectations models, strongly suggest that the qualitative welfare conclusions of proposition I (section II) will be robust to more complicated parameterizations of consumer preferences, production technology, and additional costs of adjustment in the system. Put somewhat differently, in the absence of classical sorts of externalities

---

[5] In chapter 5, Hansen, Epple, and Roberds provide a procedure for factoring nonsymmetric polynomials that can be extended in a straightforward manner to solve equations of the form given by (4.4).

in consumption and production, the existence of strong forms of risk aversion, richer possibilities for capital/oil substitution, real frictions in production, or all three, will not justify government intervention (excluding tariff arguments). Here we argue that, to the extent that market imperfections exist, a strategic petroleum reserve program would, at best, correspond to a second-best solution.

The most straightforward of the arguments in favor of strategic petroleum reserves is that the government enjoys a systematic cost advantage in storing oil. Although such a cost advantage could be analyzed in the context of the model discussed above, the government may not in fact enjoy such an advantage. Wright and Williams (1982), for example, suggest that government reserves are not advantageous because of differences between the physical and net costs of storage. They do agree that the bulk of privately stored oil is placed in steel tanks and that the physical costs associated with this mode of storage exceed the costs of storage in salt domes such as those that the current strategic petroleum reserve program uses in Louisiana and Texas. Private storage is more conveniently located, however, and thus allows firms more immediate access to inventories of oil. Wright and Williams argue that the value of this accessibility offsets the potential physical advantages of government storage. These sorts of considerations could be incorporated into the model discussed in section I, but it is difficult to imagine that any physical cost advantage on the part of the government would be so large as to justify the existing strategic petroleum reserve program. Furthermore, to the extent that such cost advantages exist today, they presumably existed prior to 1973. Yet the demand for a strategic petroleum reserve is essentially a post-1973 phenomenon (which has arisen in response to oil price shocks and not to relative cost advantages in storing the oil). We conclude that if a basic rationale for intervention exists, it lies elsewhere.

Others have argued that it is possible to justify strategic petroleum reserves because of the alleged existence of a government policy of imposing a ceiling on the price of energy. Such compensating government policies are essentially second best, however, in the sense that they may be dominated by simply removing artificial constraints on internal energy prices or profits, or both.

A case might be made for a government-run strategic petroleum reserve program, but its justification probably has to do with strategic game theoretic considerations of the type that we have abstracted from in this chapter but that could be analyzed within the present framework. Throughout our analysis, we have assumed that the energy price process is of the general form given by

$$P(t) = F_0 + F(L)\overline{M}(t) + J(t)$$

This was not derived as the solution to a well-defined optimization problem that energy producers solve. We also did not consider noneconomic, strategic motives as being one of the sources of shocks to the price of energy. One can easily imagine that the probability distribution of such shocks might be parameterized by the domestic aggregate stock of energy inventories, $\bar{I}(t)$. If so, as in the optimal tariff case, competitive agents will view $\bar{I}(t)$ as being noncontrollable from their individual points of view. As a result, the aggregate level of inventories in a nonintervention competitive equilibrium will be smaller than the socially desirable level. This can be easily seen in the context of our model by assuming, for example, that

$$P(t) = F_0 + F(L)\overline{M}(t) + J(t) - \tilde{F}\bar{I}(t) \tag{5.1}$$

Under such a representation of the price process, a role may exist for a dynamic government-run strategic petroleum reserve or inventory subsidy program, or both. Both the qualitative and quantitative characteristics of such a policy will generally be quite sensitive to the precise way in which aggregate inventory stocks influence the price process.

The derivation of such a model of the supply side of the energy market and the resulting optimal tariff-strategic petroleum reserve-inventory subsidy policy, in which the possibility of countervailing tariffs is taken into account, is clearly beyond the scope of this analysis. Future research regarding the potential welfare-enhancing role of a government-run strategic petroleum reserve should be directed toward such game theoretic considerations.

VI. CONCLUSION

This investigation of the welfare-enhancing role of government interventions in decentralized economies that face uncertainty regarding the price of energy began with a stochastic general equilibrium model of an economy that combines imported energy with domestic labor and capital to produce a single consumption good. Optimal allocations are defined as those that maximize the utility of the representative consumer subject to the relevant physical constraints on production and the law of motion of energy prices. The formal analysis implies that the rational expectations competitive equilibrium is optimal if and only if the conditional elasticity of energy prices with respect to domestic imports is equal to infinity. Thus, in general, government interventions aimed at exploiting the country's influence over the endogenous distribution of energy prices may be beneficial in some cases. When prices depend only on contemporaneous imports, an optimal tariff coupled with state-contingent rebates is sufficient to support an optimal equilibrium. When energy prices depend upon lagged imports, however, those policy instruments must be supplemented by an import tax in which firm-specific tax rates depend in a fixed way upon lagged imports. By searching over alternative sets of policy instruments, we are able to support a decentralized equilibrium that reproduces the time-consistent optimal solution of the social planning problem.

These results suggest that, in general, the optimality of nonintervention equilibria and the design of potentially welfare-improving government interventions depend critically on the nature of the state variables that energy prices feed back upon. The dependence of energy prices on noncontrollable stochastic variables does not, in and of itself, lead to a welfare-enhancing role for government interventions. Further research aimed at deriving this price process from an optimizing model of supply-side behavior would clearly be fruitful.

REFERENCES

Aiyagari, S. R., Z. Eckstein, and M. Eichenbaum. 1980. "Rational Expectations, Inventories, and Price Fluctuations." Discussion paper no. 363 (New Haven, Conn., Yale University Economic Growth Center).

Auerbach, A., and J. Green. 1981. "Components of Manufacturing Industries: A Structural Model of Production Processes." Draft (Cambridge, Mass., Harvard University, Department of Economics).

Blanchard, Oliver J., and C. M. Kahn. 1980. "The Solution of Linear Difference Models Under Rational Expectations," *Econometrica* vol. 48, pp. 1305–1311.

Eckstein, Z. 1981. "Rational Expectations Modelling of Agricultural Supply." Discussion paper no. 381 (New Haven, Conn., Yale University, Economic Growth Center).

Eichenbaum, M. 1983. "A Rational Expectations Equilibrium Model of the Cyclical Behavior of Inventories of Finished Goods and Employment," *Journal of Monetary Economics* vol. 12, no. 2, pp. 259–278.

Epple, D., L. P. Hansen, and W. Roberds. 1983. "Linear Quadratic Games of Resource Depletion. Draft (Pittsburgh, Pa., Carnegie-Mellon University).

Hansen, L. P., and T. J. Sargent. 1980. "Formulating and Estimating Dynamic Linear Rational Expectations Models," *Journal of Economic Dynamics and Control* vol. 2, no. 1, pp. 7–46.

_____. 1981. "Linear Rational Expectations Models for Dynamically Interrelated Variables," in R. E. Lucas, Jr., and T. J. Sargent, eds., *Rational Expectations and Econometric Practice* (Minneapolis, Minn., University of Minnesota Press).

Kydland, F. E., and E. C. Prescott. 1977. "Rules Rather Than Discretion: The Inconsistency of Optimal Plans," *Journal of Political Economy* vol. 85, no. 3, pp. 473–493.

Lucas, R. E., Jr. 1976. "Econometric Policy Evaluation: A Critique," in K. Brunner and A. H. Meltzer, eds., *The Phillips Curve and Labor Markets*, *Carnegie-Rochester Conference on Public Policy 1*. (Amsterdam, North-Holland).

——, and E. C. Prescott. 1971. "Investment Under Uncertainty," *Econometrica* vol. 39, no. 51, pp. 659–681.

——, and T. J. Sargent. 1981. "Introduction," in R. E. Lucas and T. J. Sargent, eds., *Rational Expectations and Econometric Practice* (Minneapolis, Minn., University of Minnesota Press).

Nichols, A. L., and R. J. Zeckhauser. 1977. "Stockpiling Strategies and Cartel Prices," *Bell Journal of Economics* vol. 8, no. 1, pp. 66–96.

Nordhaus, W. D. 1974. "The 1974 Report of the President's Council of Economic Advisors: Energy in the Economic Report," *American Economic Review* vol. 64, no. 4, pp. 558–567.

Sargent, T. J. 1981. "Interpreting Economic Time Series," *Journal of Political Economy* vol. 89, no. 2, pp. 213–248.

——. 1979. *Macroeconomic Theory* (New York, Academic Press).

Teisberg, T. J. 1981. "A Dynamic Programming Model of the U.S. Strategic Petroleum Reserves," *Bell Journal of Economics* vol. 12, no. 2, pp. 526–546.

Tolley, G. S., and J. D. Wilman. 1977. "The Foreign Dependence Question," *Journal of Political Economy* vol. 85, pp. 323–347.

Whiteman, Charles, 1983. *Linear Rational Expectations Models: A Users Guide* (Minneapolis, Minn., University of Minnesota Press).

Wright, B. D., and J. C. Williams. 1982. "The Role of Public and Private Storage in Managing Oil Import Disruptions," *Bell Journal of Economics* vol. 13, no. 2, pp. 341–353.

4

Inventories and Quantity-Constrained Equilibria in Regulated Markets: The U.S. Petroleum Industry, 1947–1972

Zvi Eckstein and Martin S. Eichenbaum

The U.S. petroleum industry has been heavily regulated during much of its history. Prior to 1973, producers of crude petroleum operated under a variety of quantity constraints imposed and administered by state and federal agencies. Although price control per se was excluded as an official policy of the Interstate Oil Compact Commission, many observers such as Epple (1975) and deChazeau and Kahn (1959) have claimed that those quantity constraints that were in effect from 1947 to 1973 did, in fact, set domestic crude petroleum prices.

This might be of little relevance for present policy debates were it not for the fact that inferences regarding the price elasticity of production rely heavily on data from that period. The existence of market interventions, such as prorationing or sales controls, obscures producer responses to the various market incentives that would obtain under deregulated environments. Because of this, the data from a regulated period are of little use in assessing the behavior of a given industry under different regimes, unless the analyst explicitly identifies the effects of regulation and distinguishes them from the effects of market incentives, per se.

Zvi Eckstein is Assistant Professor of Economics, Yale University and Tel Aviv University. Martin S. Eichenbaum is Assistant Professor of Economics, Carnegie-Mellon University.

These points are, of course, related to the more general contention that the ability of nonstructural models to imitate the behavior of data over some sample period has little to do with the models' ability to evaluate the effects of policy regime changes.[1] The ability to make such conditional forecasts requires a structural model that takes into account the fact that the behavior of economic agents will change when their constraints change. Clearly the existence of a particular type of regulatory regime qualifies as a widely known and well-understood policy rule that constrains the behavior of energy producers and consumers.

Here we argue, by way of example, that certain stylized facts regarding the relationship between prices and output in the U.S. petroleum industry during the period 1947 to 1972 can be interpreted as a direct consequence of the regulatory policies that were in effect and were not necessarily due to the fundamental nature of the industry's supply parameters. We support this contention by developing a dynamic, structural model of an industry that produces and sells a storable good subject to regulatory constraints. We first derive and analyze the rational expectations noninterventionist competitive equilibrium. This equilibrium is then contrasted with the equilibrium when the industry operates under production and hypothetical sales control regimes that are designed to support arbitrary target prices. As it turns out, both of these regulatory regimes are successful in the sense that market prices move randomly about the same target price. As a consequence, the behavior of the industry under both regimes is consistent with a time series on prices, output, sales, and inventories in which prices do not influence and are not influenced by output, sales, or inventories. The data would not in general, however, exhibit these features in a deregulated environment.

At the same time, the industry equilibrium under a production control regime differs importantly from that under sales control. Prices fluctuate more under the production control regime, but industry operating costs are lower in the sales control regime. Hence the sales control regime minimizes the inefficiencies associated with the objective of maintaining a given target price. Although our results regarding the relative desirability of the two modes of regulation are obtained for specific cost functions, they are fairly robust to changes in the functional forms assumed here. The essential differences between the two regulatory regimes arise from the fact that in the production rule regime the regulatory agency must forecast industrywide inventories, while it need not do so in the sales control regime. More generally, the equilibrium laws of motion of production and inventories are extremely sensitive to the precise specifi-

---

[1] See Lucas (1976) and Sargent (1981).

cation of the behavior of the regulatory agency. Thus, for example, inventories under the sales control regime exhibit a far more complex dynamic structure than that which emerges under the production control regime.

Taken as a whole, the models discussed here serve to support the contention that knowledge of firm decision rules or the equilibrium laws of motion of an industry under regulated environments does not allow prediction of the response of the industry to deregulation or, more generally, to changes in the stochastic process governing prices. Dynamic structural models that incorporate optimizing behavior on the part of economic agents and explicit characterizations of their constraints, including a specification of the regulatory regime that confronts such agents, can be used to address such issues, however. Given estimates of the relevant policy-invariant parameters, calculation of the equilibrium laws of motion corresponding to a wide variety of regimes is possible.

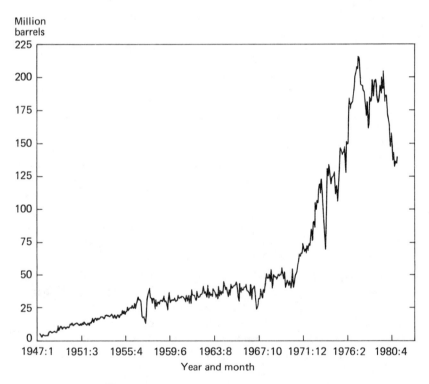

Figure 4-1.   Net U.S. imports of petroleum

I. THE U.S. PETROLEUM INDUSTRY PRIOR TO 1973

Current public concern about energy supplies is in sharp contrast to that prior to 1973. In the early years after World War II, the United States was essentially self-sufficient in crude oil supplies. As can be seen from figures 4-1, 4-2, 4-3, 4-4, and 4-5 this changed gradually during the fifties as exports declined and imports of oil began to rise.

Before 1973, concern—largely by members of the petroleum industry —was focused on the price effects of abundance, not on problems of shortage. As a result, the U.S. government in 1959 imposed an oil import quota limiting imports to a mandatory 9 percent of estimated domestic demand. The quotas were gradually increased over time, reaching ap-

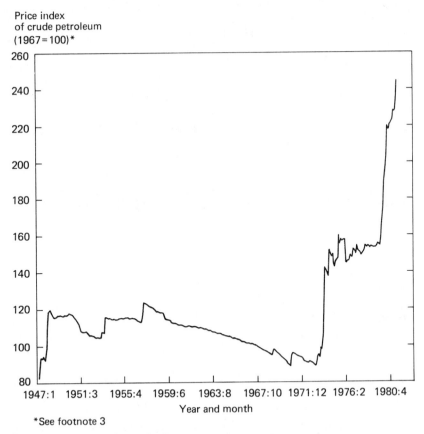

Figure 4-2.   Price of petroleum

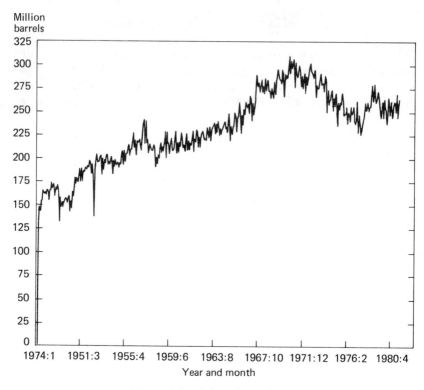

Figure 4-3.   Sales of petroleum

proximately 23 percent of total domestic demand by 1972. By April 1973, import quotas were discontinued and a tariff was briefly introduced.[2] For the purpose of our analysis, the primary significance of U.S. import policy was that, during this period, it attempted to segment the U.S. market from the world market. For this reason, as well as for simplicity, we abstract from the international aspect of the problem.

Considerable excess capacity for crude oil production developed during the early sixties. State agencies found that increasingly stringent limitations were required to prevent the price of crude petroleum from falling. Many states, for example, required buyers of crude petroleum to submit a deposition informing state regulatory agencies of their intended purchases at the going price. The agencies then distributed production or

---

[2] Bohi and Russell (1978), in their comprehensive history and analysis of U.S. oil import policy, emphasize the basic continuity of oil import policy during the period under discussion.

sales allocations to the various producers of crude petroleum (see Epple, 1975).

Though the domestic price of crude petroleum was higher than the world price between 1959 and 1973, nominal prices were relatively stable with negligible changes for periods as long as five years. As the figures indicate, the real domestic price of petroleum, while exhibiting a downward trend, behaved in a very smooth way.

We estimated two ninth-order vector autoregressions (VAR) using data from 1947:1 to 1972:4 in order to check whether the time series are consistent with the characterization of the pre-1973 U.S. petroleum industry as being effectively segmented from the world market. The data consisted of quarterly observations on[3]

domestic real prices of petroleum (PETPR)

total domestic stocks of petroleum (INV)

total domestic production of petroleum (PROD)

total net imports of petroleum (IMP)

real gross national product (GNP)

real sales of domestic crude petroleum (SALE)

Table 4-1 reports the results of the various exclusions tests conducted on a VAR including all series except sales, while table 4-2 reports similar results for a VAR that includes all series except production. Notice from table 4-1 that, for the period under consideration, imports do not appear to Granger-cause any of the relevant variables in the system, although both production and GNP (in addition to lagged imports) seem to Granger-cause imports.[4] This result appears to be consistent with the widely held view that U.S. import policy successfully insulated the domestic economy from the world economy during the period under consideration. Furthermore, table 4-1 indicates that domestic real petroleum prices apparently did not Granger-cause petroleum inventories,

---

[3] Data are from U.S. Department of Commerce, *Business Statistics*, various issues. The petroleum price is an index of the wholesale price of crude petroleum that is based on buyer's posted prices of crude petroleum in thirteen states (1967 = 100). The real petroleum price (PETPR) is the above price divided by the monthly CPI. Net imports (IMP) are imports of crude petroleum and unfinished oil minus exports of crude petroleum in millions of barrels. Sales (SALE), production (PROD), and stocks (INV) are all crude petroleum in millions of barrels. The inventory series does not include strategic petroleum reserves. The sales data are approximated by adding the change in stocks of crude petroleum to the production of crude petroleum. GNP is real gross domestic product in millions of 1967 dollars.

[4] The random variable Y is said to Granger-cause the random variable x if, given all past values of x, past values of Y help to predict x.

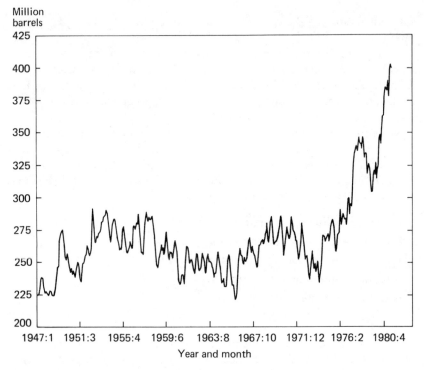

Figure 4-4.   Stocks of petroleum

TABLE 4-1.   F-STATISTIC VALUES AND MARGINAL SIGNIFICANCE LEVELS (MS)
OF EXCLUDING NINE LAGS OF SPECIFIED VARIABLES

| | \multicolumn{10}{c}{Lags excluded} |
| | PETPR | | INV | | PROD | | IMP | | GNP | |
Equation	F	MS	F	MS	F	MS	F	MS	F	MS
PETPR	22.07	.7E-10	.41	.92	.83	.59	.95	.49	1.53	.16
INV	1.61	.13	5.47	.3E-04	3.21	.4E-02	1.32	.25	1.01	.44
PROD	1.61	.14	1.47	.18	3.29	.3E-02	1.31	.25	1.85	.8E-01
IMP	.47	.88	1.49	.17	3.49	.2E-02	4.45	.3E-03	3.25	.35E-02
GNP	.63	.76	.42	.91	1.10	.38	.58	.80	50.44	0

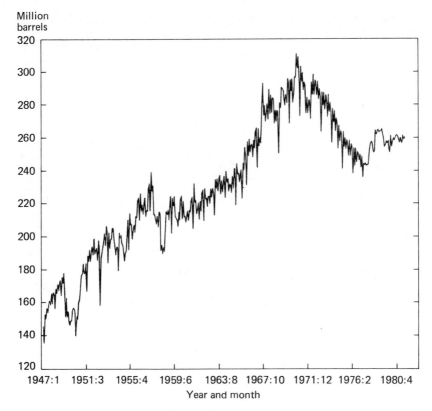

Figure 4-5.   Production of petroleum

production, imports, or domestic stocks, or GNP; nor did those variables Granger-cause domestic real petroleum prices. Similar conclusions regarding price behavior emerge from table 4-2.

These results have no implications for the supply characteristics of the petroleum industry, however. Even abstracting from the usual demand and supply identification problem, in the present context the effects of government regulations cannot be disentangled from the response of agents to economic incentives.

To confirm that the VAR results are consistent with the regulatory policies in effect during the period for which the vector autoregression was estimated, we constructed a dynamic structural model of an industry operating under regulations that in some aspects are similar to those affecting the U.S. petroleum industry during the prorationing period. We then argue that the cross-equation constraints imposed by the hypothesis of rational expectations and an explicit specification of the regulatory agency's decision rule resolves the identification problem, at least in

TABLE 4-2.   F-STATISTIC VALUES AND MARGINAL SIGNIFICANCE LEVELS (MS)
OF EXCLUDING NINE LAGS OF SPECIFIED VARIABLES

| | PETPR | | INV | | SALE | | IMP | | GNP | |
Equation	F	MS	F	MS	F	MS	F	MS	F	MS
PETPR	24.30	.6E-10	.59	.79	1.31	.25	.93	.50	1.56	.15
INV	1.05	.41	4.95	96E-04	1.81	.09	.80	.61	.87	.55
IMP	.90	.52	1.26	.28	2.89	.008	.95	.48	4.02	.6E-03
SALE	.85	.56	1.19	.32	3.81	.001	1.01	.44	1.43	.19
GNP	.74	.66	.28	.97	1.04	.41	.51	.86	45.60	.2E-11

Lags excluded (header spanning PETPR, INV, SALE, IMP, GNP)

principle. In order to make these arguments in as simple a way as
possible, we abstract from the international aspects of the problem and
concentrate on modeling regulation of the domestic industry.

Because we are interested in investigating the equilibria corresponding
to the various regimes considered, we restrict ourselves to a model that
provides us with a mapping from the structural parameters to firm
decision rules, as well as to the equilibrium laws of motion of the market
and government-determined variables of the system. This requires, by
and large, that we specify agents' objective functions and constraints in a
way that allows use of the principle of certainty equivalence. Although
this approach certainly imposes restrictions upon the analysis, it does
allow specification of the model at the level of private economic agents,
who face and solve dynamic stochastic optimization problems, as well as
derivation of explicit representations of the resulting equilibrium.

II. THE MODEL

The actual supply process in the petroleum industry is both complicated
and dynamic in that it involves exploration for and development of wells,
as well as extraction of oil. Rather than attempting to model explicitly all
aspects of this complicated phenomenon, we have used a simpler model,
which we believe suffices to illustrate our main contentions. In particular,
we consider an industry that produces a single commodity called oil. We
abstract from the exhaustible nature of oil, because the explicit consideration of this characteristic in a model such as that of Epple and Hansen
(1979), in which extraction costs increase linearly as total reserves fall,
would substantially complicate our exposition but would not affect our
qualitative results.

We define the following variables:

N = number of firms in the industry
$q(t)$ = output of the representative firm at time t
$Q(t) = Nq(t)$ = total output of the industry at time t
$i(t)$ = inventories of output of the representative firm at the end of time t
$I(t) = Ni(t)$ = total inventories of the industry at time t
$s(t)$ = sales of the representative firm at time t
$S(t) = Ns(t)$ = total sales of the industry at time t
$Y(t)$ = aggregate income at time t
$P(t)$ = price of output at time t
$T(t)$ = a random shock to demand at time t
$ci(t)$ = inventory costs of the representative firm at time t
$cq(t)$ = production costs of the representative firm at time t
β = the discount factor that is between zero and one
$\Omega(t)$ = the information set of the representative producer at time t, which
   includes the values of all the variables in the model

The market and each firm in the industry are subject, respectively, to the quantity balance equations,

$$S(t) = Q(t) - I(t) + I(t-1) \qquad (2.1)$$

and

$$s(t) = q(t) - i(t) + i(t-1) \qquad (2.2)$$

The representative firm's production and inventory-holding costs are given, respectively, by

$$cq(t) = a(t)q(t) + \frac{b}{2}q^2(t) + \frac{c}{2}[q(t) - q(t-1)]^2 \qquad (2.3)$$

$$ci(t) = d(t)i(t) + \frac{e}{2}i^2(t) + \frac{f}{2}[\alpha s(t) - i(t-1)]^2 \qquad (2.4)$$

where

$$a(t) = a + \varepsilon_a(t)$$
$$d(t) = d + \varepsilon_d(t)$$

and a, b, c, d, e, and f are positive scalars. $\varepsilon_d(t)$ and $\varepsilon_a(t)$ are zero mean, serially and contemporaneously uncorrelated stochastic processes with $E\varepsilon_d^2(t) = \sigma_d^2$ and $E\varepsilon_a^2(t) = \sigma_a^2$. Notice that the production cost function embodies the notion that adjusting production levels is costly. The inventory-holding cost function embodies two types of costs. The term $d(t)i(t) + (e/2)i^2(t)$ is intended to capture the nature of the various static, albeit stochastic, inventory cost functions that have been used in the literature. The dynamic cost term $(f/2)[\alpha s(t) - i(t-1)]^2$ has not been widely used in economic models, however, and requires some further explanation. In principle, this term is intended to capture the need for operating stocks that are immediately accessible. Our representation of these costs assumes that some optimal ratio of sales to beginning-of-period inventories, $s(t)/i(t-1) = 1/\alpha$ exists. The firm is penalized for deviations from this ratio. The penalty is formulated in a fairly simple way so the model can capture nonspeculative motives for holding inventories in a manner that allows exploitation of the property of certainty equivalence.

Let $E_t(\cdot) = E[\cdot | \Omega_t]$ represent the linear least squares projection operator conditioned on information known at time t.[5] Then the problem of the representative firm is to choose contingency plans for $q(t)$ and $i(t)$ so as to maximize the expected present value of its profits; that is,

$$E_0 \sum_{t=0}^{\infty} \beta^t \{ P(t)s(t) - cq(t) - ci(t) \} \qquad (2.5)$$

subject to (2.2), (2.3), (2.4), $q(-1)$, and $i(-1)$.

This problem is not well posed until we attribute to the firm views about how prices, $P(t)$, evolve over time. The actual stochastic process that governs the evolution of prices over time, however, depends not only on consumer preferences but also on the regulations to which the firm and the industry are subject. Hence the decision rules of firms for setting $q(t)$ and $i(t)$, as well as the industrywide equilibrium laws of motion for $Q(t)$ and $I(t)$, will depend very much on the institutional features of the model.

This analysis will focus on the equilibrium movements of industry sales, production, inventories, and prices when the industry is subject to sales or production controls imposed by a regulatory agency in order to achieve a target price path $\overline{P}(t)$. Although the analysis is conducted for arbitrary specifications of $\{\overline{P}(t)\}_{t=0}^{\infty}$, it is clear that, in the absence of subsidies to the firms in this industry, the target price path cannot imply a negative expected present value of profits for firms. Thus, although the

---

[5] Conditional expectations and linear least squares projections will coincide if the underlying stochastic processes are Gaussian.

regulatory agency can use its allocation rule for production or sales to keep new firms from entering the industry, it cannot prevent existing firms from leaving the industry.

Notice that the model contains no welfare justification that rationalizes government intervention in this industry. Given the absence of externalities or other sources of nonoptimality, a target price policy, whether implemented via production or sales allocations, should be interpreted as an exogenous ad-hoc rule. Such a framework seems to be consistent with the circumstances of the petroleum industry during the 1947–1972 period and of the many markets presently subjected to quantity regulations in an effort to achieve various price targets.

Assuming the regulatory agency aims to hold the level of supply equal to demand at the prevailing or target price, the model must incorporate some explicit representation of demand behavior, because movements in demand influence regulatory decisions and therefore firm decisions. For this reason, as well as to derive the nonintervention equilibrium, we assume that the inverse market demand curve for the output of this industry is given by

$$P(t) = B_0 - B_1 S(t) + B_2 Y(t) + T(t) \tag{2.6}$$

where $B_0, B_1, B_2 > 0$.

The autoregressive representation for the joint $\{Y(t), T(t)\}$ process is given by

$$\begin{bmatrix} Y(t) \\ T(t) \end{bmatrix} = \begin{bmatrix} A_1(L) & 0 \\ 0 & A_2(L) \end{bmatrix} \begin{bmatrix} Y(t-1) \\ T(t-1) \end{bmatrix} + \begin{bmatrix} \varepsilon_y(t) \\ \varepsilon_T(t) \end{bmatrix} \tag{2.7}$$

and

$$\begin{bmatrix} A_1(L) & 0 \\ \\ 0 & A_2(L) \end{bmatrix} = \begin{bmatrix} \sum_{j=1}^{\gamma_y} A_{1J} L^J & 0 \\ \\ 0 & \sum_{J=1}^{\gamma_T} A_{2J} L^J \end{bmatrix} \tag{2.8}$$

The lag operator L is defined by $L^J X(t) = X(t-J)$, $Y(t) - E[Y(t)|Y(t-1), T(t-1), Y(t-2), T(t-2), \ldots] = \varepsilon_y(t)$ and $T(t) - E[T(t)|Y(t-1), T(t-1), Y(t-2), T(t-2), \ldots] = \varepsilon_T(t)$. In addition, we assume that $E[\varepsilon_y(t), \varepsilon_T(t)] = 0$ and $E[\varepsilon_y(t), \varepsilon_T(t)]' [\varepsilon_y(s), \varepsilon_T(s)] = [0]$ for all t not equal to s. Hence $\{\varepsilon_y(t), \varepsilon_T(t)\}'$ is the one-step-ahead linear least squares forecast error associated with the linearly indeterministic covariance stationary $\{Y(t), T(t)\}$ process.[6] In addition, we assume that $\varepsilon_y(t)$ and $\varepsilon_T(t)$ are contemporaneously uncorrelated. This assumption is made only for convenience. Notice that (2.7) embodies the assumption that $Y(t)$, as well as $T(t)$, is not Granger-caused by the other variables in the model, which is consistent with the data presented in section I.

We assume that the regulatory agency knows the parameters of the market demand curve, B_0, B_1, and B_2. It does not control market prices directly, however. Instead, at the end of period $t-1$ it announces its period t controls, whether these be sales or production levels for each firm. Thus, at time $t-1$, the agency must forecast those variables that affect period t prices. These forecasts are modeled as being rational; that is, the agency regulates the industry using its knowledge of the true process governing the relevant variables. For convenience, we assume that the regulatory agency and firms have the same information set, $\Omega(t)$, which includes $\{Q(t), Q(t-1), \ldots, S(t), S(t-1), \ldots P(t), P(t-1), \ldots, \bar{P}(t), \bar{P}(t-1), \bar{P}(t+1), \ldots, Y(t), Y(t-1), \ldots, T(t), T(t-1), \ldots\}$, as well as $T(t+1)$. The assumption that $T(t+1)$ is contained in $\Omega(t)$ is made only for algebraic convenience.

III. THE NONINTERVENTION COMPETITIVE EQUILIBIUM

The representative firm seeks to maximize the expected discounted value of its profits, given by (2.5), subject to (2.2) through (2.4), (2.6) through (2.7), $q(-1)$, and $i(-1)$ and the laws of motion of $a(t)$ and $d(t)$.[7] The maximization is over contingency plans for setting $q(t)$ and $i(t)$ as linear functions of the elements of $r(t)$. The first-order necessary conditions to this problem are given by

$$\beta c E_t q(t+1) - \left[c(1+\beta) + b + f\alpha^2 \right] q(t) + cq(t-1)$$
$$+ f\alpha^2 i(t) - f\alpha(\alpha-1)i(t-1) = a(t) - P(t) \tag{3.1}$$

$$\beta f\alpha(\alpha-1)E_t i(t+1) - \left[e + f\alpha^2 + \beta f(\alpha-1)^2 \right] i(t)$$
$$+ f\alpha(\alpha-1)i(t-1) - \beta f\alpha(\alpha-1)E_t q(t+1) + f\alpha^2 q(t)$$
$$= P(t) - \beta E_t P(t+1) + d(t) \tag{3.2}$$

---

[6] For most of this analysis, this assumption can be relaxed and replaced by the assumption that $[Y(t), T(t)]$ is of mean exponential order less than $1/\beta$.

[7] See Hansen and Sargent (1980) for a more detailed discussion of the underlying optimization theory.

A rational expectations nonintervention competitive equilibrium may be defined as a stochastic process for prices, industrywide output, and inventories such that all individuals in the market behave optimally, markets clear at each point in time, and agents correctly perceive the endogenous law of motion of prices, as well as the stochastic process governing the evolution over time of those variables that affect firms' objective functions but that they cannot control.[8]

As Sargent (1981) points out, the rational expectations competitive equilibrium for such models solves a particular type of social planning problem. If we normalize the number of firms in the industry to one, so that $i(t) = I(t)$ and $q(t) = Q(t)$, then the equilibrium laws of motion for $Q(t)$ and $I(t)$ may be obtained by solving the following problem, which consists of maximizing the expected discounted area under the demand curve for final consumption of the good minus the total social costs associated with inventories and producing the good:

Maximize

$$
E_0 \sum_{t=0}^{\infty} \beta^t \bigg\{ \big[B_0 + B_2 Y(t) + T(t) \big] \big[Q(t) - I(t) + I(t-1) \big]
$$

$$
- \frac{B_1}{2} \big[Q(t) - I(t) + I(t-1) \big]^2 - a(t)Q(t) - \frac{b}{2} Q^2(t)
$$

$$
- \frac{c}{2} \big[Q(t) - Q(t-1) \big]^2 - d(t)I(t) - \frac{e}{2} I^2(t)
$$

$$
- \frac{f}{2} \big[\alpha Q(t) - \alpha I(t) + (\alpha - 1)I(t-1) \big]^2 \bigg\} \tag{3.3}
$$

subject to (2.7), (2.8), $Q(-1)$, $I(-1)$, and the laws of motion governing the behavior of $a(t)$ and $d(t)$. The maximization is over contingency plans setting $Q(t)$ and $I(t)$ as linear functions of the elements of the planner's information set at time t. Sargent (1981) establishes, in a more general context, that the solution of this problem will be of the form,

$$
Q(t) = F_1 Q(t-1) + F_2 I(t-1)
$$

$$
+ \sum_{J=0}^{\gamma_y - 1} F_{3,J} Y(t-J) + \sum_{J=0}^{\gamma_T - 1} F_{4,J} T(t+1-J)
$$

$$
+ F_5 \varepsilon_a(t) + F_6 \varepsilon_d(t) + F_0 \tag{3.4}
$$

---

[8] See Sargent (1981) for a more formal definition of equilibrium in such models.

and

$$I(t) = G_1 Q(t-1) + G_2 I(t-1)$$

$$+ \sum_{J=0}^{\gamma_y - 1} G_{3,J} Y(t-J) + \sum_{J=0}^{\gamma_T - 1} G_{4,J} T(t+1-J)$$

$$+ G_5 \varepsilon_a(t) + G_6 \varepsilon_d(t) + G_0 \tag{3.5}$$

Hansen and Sargent (1980) discuss how to calculate the coefficients of the above equilibrium laws of motion for given values of the structural parameters of the model. Here, we point out that changes in those parameters, including changes in the demand parameters, cause systematic quantitative changes in the parameters of (3.4) and (3.5). In this analysis, we consider the impacts of different types of government policies on the qualitative features of the equilibrium laws of motion for output and inventories.

IV. THE CONSTRAINED EQUILIBRIUM UNDER PRODUCTION CONTROL

Now, we introduce two regulatory regimes, both designed to enable the authorities to meet their objective of supporting a given target price path $\bar{P}(t)$. Although the most straightforward instrument for accomplishing such a goal is a sales control policy, we begin by considering a production control regime because most observers, such as Epple (1975), agree that the government, in effect, actually controlled petroleum industry production rather than sales.

Let $\bar{Q}(t)$ be the level of production that at time $t-1$ is expected to equate the time t market price, $P(t)$, with the target price, $\bar{P}(t)$. Given knowledge of the inverse market demand curve (2.6), the regulatory agency can determine that

$$\bar{Q}(t) = E_{t-1} I(t) - I(t-1) + \frac{1}{B_1} \left[B_0 - \bar{P}(t) + B_2 E_{t-1} Y(t) + T(t) \right] \tag{4.1}$$

where $E_{t-1} Y(t) = A_1(L) Y(t-1)$, and $E_{t-1} I(t)$ is taken with respect to the true equilibrium process of $I(t)$. Notice that the regulatory agency is assumed to forecast rationally the endogenous variable $I(t)$, as well as the exogenous variable $Y(t)$. Substituting (4.1) back into the market demand curve (2.6) implies that, if an equilibrium exists, actual prices at time t are given by

$$P(t) = \bar{P}(t) + B_2\left[Y(t) - E_{t-1}Y(t)\right] + B_1\left[I(t) - E_{t-1}I(t)\right] \qquad (4.2)$$

so that

$$E_{t-1}P(t) = \bar{P}(t) \text{ for all } t \qquad (4.3)$$

Hence this regime is capable of equating conditionally expected market prices to target prices.

Under these circumstances, the problem of the representative firm is to maximize the expected discounted value of its profits, (2.5), by choice of a contingency plan for $i(t)$ subject to knowledge of $\{\bar{P}(t)\}_{t=0}^{\infty}$, (2.4), $i(-1)$, and the constraint that its production at time t, $\bar{q}(t)$, be equal to $\bar{Q}(t)/N$, where the law of motion of $\bar{Q}(t)$ is given by (4.1).

Because the firm views the sequences $\{\bar{q}(t)\}_{t=0}^{\infty}$ and $\{\bar{P}(t)\}_{t=0}^{\infty}$ as being noncontrollable, it in effect maximizes

$$E_0 \sum_{t=0}^{\infty} \beta^t\bigg\{ P(t)[-i(t) + i(t-1)] - d(t)i(t) - \frac{e}{2}i^2(t)$$

$$-\frac{f}{2}\left[\alpha\bar{q}(t) - \alpha i(t) + (\alpha - 1)i(t-1)\right]^2\bigg\} \qquad (4.4)$$

subject to $\bar{q}(t) = \bar{Q}(t)/N$, $\{\bar{P}(t)\}_{t=0}^{\infty}$, (2.4), (4.1), and $i(-1)$ given, by choice of contingency plan for $i(t)$, $t = 0, 1, \ldots$.

The first-order necessary conditions for maximizing (4.4) consist of the following stochastic Euler equation, as well as the associated transversality condition:

$$\beta f\alpha(\alpha - 1)E_t i(t+1) + \phi i(t) + f\alpha(\alpha - 1)i(t-1) = d(t) - f\alpha^2\bar{q}(t)$$

$$+ \beta f\alpha(\alpha - 1)E_t\bar{q}(t+1) - \beta E_t P(t+1) + P(t) \qquad (4.5)$$

where $\phi = -[e + f\alpha^2 + \beta f(\alpha - 1)^2]$.

Again, as in the case of the noninterventionist equilibrium, this problem is not well posed until we attribute to the firm views regarding the evolution over time of those variables, such as $\bar{q}(t)$ and $I(t)$, that affect its objective function but that it cannot control. Unlike the nonintervention equilibrium, this problem requires specifying target prices, as well as the stochastic process governing market prices and the firm's own noncontrollable production levels.

Assuming that the regulatory agency allocates production evenly among the identical firms of this industry, we have that

$$\bar{q}(t) = \frac{\bar{Q}(t)}{N} \tag{4.6}$$

and from (4.2) that

$$P(t) = \bar{P}(t) + B_2 \varepsilon_y(t) + B_1 [I(t) - E_{t-1}I(t)] \tag{4.2'}$$

In addition, we assume that firms and the regulatory agency view $I(t)$ and $Q(t)$ as evolving according to

$$I(t) = \gamma_0 + \gamma_1 I(t-1) + \psi(L)\dot{Y}(t) + \rho(L)T(t+1) + \gamma_5 d(t) \tag{4.7}$$

and

$$\bar{Q}(t) = D_0 + D_1(L)Y(t) + D_2(L)T(t+1) \tag{4.8}$$

where $\psi(L)$, $\rho(L)$, $D_1(L)$, and $D_2(L)$ are finite-ordered polynomials in the lag operator.[9]

Given these views, the firm maximizes (2.5) subject to (2.4), (4.2), (4.6), (4.7), and (4.8) over linear contingency plans for $i(t)$ of the form

$$i(t) = E_1 + E_2 i(t-1) + E_3(L)Y(t) + E_4(L)T(t+1)$$
$$+ E_5 I(t-1) + E_6 d(t) \tag{4.9}$$

DEFINITION. *A rational expectations competitive equilibrium under a production-control regime is five linear functions (4.2), (4.6), (4.7), (4.8), and (4.9) such that*

(*i*) *given the aggregate laws of motion for inventories and output, (4.7) and (4.8), as well as the sequence of target prices* $\{\bar{P}(t)\}_{t=0}^{\infty}$, *the contingency plan (4.9) solves the firm's problem subject to the constraints (4.6) placed upon its production levels.*

(*ii*) *The contingency plans (4.9) of the representative firm and its production levels imply the laws of motion for industrywide inventories and output, (4.7) and (4.8), so that*

$$Ni(t) = I(t) \text{ and } Nq(t) = Q(t).$$

(*iii*) *the aggregate laws of motion, (4.7) and (4.8), imply that the law of motion for market prices satisfies (4.2).*

---

[9] The absence of any terms in (4.8) explicitly involving t reflects the assumption that $\bar{P}(t)$ is constant over time.

As the actual calculation of the above equilibrium is somewhat involved, here we only trace out the necessary steps. The appendix contains a more detailed exposition of the derivation. In brief, to obtain the rational expectations equilibrium, we note that expectations in (4.5) are taken with respect to the true stochastic process governing $\bar{q}(t)$ and $P(t)$. Multiplying both sides of (4.5) by N and substituting (4.1), (4.2), and (4.5) into the resulting equation, we obtain

$$I(t) = \mu_0 E_{t-1} I(t) + \mu_1 I(t-1) + \mu_2 + \delta(L)Y(t)$$
$$+ \mu_3 T(t) + \mu_4 T(t+1) + \mu_5 d(t) \tag{4.10}$$

where, for simplicity, we have set $\bar{P}(t) = \bar{P}$ for all t. The coefficients μ_0 to μ_5, as well as $\delta(L)$ are defined in terms of the underlying structural parameters of the model in the appendix.

In order to establish the conditions under which a rational expectations equilibrium exists, as well as to derive its solution, we begin with a guess regarding the equilibrium law of motion for $I(t)$, given by (4.7). Taking conditional expectations on both sides of (4.7),

$$E_{t-1} I(t) = \gamma_0 + \gamma_1 I(t-1) + (\psi(L) - \psi_0)Y(t) + \psi_0 A_1(L)Y(t-1)$$
$$\times (\rho(L) - \rho_0)T(t+1) + \rho_0 A_2(L)T(t) + \gamma_5 d \tag{4.11}$$

Substituting (4.11) into (4.10), we obtain

$$I(t) = [\mu_2 + \mu_0 \gamma_0 + \mu_0 \gamma_5 d] + [\mu_0 \gamma_1 + \mu_1] I(t-1)$$
$$+ [\mu_0(\psi(L) - \psi_0) + \mu_0 \psi_0 A_1(L)L + \delta(L)] Y(t)$$
$$+ [\mu_0(\rho(L) - \rho_0) + \mu_0 \rho_0 A_2(L)L + \mu_3 L + \mu_4] T(t+1)$$
$$+ \mu_5 d(t)$$

The solution for the equilibrium law of motion of $I(t)$, (4.7), is obtained by equating coefficients in (4.7) and (4.11). Hence

$$\gamma_1 = \frac{\mu_1}{1 - \mu_0} \tag{4.12a}$$

$$\gamma_5 = \mu_5 \tag{4.12b}$$

$$\gamma_0 = \frac{1}{1 - \mu_0}(\mu_2 + \mu_0 \gamma_5 d) \tag{4.12c}$$

$$\psi(L) = \mu_0(\psi(L) - \psi_0) + \mu_0 \psi_0 A_1(L)L + \delta(L) \tag{4.12d}$$

$$\rho(L) = \mu_0 \rho_0 A_2(L)L + \mu_3 L + \mu_0(\rho(L) - \rho_0) + \mu_4 \tag{4.12e}$$

Notice that for (4.7) to be a solution consistent with the firm's maximization problem, $\{I(t)\}_{t=0}^{\infty}$ must be of mean exponential order less than
$1/\sqrt{\beta}$. Given our assumption that $\{Y(t)\}_{t=0}^{\infty}$ and $\{T(t)\}_{t=0}^{\infty}$ are covari-
ance stationary, this simply requires that $|\gamma_1| < 1/\sqrt{\beta}$ or from (4.12a),
$|\mu_1/1 - \mu_0| < 1/\sqrt{\beta}$. Substituting for μ_0 and μ_1, we have that a necessary and sufficient condition for a rational expectations equilibrium to
exist is that

$$\left| \frac{f\alpha}{e - \beta f(\alpha - 1)} \right| < \frac{1}{\sqrt{\beta}} \tag{4.13}$$

In order to complete the solution to (4.12), we must equate coefficients
on each lag of the right- and left-hand sides of (4.12d) and (4.12e). Doing
this for L^0, we obtain $\psi_0 = \delta$ and $\rho_0 = \mu_4$, where δ_0 is the coefficient of
L^0 in $\delta(L)$, defined by (A.8), and μ_4 is defined by (A.6). Using these
results, we may express the coefficients in $\psi(L)$ and $\rho(L)$ as exact
functions of the structural parameters of the model, including those
governing the evolution of $Y(t)$ and $T(t)$ over time.

Hence

$$\psi_0 = \delta_0$$

$$\psi_1 = \frac{1}{1 - \mu_0} \delta_1$$

$$\psi_J = \frac{1}{1 - \mu_0} [\delta_0 \mu_0 A_{1J-1} + \delta_J], \qquad J = 2, 3, \ldots \tag{4.14}$$

and

$$\rho_0 = \mu_4$$

$$\rho_1 = \frac{1}{1 - \mu_0} \mu_3$$

$$\rho_J = \frac{1}{1 - \mu_0} [\mu_0 \mu_4 A_{2J-1} + \delta_J], \qquad J = 2, 3, \ldots \tag{4.15}$$

Having calculated the solution for $I(t)$, as represented by (4.7), the
expectations conditional on information available at time $(t - 1)$ may be
substituted into (4.1) to obtain the law of motion for aggregate production, (4.8), in terms of the fundamental structural parameters of the
model.

V. THE CONSTRAINED EQUILIBRIUM UNDER SALES CONTROL

The regulatory agency may choose to meet its objective of supporting a given price path through either of two sales control regimes. One allows for some flexibility in actual market prices and the other involves no deviations from the desired price process. It is clear that the definitions of equilibrium and the actual equilibrium laws of motion of the system will be quite different in these two regimes. In the first regime, planned and actual inventories differ by a number that is proportional to the one-step-ahead error in forecasting income at time t based on information available at time $t - 1$, while in the second regime planned and actual inventories are identical.

Sales Control with Fluctuating Prices

Under this regime, the regulatory agency at time $t - 1$ sets the time t level of industrywide sales $S(t)$ in trying to meet its price objective $\bar{P}(t)$. Let $\bar{S}(t)$ be the level of sales such that

$$\bar{P}(t) = B_0 - B_1 \bar{S}(t) + B_2 E_{t-1} Y(t) + T(t)$$

where $E_{t-1}Y(t)$ is the best linear forecast of $Y(t)$, given information at time $t - 1$; that is, $E_{t-1}Y(t) = E[Y_t | \Omega_{t-1}] = A_1(L)Y(t - 1)$. For any given target price $\bar{P}(t)$, the regulatory agency can find the level of time t sales such that $E[P(t)|\Omega(t - 1)] = \bar{P}(t)$ from (2.6) or

$$\bar{S}(t) = \frac{1}{B_1} \left[B_0 - \bar{P}(t) + B_2 A_1(L)Y(t - 1) + T(t) \right] \qquad (5.1)$$

Given that the target price $\bar{P}(t)$ is not a function of the firms' production and/or inventory decisions, the target price policy can be supported by setting $\bar{s}(t) = \bar{S}(t)/N$ for each firm. In this case, the actual market price at time t can be found by substituting (5.1) into (2.6), so that

$$P(t) = \bar{P}(t) + u(t) \qquad (5.2)$$

where $u(t) = B_2 \varepsilon_y(t)$ is a white noise that is proportional to the innovation in the $Y(t)$ process. Hence, as in the production control regime, we have that $E_{t-1}P(t) = \bar{P}(t)$ for all t. Unlike the former regime, however, the regulatory agency can implement the required controls without forecasting the endogenous behavior of the agents it is regulating. It is, of course, the absence of this simultaneity that leads to the relatively more straightforward operating rule of the regulatory agency in the sales regime.

Under these circumstances, the problem of the representative firm is to maximize the expected value of its profits subject to the stochastic constraint on industrywide sales $S(t)$, which is given by (5.1), the allocation rule $\bar{s}(t) = \bar{S}(t)/N$ for all $t = 1, 2, \ldots$, and the firm quantity-balance condition

$$q(t) = \bar{s}(t) + i(t) - i(t-1) \tag{5.3}$$

Substituting (5.3), (2.3), and (2.4) into (2.5), the firm's problem is to choose a contingency rule for setting $i(t)$ as a function of the elements of its information set $\Omega(t)$ to maximize

$$E_0 \sum_{t=0}^{\infty} \beta^t \Big\{ P(t)\bar{s}(t)$$

$$- a(t)[\bar{s}(t) - i(t-1) + i(t)] - \frac{b}{2}[\bar{s}(t) - i(t-1) + i(t)]^2$$

$$- \frac{c}{2}[\bar{s}(t) - 2i(t-1) + i(t) - \bar{s}(t-1) + i(t-2)]^2$$

$$- d(t)i(t) - \frac{e}{2}i(t)^2 - \frac{f}{2}[a\bar{s}(t) - i(t-1)]^2 \Big\} \tag{5.4}$$

subject to $i(-1)$ and $i(-2)$ given, as well as (5.1), the regulatory agency's rule for setting $\bar{S}(t)$, and the allocation rule for determining $\bar{s}(t)$.

The first-order necessary conditions for this problem consist of the following Euler equation, as well as the associated transversality condition:

$$- \beta^2 c E_t i(t+2) + \beta \phi_1 E_t i(t+1) + \phi_0 i(t) + \phi_1 i(t-1) - ci(t-2)$$
$$= d(t) + a(t) - \beta E_t a(t+1)$$
$$+ E_t \big[- c\bar{s}(t-1) + g_1 \bar{s}(t) + g_2 \bar{s}(t+1) + \beta^2 c\bar{s}(t+2) \big] \tag{5.5}$$

where

$$\phi_1 = b + 2c(1 + \beta)$$
$$\phi_0 = -(\beta f + \beta^2 c + 4c\beta + b + c + e + \beta b)$$
$$g_1 = b + c + 2\beta c$$
$$g_2 = -\beta(b + 2c + f\alpha + \beta c)$$

Given our assumptions about the underlying parameters of the model, the unique optimal solution to (5.5) that obeys the transversality condition is given by

$$(1 - \lambda_1 L)(1 - \lambda_2 L)i(t) = -\frac{\lambda_1 \lambda_2 E_t}{c} \sum_{k=0}^{\infty} \lambda_3^{-J} L^{-J} \left\{ \sum_{J=0}^{\infty} \lambda_4^{-J} M(t + J) \right\}$$

(5.6)

where

$$M(t + J) = E_t \big[a(t + J) - \beta a(t + J + 1) + d(t + J) - c\bar{s}(t + J - 1)$$

$$+ g_1 \bar{s}(t + J) + g_2 \bar{s}(t + J + 1) + \beta^2 c\bar{s}(t + J + 2) \big]$$

and λ_1, λ_2, λ_3 and λ_4 are the four distinct roots of

$$1 - \frac{\phi_1 Z}{c\beta} - \frac{\phi_0 Z^2}{c\beta^2} - \frac{\phi_1 Z^3}{c\beta^2} + \frac{Z^4}{\beta^2} = 0$$

Because (5.5) is a Euler equation corresponding to a well-defined linear quadratic optimization problem, one can use the results of Hansen and Sargent (1981) to show that $\lambda_1 = 1/(\beta\lambda_3)$ and $\lambda_2 = 1/(\beta\lambda_3)$ do not exceed $1/\sqrt{\beta}$ in modulus.

Now (5.6) is not yet a decision rule because terms like $E_t \bar{s}(t + J)$, $J > 0$ must be expressed as functions of the elements of the firm's information set at time t, $\Omega(t)$. For simplicity, assume that $\bar{P}(t) = \bar{P}$ for all t. By using the fact that $d(t) = d + \varepsilon_d(t)$, $a(t) = a + \varepsilon_a(t)$, $E\varepsilon_d(t)\varepsilon_d(s) = E\varepsilon_a(t)\varepsilon_a(s) = 0$ for all $t \neq s$, and (5.1), the decision rule for $i(t)$ can be written as

$$i(t) = (\lambda_1 + \lambda_2)i(t - 1) - \lambda_1 \lambda_2 i(t - 2) + X_0 + X_y(L)Y(t)$$

$$+ X_T(L)T(t + 1) + X_d \varepsilon_d(t) + X_a \varepsilon_a(t)$$

(5.7)

where

$$X_y(L) = \sum_{J=0}^{\gamma_y - 1} X_{yJ} L^J, \quad X_T(L) = \sum_{J=0}^{\gamma_T - 1} X_{TJ} L^J$$

X_a, X_d, and X_0 are functions of the underlying structural parameters of the model.[10] Given the decision rule (5.7) for $i(t)$, the production decision is given by the constraint (5.3).

As the definition of a rational expectations equilibrium under a sales control regime is virtually the same as that under the production control regime, we will not restate it here. Instead we point out that if the number of firms N is normalized to one, that definition requires, among other things, that $i(t) = I(t)$ and $q(t) = Q(t)$. Using this relationship in (5.7) yields the equilibrium law of motion for industrywide inventories

$$I(t) = (\lambda_1 + \lambda_2)I(t-1) - \lambda_1\lambda_2 I(t-2) + X_0 + X_y(L)Y(t)$$
$$+ X_T(L)T(t+1) + X_d\varepsilon_d(t) + X_a\varepsilon_a(t) \qquad (5.8)$$

If, for simplicity, one considers $\hat{P}(t)$, the deviation of $P(t)$ from its deterministic component $\overline{P}(t)$, we have from (5.2), that $u(t) = B_2\varepsilon_y(t)$. It is immediately evident that $P(t) - \overline{P}(t)$ is not Granger-caused by the deviations of sales, production, or inventories from their deterministic components. There is no reason to believe, however, that the absence of a Granger-causality result will survive the change of regimes. In fact, that result obtains precisely because of the regulations that define the interventionist regime. Hence output could be Granger-caused by prices in a deregulated environment.

In sum, this example demonstrates why the F-tests on an unconstrained vector autoregressive system or the implied dynamics revealed, say, by the corresponding moving average representation may contain very little information about the possible effects of deregulation. More generally, estimates of "structural" models that abstract from the effects of regulation may lead to possibly misleading policy implications if, in fact, economic agents face nontrivial constraints arising from the behavior of government agencies. This problem would seem to be particularly important in the context of certain U.S. energy-related markets.

Sales Control with Fixed Prices

An alternative sales control regime equates, identically, market prices to target prices at the cost of inducing unplanned inventories of finished goods. Let $I^P(t)$ denote industrywide planned inventories of finished goods, with $i^P(t)$, the representative firm's planned inventories of finished goods, being equal to $I^P(t)/N$. One way to implement the

---

[10] The precise relationship, which may be obtained by a straightforward but tedious application of results in Hansen and Sargent (1981), is contained in an appendix available upon request.

fixed price regime is to insist that firms supply, from inventory, additional units of the good in the event of higher than anticipated demand or to accumulate additional inventories in the event of lower than anticipated demand. Hence actual inventories $I(t)$ will, in general, be different from planned inventories at both the firm and industry levels, so that $I(t) = I^P(t) + I^U(t)$, where $I^U(t)$ represents unplanned inventories at time t. Actual sales at time t, $S(t)$, are given by $\bar{S}(t) + V(t)$, where $\bar{S}(t)$, defined by (5.1), is equal to the amount of sales which at time $(t-1)$ is expected to support the price $\bar{P}(t)$, and $V(t)$ is equal to the unplanned change in inventories, $[I(t) - I^P(t)] - I(t-1)$. This assumes, of course, that production does not occur instantaneously so that unplanned sales cannot be accommodated by changes in production plans. If $P(t) = \bar{P}(t)$ for all t, we have from (2.6) that

$$B_0 - B_1[\bar{S}(t) + V(t)] + B_2 Y(t) + T(t) = \bar{P}(t) \tag{5.9}$$

Moreover, from (5.1)

$$\bar{S}(t) = \frac{1}{B_1}[B_0 - \bar{P}(t) + B_2 E_{t-1} Y(t) + T(t)]$$

Hence

$$V(t) = \frac{B_2}{B_1}\varepsilon_y(t) \tag{5.10}$$

Because $\bar{S}(t) = Q(t) - I^P(t) + I(t-1)$ and $S(t) = \bar{S}(t) + V(t) = Q(t) - I(t) + I(t-1)$, we have that

$$I(t) - I^P(t) = V(t) \tag{5.11}$$

and

$$i(t) - i^P(t) = V(t)/N \tag{5.12}$$

Hence at either the firm or industry level, unanticipated sales, whether positive or negative, are matched by unanticipated inventories, which are proportional to the one-step-ahead forecasting error in predicting demand. This error is in turn proportional to the one-step-ahead forecast error in income.

The obvious question is the enforceability of this scheme. Two points may be made here: (1) By hypothesis the regulatory agency predicts $S(t)$ optimally to support $\bar{P}(t)$, so that $E[I(t) - I^P(t)] = E[V(t)] = 0$ and

$E[V(j)V(t)] = 0$ for all $j \neq t$. Hence, on average, firms do not expect unplanned inventory changes to occur. Furthermore, to the extent that such changes do occur, they are not serially correlated, so both the unconditional and conditional expected values of unplanned inventory changes are zero. (2) The regulatory agency fixes prices so that firms cannot, in principle, raise or reduce prices. Moreover, because it is the regulatory agency that rations sales, it is in principle able to enforce the rule against price-cutting or price increases.

Given the above considerations, the problem of the representative firm is identical to (5.4), with the proviso that $i(t)$ is replaced by $i^P(t) + V(t)/N$ for all t. Notice that the relevant constraint on production, $q(t)$, is now $q(t) = \bar{s}(t) + i^P(t) - i(t-1) + V(t)/N = \bar{s}(t) + i^P(t) - i^P(t-1) + V(t)/N - V(t-1)/N$.

It can be verified that the Euler equation for this problem is virtually the same as the corresponding Euler equation in the previous sales control regime, except for additional terms in $V(t)$. Moreover, the equilibrium laws of motion for $I(t)$ will be the same as (5.8), except for additional linear terms in current and lagged values of $V(t)$. Hence the fixed-price regime results in an inventory process with higher variance than that under the fluctuating-price sales control regime; a systematic tradeoff exists between the variance of prices and the variance of inventories.

VI. COMPARING REGIMES

From the regulatory agency's point of view, $E_{t-1}P(t)$ is $\overline{P}(t)$ under both the production and sales control regimes. The production control regime, however, requires forecasting inventories at time t, as well as forecasting future income. Because inventory decisions are made after the production constraint is announced, actual inventories will most likely deviate (randomly) from forecast inventories. Hence the actual price in the production control regime will have an additional error component compared to that of the actual price in the sales control case. To prove this, recall the price processes under the two regimes, equations (5.2) and (4.2), for the sales and production control regimes, respectively.

$$P_s(t) = \overline{P} + B_2[Y(t) - E_{t-1}Y(t)] \qquad (6.1)$$

and

$$P_Q(t) = \overline{P} + B_2[Y(t) - E_{t-1}Y(t)] + B_1[I(t) - E_{t-1}I(t)] \qquad (6.2)$$

where $\{P_s(t)\}_{t=0}^{\infty}$ is the actual price process under the sales control regime, $\{P_Q(t)\}_{t=0}^{\infty}$ is the actual price process under the production control regime. We have assumed for simplicity that $\bar{P}(t) = \bar{P}$ for all t under both regimes.

It follows that the variance of prices in the sales control regime is

$$\text{Var}[P_s(t)] = B_2^2 E[\varepsilon_y^2(t)] \tag{6.3}$$

and the variance of prices in the production control regime is

$$\text{Var}[P_Q(t)] = (B_2 + \psi_0 B_1)^2 E[\varepsilon_y^2(t)] + (B_1\gamma_s)^2 E[\varepsilon_d^2(t)]$$
$$+ (B_1\rho_0)^2 E[\varepsilon_T^2(t)] \tag{6.4}$$

which follows from our assumption that $E[\varepsilon_y(t)\varepsilon_d(t)] = E[\varepsilon_y(t)\varepsilon_T(t)] = 0$ for all t. Hence a sufficient condition for $\text{Var}[P_Q(t)]$ to be greater than $\text{Var}[P_s(t)]$ is that ψ_0 be greater than 0. Moreover, the higher is the variance of the innovation in the stochastic process $\{T(t)\}$, $\varepsilon_T(t)$, and the higher is the variance in inventory holding costs, $\varepsilon_d(t)$, the higher is the variance of prices in the production control regime relative to the variance of prices in the sales control regime.

Although the variance of prices, under our assumptions, will be higher under the production control than under the sales control regime, this mode of regulation implies an essentially nondynamic decision problem for the representative firm. Under a production control regime, the firm can only control inventory levels in order to minimize inventory costs. In contrast, the sales control regime allows firms to choose both production levels and inventory levels in order to minimize total operating costs subject to their sales constraint. As a result, the equilibrium law of motion of inventories under the sales control regime exhibits a much richer and more complex dynamic structure that reflects both the underlying dynamics of the production process, as well as the costs and benefits of holding inventories. Hence under the sales control regime, the equilibrium law of motion for inventories (5.8) is a second-order difference equation in $I(t)$, while under the production control regime, the equilibrium inventory process involves only one lagged value of inventories.

Overall then, prices fluctuate more in the production control case, while inventories exhibit less interesting and simpler dynamics. This is accomplished, however, at the cost of higher operating costs for the industry, even though average sales are the same under the two modes of regulation. Hence the sales regime is easier to implement and implies both lower industrywide operating costs and lower variance in the equilibrium price process.

Why, then, do governments tend to control production rather than sales? Presumably, the answer has to do with nonprice objectives of regulatory agencies, the acceptability of modes of regulation under existing laws, and the enforceability of the various regimes. Although these aspects have been neglected here, the framework of our analysis may be useful in addressing these issues.

At a different level, the important differences among the equilibria corresponding to the three regimes considered here are illustrative of a much more significant point: the data from a period in which one of the regimes is in effect are of little use in assessing the effects of moving to a new policy regime, unless the analyst explicitly takes into account the effects of the policy rule in force. Put somewhat differently, in order to conduct policy analysis, both the theoretical model as well as the estimation strategy used must be geared toward identifying the structural policy-invariant parameters of the model. Imagine that the analyst believes that the data to be used emerged from a period in which the production control regime was in effect. Then, the equilibrium laws of motion for inventories, output, and prices (in terms of deviations from deterministic components) are given by

$$I(t) = \gamma_1 I(t-1) + \psi(L)Y(t) + \rho(L)T(t+1) + \gamma_5 \varepsilon_d(t) \tag{6.5}$$

$$Q(t) = D_1(L)Y(t) + D_2(L)T(t+1) \tag{6.6}$$

$$P(t) = \varepsilon_p(t) \tag{6.7}$$

where

$$\varepsilon_p(t) = (B_2 + \psi_0 B_1)\varepsilon_y(t) + B_1 \gamma_5 \varepsilon_d(t) + B_1 \rho_0 \varepsilon_T(t)$$

The model predicts that, under deregulation, the equilibrium laws of motion are given by

$$I(t) = F_1 I(t-1) + F_2 Q(t-1) + F_3(L)Y(t) + F_4(L)T(t+1)$$
$$+ F_5 \varepsilon_d(t) + F_6 \varepsilon_a(t) \tag{6.8}$$

$$Q(t) = G_1 I(t-1) + G_2 Q(t-1) + G_3(L)Y(t) + G_4(L)T(t+1)$$
$$+ G_5 \varepsilon_d(t) + G_6 \varepsilon_a(t) \tag{6.9}$$

$$P(t) = -B_1 Q(t) + B_1[I(t) - I(t-1)] + B_2 Y(t) + T(t) \tag{6.10}$$

The unregulated model can be easily modified to allow for prices to Granger-cause output.[11] Eichenbaum (1984), in a nonenergy market related context, implements such a model on U.S. industry-level time series data.

Inspection of equations (6.5)–(6.10) points out how misleading it would be to predict the effects of deregulation on the basis of estimates of $\{\gamma_1, \psi(L), \rho(L), \gamma_5, D_1(L), D_2(L)\}$. It is clear that to undertake an analysis of the effects of different regulatory policies on this industry, the relevant objects of estimation must be $\{a, b, c, d, e, f\}$, the structural parameters of the firm's objective function, as well as $\{A_{11}, \ldots, A_{1\gamma_y}, A_{21}, \ldots, A_{2\gamma_T}\}$, the parameters governing the stochastic process $\{Y(t), T(t)\}$ and $\{B_0, B_1, B_2\}$, the parameters of demand behavior. In fact, one of our main purposes is to point out that, although such parameters as $\{a, b, c, d, e, f\}$ may be regarded as being in principle invariant to policy regimes, such estimates as $\{\gamma_0, \gamma_1, \gamma_5, \psi(L),$ $\rho(L), D_0, D_1(L), D_2(L)\}$ depend crucially upon the precise policy regime in effect. To proceed with estimation, the researcher must take a stand on which regulatory regime was in effect during the period the data represent. Having done this, error terms must be included in the model in the form of unobserved (from the econometrician's point of view) components to costs or demand—for example, $T(t)$, $\varepsilon_d(t)$, and $\varepsilon_a(t)$—or measurement error. Given a model of the error term, the parameters of the model may be estimated by some method such as maximum likelihood. By explicitly parameterizing demand, identifying the policy regime in effect, and allowing for fairly rich driving processes, such as $Y(t)$ and $T(t)$, it is possible to estimate the structural parameters of the model without identification necessarily depending on movements in prices.

VII. CONCLUSION

This chapter argues, by way of example, that the low responsiveness of output to prices observed in the data pertaining to the pre-1973 U.S. petroleum industry can be interpreted to be a direct consequence of the regulatory policies that were in effect. This conclusion is based on a consideration of the equilibrium of an industry operating under various government-imposed constraints designed to support a given target price path. Both the production control regime and the flexible price sales control regime models are consistent with the observation that prices did

---

[11] This is accomplished by assuming that serially correlated shocks to the industry demand curve are unobserved by the econometrician.

not Granger-cause, nor were they Granger-caused by, output and inventories in the U.S. petroleum industry prior to 1973.

Our results suggest that regulatory policies can often mask the response of supply decisions to market incentives. The combination of explicit hypotheses regarding regulatory regimes and the assumption of rational expectations can, in principle, solve this identification problem. Under circumstances in which regulations are viewed as if their purpose were to stabilize price movements, it is tempting to view prices as being determined by nonmarket forces. Adopting such an attitude is tantamount to abstracting from the cross-equation constraints that arise from optimizing agents' expectations regarding future regulatory decisions and the actual feedback to and from agents' decision rules and government policy rules. The examples in this chapter point out that such a procedure may reveal very little about the fundamental supply characteristics of the industry in question and offer unreliable guidance about the possible effects of changes in regulatory policy.

APPENDIX A

Here we derive equation (4.10) in terms of the underlying parameters of the model. Multiplying both sides of (4.5) by $N = 1$ and using equations (4.1) and (4.2), as well as the fact that $Ni(t) = I(t)$ and $Nq(t) = \bar{Q}(t)$, we have that

$$
\begin{aligned}
&[\phi + \beta f\alpha(\alpha - 1) - B_1] I(t) + (f\alpha^2 + B_1) E_{t-1} I(t) - f\alpha I(t-1) \\
&= d(t) + \frac{B_0}{B_1} [Bf\alpha(\alpha - 1) - f\alpha^2] + \left(\frac{f\alpha^2}{B_1} + 1\right) \bar{P}(t) \\
&\quad - \left[\beta + \frac{\beta f\alpha(\alpha - 1)}{B_1}\right] \bar{P}(t+1) - \left(B_2 + \frac{B_2}{B_1} f\alpha^2\right) A_1(L) Y(t-1) \\
&\quad + \left[\frac{\beta B_2 f(\alpha - 1)\alpha}{B_1}\right] A_1(L) Y(t) + B_2 Y(t) \\
&\quad - \frac{f\alpha^2}{B_1} T(t) + \frac{\beta f(\alpha - 1)\alpha}{B_1} T(t+1)
\end{aligned} \tag{A.1}
$$

Given that $\bar{P}(t) = \bar{P}$ for all t, μ_0 to μ_5 of (4.10) are given by

$$\mu_0 = -\left[f\alpha^2 + B_1\right]\mu_5 \tag{A.2}$$

$$\mu_1 = f\alpha\mu_5 \tag{A.3}$$

$$\mu_2 = \left\{ \frac{B_0}{B_1}\left[\beta f\alpha(\alpha - 1) - f\alpha^2\right] + \left(\frac{f\alpha^2}{B_1} + 1\right)\bar{P} \right.$$
$$\left. + \left[\beta - \beta\frac{f\alpha(\alpha - 1)}{B_1}\right]\bar{P}\right\}\mu_5 \tag{A.4}$$

$$\mu_3 = \frac{-f\alpha^2}{B_1}\mu_5 \tag{A.5}$$

$$\mu_4 = \frac{\beta f\alpha(\alpha - 1)}{B_1}\mu_5 \tag{A.6}$$

$$\mu_5 = \frac{1}{\phi + \beta f\alpha(\alpha - 1) - B_1} \tag{A.7}$$

$$\delta(L) = \mu_5\left\{ -\left[B_2 + \frac{B_2}{B_1}f\alpha^2\right]A_1(L)L + \frac{B_2}{B_1}\beta f(\alpha - 1)\alpha A_1(L) + B_2\right\} \tag{A.8}$$

$$\phi = -\left[e + f\alpha^2 + \beta f(\alpha - 1)^2\right] \tag{A.9}$$

REFERENCES

Bohi, D. R., and M. Russell. 1978. *Limiting Oil Imports* (Baltimore, Md., Johns Hopkins University Press for Resources for the Future).

deChazeau, Melvin G., and Alfred E. Kahn. 1959. *Integration and Competition in the Petroleum Industry* (New Haven, Conn., Yale University Press).

Eichenbaum, Martin. 1983. "A Rational Expectations Equilibrium Model of the Inventories of Finished Goods and Employment," *Journal of Monetary Economics* vol. 12, no. 2, pp. 259–278.

_____. 1984. "Some Evidence of the Smoothing Properties of Inventories of Finished Goods," *Journal of Monetary Economics*, forthcoming.

Epple, Dennis N. 1975. *Petroleum Discoveries and Government Policy: An Econometric Study of Supply* (Cambridge, Mass., Ballinger Publishing Company).

_____, and L. P. Hansen. 1979. "An Econometric Framework for Modeling Exhaustible Resources Supply," draft (Pittsburgh, Pa., Carnegie-Mellon University, GSIA).

Hansen, Lars P. 1980. "Large Sample Properties of Generalized Method of Moment Estimators," *Econometrica* vol. 50, no. 4, pp. 1029–1054.

————, and Thomas J. Sargent. 1980. "Formulating and Estimating Dynamic Linear Rational Expectations Models," *Journal of Economics Dynamics and Control* vol. 2, no. 1, pp. 7–46.

————. 1981. "Linear Rational Expectations Models for Dynamically Interrelated Variables," in R. E. Lucas and T. J. Sargent, eds., *Rational Expectations and Econometric Practice* (Minneapolis, Minn., University of Minnesota Press).

Lucas R. E., Jr. 1976. "Econometric Policy Evaluation: A Critique," in K. Brunner and A. H. Meltzer, eds., *The Phillips Curve and Labor Markets*, Carnegie-Rochester Conferences on Public Policy, vol. 1 (Amsterdam, North-Holland Press).

————, and E. C. Prescott. 1971. "Investment Under Uncertainty," *Econometrica* vol. 39, no. 5, pp. 659–681.

Sargent, Thomas J. 1981. "Interpreting Economic Time Series," *Journal of Political Economy* vol. 89, no. 2, pp. 213–248.

5
Linear-Quadratic Duopoly Models of Resource Depletion

Lars Peter Hansen, Dennis Epple,
and William Roberds

This chapter contains some methods for quantitatively analyzing multiple-agent models of dynamic games in which at least one agent takes into account its influence on the aggregate environment. We confine our attention to models in which the agents solve stochastic, quadratic optimization problems subject to linear constraints. A convenient feature of such models is that the equilibrium laws of motion are linear in the relevant state variables and can be deduced easily. Consequently, we can obtain tractable characterizations of the empirical implications of the models under alternative rules for how the agents interact.

Our approach to solving such models is first to deduce the stochastic Euler equations for each of the agents and then to solve simultaneously these stochastic Euler equations subject to the respective transversality conditions. Because the stochastic Euler equations are time invariant, we use the solution strategy suggested by Sargent (1979), Taylor (1979b), Hansen and Sargent (1981), and Whiteman (1983) that involves factoring the characteristic function of the system of stochastic difference equa-

Lars Peter Hansen is Professor of Economics, University of Chicago. Dennis Epple is Professor of Economics, Carnegie-Mellon University. William Roberds is with the Research Department of the Federal Reserve Bank of Minneapolis.

tions. The procedure we propose for obtaining the factorization, however, is different from those suggested previously.

Our solution approach is meant to be complementary to the recursive procedures suggested by Kydland (1977), Kydland and Prescott (1980), and Chow (1981) for solving models of dynamic games. For certain problems, our methods will be computationally more convenient than recursive methods. Computational costs are of some concern when an investigator is ultimately interested in obtaining estimates of parameters via numerical search procedures that require that the model be solved a large number of times. In addition to computational costs, however, our nonrecursive procedures can be more revealing in some dimensions when comparing the dynamics across alternative games.

Although our methods can be applied to a variety of dynamic game situations that might occur, for instance, in studying macroeconomic policy making, our discussion is conducted in the context of a resource depletion example. Not only does this example provide a useful forum for illustrating our solution proposals, but it is also of interest in its own right. The substantive economic analysis here provides the theoretical support for the empirical investigations of Epple (1984) in his study of oil and gas exploration and Roberds (1984) in his study of the depletion of Canadian nickel.

The key dynamic ingredient in our resource depletion models is the specification of marginal exploitation costs as an increasing function of the cumulative amount of the resource exploited. In contrast to exhaustible resource models, we do not impose a finite resource stock constraint. Our models can be expanded to include other forms of endogenous dynamics such as adjustment costs, gestation lags, or intertemporal specifications of demand. For ease of comparison, however, our specification of resource exploitation costs is the sole source of endogenous dynamics in our models. We do permit exogenous dynamics in the form of serially correlated demand and supply shocks.

For simplicity, we consider two-player dynamic games, although our methods can be extended easily to analyze n-player games. Our players are resource suppliers that are endowed with possibly different specifications of cost parameters and that face a sequence of one-period demand functions. Uncertainty enters into the environment via stochastic shifts in exploitation costs and in the one-period demands. In making intertemporal decisions, each player forecasts future values of the demand and supply shocks optimally using current and past values of a set of stochastic forcing variables.

One of our principal tasks is to compare the behavior of the two suppliers when they play alternative dynamic games. We consider three games in which each supplier is treated symmetrically and three games in which one player is dominant in some sense. The specification of the dominant player games relies heavily on the work of Kydland (1977) and Kydland and Prescott (1977, 1980).

I. MODEL SPECIFICATIONS

In this section, we specify the dynamic quadratic objective functions for two suppliers of an exhaustible resource, the linear market demand function, and the linear laws of motion for the stochastic forcing variables. The specifications are simple in order to facilitate the calculation of dynamic equilibrium solutions, but they do capture important features of the resource depletion problem. Although we assume two suppliers, some specifications apply to a larger class of suppliers whose behavior can be summarized by fictitious representative players.

First, we specify the dynamic objective function of supplier i. Later in this section we will discuss the constraints faced by each supplier. Supplier i's objective is to maximize:

$$E_0 \sum_{t=0}^{\infty} \beta^t \Big\{ p_t\big[(1-L)r_{it}\big] - s_{it}\big[(1-L)r_{it}\big] - \tfrac{1}{2}\big[(1-L)r_{it}\big]^2 \theta_i$$

$$-\pi_i\big[\tfrac{1}{2}(1-L)r_{it} + r_{it-1}\big]\big[(1-L)r_{it}\big]\Big\} \tag{1.1}$$

where r_{it} is the cumulative amount of resource extracted by player i from time period zero through time period t, p_t is the price of the resource at time period t, s_{it} is a random shock to the extraction cost of player i at time t, β is a discount factor between zero and one, θ_i and π_i are positive extraction cost parameters for player i, L is the lag operator, and E_t is the expectations operator conditioned on information available at time t. Player i is allowed to make period t decisions contingent on information available at time t. The content of this information will be made precise in subsequent discussion. In (1.1), $r_{it,-1}$ is normalized to be zero.[1]

The objective given in (1.1) can be viewed as a discounted sum of current and future revenues from selling a resource minus costs associated with extracting the resource. For instance, $p_t[(1-L)r_{it}]$ is the revenue from selling the resource at time t and the remaining component to the period t reward is the negative of the time t cost of extracting the

---

[1] The impact of extraction prior to time zero is captured in the supply shock s_{it} because this shock can have a positive mean.

resource. Hence the marginal time period t cost of extracting $(1 - L)r_{it}$ units of the resource is given by $s_{it} + \theta_i(1 - L)r_{it} + \pi_i r_{it}$. The cost parameter π_i captures the notion that marginal extraction costs increase as the cumulative stock extracted increases. Therefore extraction today not only increases the costs incurred today but also costs incurred in future time periods. This characteristic serves to define a nonrenewable resource, and a finite physical resource stock constraint is not imposed. A limitation of the analysis is that $(1 - L)r_{it}$ is not required to be nonnegative.

Manipulating the quadratic cost terms in the objective function (1.1) produces the following alternative expression for the discounted costs:

$$\sum_{t=0}^{\infty} \beta^t \left\{ \tfrac{1}{2}\left[(1 - L)r_{it}\right]^2 \theta_i + \tfrac{1}{2}(r_{it})^2 \pi_i(1 - \beta) + s_{it}\left[(1 - L)r_{it}\right] \right\}$$

Therefore the objective function for supplier i can be represented as

$$E_0 \sum_{t=0}^{\infty} \beta^t \Big\{ p_t\left[(1 - L)r_{it}\right] - s_{it}\left[(1 - L)r_{it}\right] - \tfrac{1}{2}\left[(1 - L)r_{it}\right]^2 \theta_i$$
$$- \tfrac{1}{2}(r_{it})^2 \pi_i(1 - \beta)\Big\} \tag{1.2}$$

which is a more convenient representation of supplier i's objective than is (1.1).

Each supplier faces a set of linear constraints. The inverse demand function for the resource is given by

$$p_t = d_t - \delta\left[(1 - L)r_{1t} + (1 - L)r_{2t}\right] \tag{1.3}$$

where d_t is a stochastic demand shock and δ is a demand parameter that is assumed to be positive.[2]

The stochastic forcing variables (d_t, s_{1t}, s_{2t}) are elements of a vector X_t that has a law of motion given by

$$\Xi(L)X_t = \phi(L)U_t \tag{1.4}$$

---

[2] The demand function (1.3) is linear with a stochastic choke price d_t. Recall that $(1 - L)r_{it}$ is not required to be nonnegative. Hence an equilibrium is possible in which resource consumption is negative in some time periods with prices above d_t. Many stochastic specifications of this model will have negative resource consumption at some points in time, but this phenomenon seems more likely to occur far away from the initial time period when the impact of the cumulative extraction is very pronounced. Also, for the deterministic versions of the model that we have studied numerically, $(1 - L)r_{it}$ stays nonnegative over the entire infinite horizon for both players. Nonetheless, we have not investigated thoroughly the pervasiveness of negative production and consumption for stochastic versions of the model.

for $t = 0, 1, \ldots$, where $\Xi(Z)$ is a scalar polynomial with zeros that are greater than $\sqrt{\beta}$ in absolute value and $\phi(Z)$ is matrix polynomial in Z. For $t = 0, 1, \ldots$, the vector U_t satisfies

$$E_{t-1}(U_t) = K$$

and

$$E_0(U_t'U_t) < B$$

where K and B are in the information set at time zero. Because $\Xi(Z)$ can have zeros that are less than 1 in absolute value, specification (1.4) allows for certain forms of stochastic growth. For convenience, this analysis uses a moving average representation of the forcing process X. Relation (1.4) can be extended to hold for all time t by, among other things, letting X_t and U_t be zero for all t less than some negative integer. Then, we can solve for X_t and obtain the moving average representation

$$X_t = \left[\frac{\phi(L)}{\Xi(L)} \right] U_t \tag{1.5}$$

which is always well defined, given that at any time t only a finite number of current and past values of U_t are different from zero. Both suppliers observe current and past values of U_t at time t and are allowed to make decisions at time t contingent on that information.

Completing the specification of the model requires stipulating the dynamic game the two suppliers are assumed to play. Such a stipulation includes each player's perception of the stochastic laws of motion for prices and the decisions of the other player. We consider three games in which each player is treated symmetrically and three games in which the second player is dominant in some sense. The three symmetric games are:

A. *Competitive Equilibrium*: Each supplier maximizes its respective objective function treating prices as an uncontrollable forcing process.

B. *Symmetric Nash Game*: Each supplier maximizes its respective objective function taking into account its own influence on prices but treating the decisions of the other supplier as an uncontrollable forcing process.

C. *Collusive Game*: The two suppliers collude and maximize the sum of the two objective functions given in (1.2), taking into account their influence on prices.

The specification of the symmetric Nash game warrants further elaboration. Player i substitutes the inverse demand function into i's objective function (1.2). Then at time period 0 player i selects a sequence of decision rules for r_{it} that are functions of U_s for s less than or equal to t and of the initial conditions. Player i chooses these decision rules by maximizing (1.2) subject to the other player's sequence of decision rules. This solution approach allows each player to respond to movements in the stochastic forcing processes but not to take into account the influence on the other player's decisions. The decision rules obtained in this manner will not be valid for subgames initiated at future time periods with beginning-period cumulative resource extractions that are different from those obtained in the equilibrium solution. In this sense, the equilibrium concept is not subgame perfect. The decision rules will remain valid, however, for those subgames initiated with the beginning period cumulative resource extractions obtained in equilibrium. This Nash game may be viewed as a stochastic counterpart to the symmetric open-loop game described by Kydland (1975) and Reinganum and Stokey (1983), among others.

In section III, we show how to calculate the stochastic equilibria for three games in which the second player is dominant in some sense. In all of these games, the first player maximizes its objective function, taking prices as an uncontrollable forcing process. The strategies of the second player are:

D. *Nash-Competitive Game*: The second supplier maximizes its objective function, taking into account its influence on prices but treating the decisions of the first player as an uncontrollable forcing process.

E. *Dominant-Competitive Game*: The second supplier maximizes its objective function taking into account its influence both on prices and on the decisions of the first player.

F. *Dominant-Competitive, Time-Consistent Game*: The second supplier maximizes its objective function, taking into account its influence on the current and future prices and decisions of the first supplier but systematically ignoring its influence on past prices and decisions of the first supplier.

The distinctions between games E and F are explained more fully in section III.

II. SYMMETRIC GAMES

All of the games considered in this chapter can be solved using nonrecursive procedures. Our solutions to the symmetric games do not require that we deduce the equilibrium decision rules for each individual player. Instead, we calculate the equilibrium by solving a system of stochastic difference equations obtained from the Euler equations of each player. If desired, the individual decision rules can be derived using our calculation of the equilibrium law of motion for prices and quantities, although we do not elaborate on such calculations.

The solutions to all three symmetric games are also solutions to quadratic control problems. Furthermore, these control problems have a common form, so that by solving one control problem and varying the parameters of that problem we can obtain the solutions to all three games. The solution to the following stochastic control problem gives the solution to the symmetric games. Suppose a fictitious agent solves the problem of maximizing

$$E_0 \sum_{t=0}^{\infty} \beta^t \left\{ S_t'[(1-L)R_t] - \tfrac{1}{2}[(1-L)R_t]'\theta[(1-L)R_t] - \tfrac{1}{2}R_t'\pi R_t \right\}$$

$$(2.1)$$

where $R_t = (r_{1t}, r_{2t})'$

$$\pi = \begin{bmatrix} (1-\beta)\pi_1 & 0 \\ 0 & (1-\beta)\pi_2 \end{bmatrix}$$

$$\theta = \begin{bmatrix} \theta_1 & 0 \\ 0 & \theta_2 \end{bmatrix} + \Omega$$

S_t is a two-dimensional, uncontrollable forcing vector, $R_{-1} = 0$, and β is a positive discount factor that is less than 1.

By selecting different specifications of the (2×2) matrix Ω, we obtain the equilibrium laws of motion for the quantities of the three symmetric games described at the end of section I. The laws of motion for the prices are obtained by substituting for R_t in the inverse demand function (1.3). All three games have the same forcing vector, given by

$$S_t = \begin{bmatrix} d_t - s_{1t} \\ d_t - s_{2t} \end{bmatrix}$$

The matrix Ω is distinct for each game. For game A (competitive equilibrium), following Lucas and Prescott (1971) and Sargent (1979), the law of motion for the equilibrium quantities can be obtained by solving a social planning problem of the form given in (2.1) with

$$\Omega^a = \begin{bmatrix} \delta & \delta \\ \delta & \delta \end{bmatrix} \qquad (2.2)$$

As shown by Jagannathan (1981), the equilibrium quantities for game B (symmetric Nash game) can be obtained by maximizing (2.1), where Ω is given by

$$\Omega^b = \begin{bmatrix} 2\delta & \delta \\ \delta & 2\delta \end{bmatrix} \tag{2.3}$$

The equilibrium quantities for game C (collusive game) are obtained by maximizing (2.1), where Ω is given by

$$\Omega^c = \begin{bmatrix} 2\delta & 2\delta \\ 2\delta & 2\delta \end{bmatrix} \tag{2.4}$$

The fact that the laws of motion of the equilibrium quantities in the three symmetric games can be obtained by maximizing (2.1) for alternative choices of Ω is very convenient in deriving comparative dynamics results.

Solution

To solve the optimization problem given in (2.1), we follow Hansen and Sargent (1981) and obtain the stochastic Euler equation system by differentiating with respect to R_t. This Euler equation system is

$$E_t\left\{\left[\theta(1-\beta L^{-1})(1-L)+\pi\right]R_t\right\} = E_t\left[(1-\beta L^{-1})S_t\right] \tag{2.5}$$

for $t = 0,1,\ldots$, where $R_{-1}=0$. The characteristic function for this system of equations can be factored as follows:

$$(1-\beta Z^{-1})(1-Z)\theta + \pi = C(\beta Z^{-1})'C(Z)$$

where $\det[C(Z)]$ is different from zero when $|Z|$ is less than $\sqrt{\beta}$ and where $C(Z)$ is a first-order matrix polynomial in Z. The decision rule for R_t is then given by

$$C(L)R_t = E_t\left[(1-\beta L^{-1})C(\beta L^{-1})'^{-1}S_t\right] \tag{2.6}$$

To implement decision rule (2.6), it is necessary to calculate the solution to an optimal forecasting problem, that is, to calculate

$$E_t\left[(1-\beta L^{-1})C(\beta L^{-1})'S_t\right]$$

In performing this computation, we again follow Hansen and Sargent (1981). Let Z_1 and Z_2 denote the two zeros of $\det[C(Z)]$. In appendix A, both of these zeros are shown to be real and greater than 1. Because

$$\left[C(Z)'\right]^{-1} = \frac{\text{adj}\left[C(Z)'\right]}{\det\left[C(Z)\right]}$$

where $\det[C(Z)] = Z_0(Z - Z_1)(Z - Z_2)$, a matrix partial fractions representation of $(1 - Z)[C(Z)']^{-1}$ is given by

$$(1 - Z)\left[C(Z)'\right]^{-1} = Q_0 + Q_1(Z - Z_1)^{-1} + Q_2(Z - Z_2)^{-1}$$

Therefore

$$(1 - \beta Z^{-1})\left[C(\beta Z^{-1})\right]^{-1} = Q_0 - \frac{Q_1 Z_1^{-1}}{\left[1 - \beta(ZZ_1)^{-1}\right]} - \frac{Q Z_2^{-1}}{\left[1 - \beta(ZZ_2)^{-1}\right]}$$

and (2.6) can be expressed as

$$C(L)R_t = Q_0 S_t - E_t \left\{ \left[\frac{Q_1 Z_1^{-1}}{(1 - \beta Z_1^{-1} L^{-1})} + \frac{Q_2 Z_2^{-1}}{(1 - \beta Z_2^{-1} L^{-1})} \right] S_t \right\}$$

Hence obtaining a decision rule for R_t expressed in terms of variables known to the players at time t requires solving the following forecasting problem:

$$E_t \left\{ \left[\frac{1}{(1 - \beta Z_i^{-1} L^{-1})} \right] S_t \right\} = E_t \left[\sum_{j=0}^{\infty} \left(\frac{\beta}{Z_i} \right)^j S_{t+j} \right] \tag{2.7}$$

for $i = 1, 2$.

To solve the optimal forecasting problems given in (2.7), we exploit the time-invariant moving average representation given in (1.5). In particular, (1.5) implies that S can be represented as a time-invariant moving average,

$$S_t = \Gamma(L)U_t$$

Hansen and Sargent (1980) show that

$$E_t \left\{ \left[\frac{1}{(1 - \beta Z_i^{-1} L^{-1})} \right] S_t \right\} = \left[\frac{L\Gamma(L) - \beta Z_i^{-1} \Gamma(\beta Z_i^{-1})}{(L - \beta Z_i^{-1})} \right] U_t$$

$$+ \frac{\beta Z_i^{-1} \Gamma(\beta Z_i^{-1}) K}{(1 - \beta Z_i^{-1})}$$

The decision rule for R_t is obtained by substituting the above solution to the forecasting problem into (2.6)

$$
\begin{aligned}
C(L)R_t = \Bigg\{ & Q_0\Gamma(L) - \beta Z_1^{-1}Q_1 \frac{\left[L\Gamma(L) - \beta Z_1^{-1}\Gamma(\beta Z_1^{-1})\right]}{(L - \beta Z_1^{-1})} \\
& - \beta Z_2^{-1}Q_2 \frac{\left[L\Gamma(L) - \beta Z_2^{-1}\Gamma(\beta Z_2^{-1})\right]}{(L - \beta Z_2^{-1})} \Bigg\} U_t \\
& + \frac{\beta Z_1^{-1}\Gamma(\beta Z_1^{-1})K}{(1 - \beta Z_1^{-1})} + \frac{\beta Z_2^{-1}\Gamma(\beta Z_2^{-1})K}{(1 - \beta Z_2^{-1})}
\end{aligned}
\tag{2.8}
$$

Hansen and Sargent (1981) elaborate on each of these steps in deriving the decision rule, and they describe some algorithms that are useful in executing the computations.

Comparative Dynamics

Relation (2.8) is convenient for formal econometric analysis and simulation. Obtaining qualitative comparative dynamic results across different games at the level of generality considered here is difficult, if not impossible. For some special cases of our model, however, dynamic comparisons can be made. These special cases entail restrictions on the parameters of the cost functions and on the stochastic process for the forcing variables. We first impose restrictions that permit ordering of the cumulative extraction path for each date t. We then relax restrictions on the cost function parameters while retaining restrictions on the stochastic process for the forcing variables. This allows us to make comparisons that hold for sufficiently large t.

First, we simplify our cost specification by requiring that π_1 equal π_2, and θ_1 equal θ_2. Premultiplying Euler equations (2.5) by the row vector [1 1] yields

$$
E_t\left\{\left[(1 - \beta L^{-1})(1 - L)\theta_a + \pi_a\right]R_{at}\right\} = E_t\left[(1 - \beta L^{-1})S_{at}\right]
\tag{2.9}
$$

where

$$
R_{at} = [1\ 1]R_t
$$
$$
S_{at} = [1\ 1]S_t
$$
$$
\theta_a = \tfrac{1}{2}[1\ 1]\theta[1\ 1]'
$$
$$
\pi_a = \tfrac{1}{2}[1\ 1]\pi[1\ 1]'
$$

The stochastic difference equation (2.9) can be solved for aggregate cumulative extraction R_{at}. To do this, we use the same solution strategy described above, except that now we have a single equation system. The characteristic function for (2.9) can be factored as follows:

$$(1 - \beta Z^{-1})(1 - Z)\theta_a + \pi_a = c_0(1 - c_1\beta Z^{-1})(1 - c_1 Z)$$

where $0 < c_1 < 1$. The stochastic process R_a satisfies

$$R_{at} = c_1 R_{at-1} + \left(\frac{1}{c_0}\right) E_t \sum_{j=0}^{\infty} (\beta c_1)^j (S_{a,t+j} - \beta S_{a,t+j+1})$$

or equivalently,

$$R_{at} = c_1 R_{at-1} + \left(\frac{1}{c_0}\right) S_{at} - \left[\frac{(\beta - \beta c_1)}{c_0}\right] E_t \sum_{j=0}^{\infty} (\beta c_1)^j (S_{at+j+1})$$

(2.10)

For the time being, we make the forecasting problem implicit in (2.10) trivial by assuming that $S_{at} = K_a > 0$ for all nonnegative t. In this case, (2.10) simplifies to the expression

$$R_{at} = c_1 R_{at-1} + \frac{(1 - \beta)(1 - c_1)K_a}{\pi_a}$$

Because $R_{a,-1}$ is zero, it follows that

$$R_{at} = \left(\sum_{j=0}^{t} c_1^j\right) \frac{(1 - \beta)(1 - c_1)K_a}{\pi_a}$$

$$= \frac{(1 - c_1^{t+1})(1 - \beta)K_a}{\pi_a}$$

(2.11)

The alternative symmetric games imply different values of c_1 but leave β, π_a, and K_a unaltered. Values of c_1 that are closer to unity imply the sequence $\{R_{at}: t = 0, 1, 2 \ldots\}$ converges more slowly to the asymptote

$$\frac{(1 - \beta)K_a}{\pi_a}$$

which is common to all games.

In light of (2.11), the time paths for the alternative games can be compared by ranking the values of c_1 for each game. Let θ_a^a denote the value of θ_a for the competitive game (game A), θ_a^b the value of θ_a for the Nash game (game B), θ_a^c the value of θ_a for the cooperative game (game C). Specifications (2.2), (2.3), and (2.4) imply that

$$\theta_a^c > \theta_a^b > \theta_a^a \tag{2.12}$$

These inequalities in turn imply that

$$c_1^c > c_1^b > c_1^a$$

Therefore,

$$R_{at}^c < R_{at}^b < R_{at}^a$$

for $t = 0, 1, \ldots$. Hence, with this simple specification of costs and trivial specification of the forcing variables, the cumulative amount of resource exploited by the players is greatest for the competitive game and least for the cooperative game at all points in time.[3] This is true even though

$$\lim_{t \to \infty} R_{at}^c = \lim_{t \to \infty} R_{at}^b = \lim_{t \to \infty} R_{at}^c = \frac{(1 - \beta) K_a}{\pi_a}$$

Next, we maintain the identical cost specification and introduce a simple stochastic structure. Suppose that $S_{at} = \Gamma_a U_t$ for all nonnegative t. Relation (2.10) now becomes

$$R_{at} = c_1 R_{at-1} + \left(\frac{1}{c_0}\right) \Gamma_a U_t - \frac{\beta(1 - c_1) K_a}{c_0(1 - \beta c_1)} \tag{2.13}$$

where $K_a = \Gamma_a K$. The inequalities in (2.12) imply that

$$c_0^c > c_0^b > c_0^a$$

Hence, when the stochastic forcing variables are serially uncorrelated, the aggregate cumulative extraction R_{at} is most responsive to an innovation in the forcing variables, that is, to $\Gamma_a U_t$, in the competitive game and least responsive in the cooperative game.

Finally, suppose that the elements of $\Gamma(Z)$ do not have any poles inside the unit circle. This condition insures that the impact of U_t on

---

[3] Relation (2.11) also can be used in comparing the price paths across the alternative games. Because the demand function (1.3) relates prices to $(1 - L) R_{at}$, the prices initially will be smallest but eventually largest for game A. Conversely, the prices initially will be largest but eventually smallest for game C.

future values of X_t in representation (1.5) ultimately dies out, so that

$$\lim_{j \to \infty} E_t S_{t+j} = \Gamma(1)K$$

In this case,

$$\lim_{j \to \infty} E_t R_{at+j} = \frac{(1 - \beta)K_a}{\pi_a}$$

for all three symmetric games where $K_a = [1 \ 1]\Gamma(1)K$. Uniform ordering of the time paths of cumulative exploitation is not possible, however, for this more general stochastic specification of S.

We now return to the case in which the cost parameters for the two suppliers are distinct. In other words, θ_1 and θ_2 may differ, as may π_1 and π_2. We consider the trivial specification of the forcing variables in which $S_t = K^* > 0$ for all nonnegative t. From (2.6), it follows that

$$C(L)R_t = (1 - \beta)\left[C(\beta)'\right]^{-1}K^* \tag{2.14}$$

Let Z_1 and Z_2 be the zeros of $\det[C(Z)]$. Notice that Z_1 and Z_2 are also zeros of the determinant of the characteristic function of (2.5) because that function can be expressed as $C(\beta Z^{-1})'C(Z)$. In appendix A, Z_1 and Z_2 are shown to be greater than 1.[4] The solution to this difference equation, (2.14), is

$$R_t = \mu_1(Z_1)^{-t} + \mu_2(Z_2)^{-t} + (1 - \beta)\pi^{-1}K^*$$

where μ_1 and μ_2 satisfy

$$C(Z_1)\mu_1 = 0$$
$$C(Z_1)\mu_2 = 0$$

and

$$\mu_1 Z_1 + \mu_2 Z_2 = -(1 - \beta)\pi^{-1}K^* \tag{2.15}$$

Without loss of generality, we assume that Z_1 is less than Z_2. In appendix A, it is shown that

$$Z_1^c < Z_1^b < Z_1^a$$

---

[4] In appendix A, we consider only the solution to the homogeneous component of the difference equation.

For all games, the elements of the vector μ_1 have the same sign while the elements of μ_2 have opposite signs. In light of (2.15), the elements of μ_1 must be negative for all games. These facts allow us to conclude that for sufficiently large values of t

$$R_t^c < R_t^b < R_t^a$$

and

$$\lim_{t \to \infty} R_t^c = \lim_{t \to \infty} R_t^b = \lim_{t \to \infty} R_t^a = (1 - \beta)\pi^{-1}K^* \qquad (2.16)$$

Hence, for sufficiently large t, we can order the cumulative amount of the resources exploited by each supplier under the three alternative symmetric games; however, the ultimate amount of the resource each of the suppliers exploits is the same for all three games.

In situations in which the stochastic forcing variables are nontrivial but the elements of $\Gamma(Z)$ do not have any poles inside the unit circle, the following analogue to (2.16) occurs for all games:

$$\lim_{j \to \infty} E_t R_{t+j} = (1 - \beta)\pi^{-1}K^*$$

where $K^* = \Gamma(1)K$. In other words, at any point in time the ultimate amount of resource each supplier would be expected to extract is the same for each of the symmetric games. As in the identical cost case, for general specifications of S, we cannot expect to order time paths of cumulative exploitation. Representation (2.8), however, does provide us with a convenient mapping from the parameters of the stochastic forcing variables, Γ and K, to the parameters governing the stochastic evolution of R. This mapping can be applied for any of the three symmetric games.

Roughly speaking, our comparative dynamics results for symmetric games conform with results obtained in studies of perfect certainty models of exhaustible resource depletion. For instance, Stiglitz (1976) and Sweeney (1977) found that a monopolist depletes the resource at a faster rate than a comparable competitive supplier. Salant (1976) found that the equilibrium rate of resource extraction in a Nash-Cournot model is between the rates obtained in monopoly and competitive models. All three of these studies rely on a fixed resource stock as being the principal source of endogenous dynamics, and they adopt a relatively simple specification of intraperiod extraction costs. In this sense, their models are not comparable to the models in this section.

III. NONSYMMETRIC GAMES

In the nonsymmetric games D, E, and F, the first supplier is competitive and views prices as a component of an uncontrollable stochastic process, while the second supplier can exert influence over prices and the decisions of the first supplier. The amount of influence the second supplier can exert is different for each of the three games.

First, consider game D, in which the second supplier takes into account its own influence on prices but treats the decisions of the first player as a stochastic forcing process. The solution method proposed in section II can be applied to this problem by letting

$$\Omega^d = \begin{bmatrix} \delta & \delta \\ \delta & 2\delta \end{bmatrix}$$

Games E and F require a different solution method. We begin by deducing expressions that specify the dependence of the first supplier's decisions on the anticipated decisions of the second supplier. When the first player is a price taker, the stochastic Euler equation system obtained by differentiating (1.2) with respect to r_{it} for i equal to 1 is

$$E_t\left\{\left[\theta_1(1 - \beta L^{-1})(1 - L) + \pi_1(1 - \beta)\right]r_{1t}\right\}$$
$$= E_t\left[(1 - \beta L^{-1})(p_t - s_{1t})\right]$$

for $t = 0, 1, \ldots$. Substituting for p_t from the inverse demand function (1.3) yields

$$E_t\left\{\left[(\theta_1 + \delta)(1 - \beta L^{-1})(1 - L) + \pi_1(1 - \beta)\right]r_{1t}\right\}$$
$$= -E_t\left[\delta(1 - \beta L^{-1})(1 - L)r_{2t}\right] + E_t(1 - \beta L^{-1})(d_t - s_{1t}) \quad (3.1)$$

We now solve (3.1) for r_1, treating r_2 as a component of the stochastic forcing process. The characteristic function for the left-hand side of (3.1) can be factored as follows:

$$(\theta_1 + \delta)(1 - \beta Z^{-1})(1 - Z) + \pi_1(1 - \beta) = \sigma_0(1 - \sigma_1 \beta Z^{-1})(1 - \sigma_1 Z)$$

where $0 < \sigma_1 < 1$. Hence the stochastic decision process for the first supplier satisfies

$$\sigma_0(1 - \sigma_1 L)r_{1t} + E_t\left\{\left[\delta\frac{(1 - \beta L^{-1})(1 - L)}{(1 - \sigma_1 \beta L^{-1})}\right]r_{2t}\right\}$$
$$- E_t\left\{\left[\frac{(1 - \beta L^{-1})}{(1 - \sigma_1 \beta L^{-1})}\right](d_{1t} - s_{1t})\right\} = 0 \quad (3.2)$$

Relation (3.2) is valuable in calculating the solutions to games E and F because it displays the dependence, in equilibrium, of the decisions of player one on current and anticipated future decisions of player two.

Solution to Game E

To determine the decision rule for the dominant player in game E, the inverse demand function (1.3) is substituted into the objective function (1.2) for the second supplier. The resulting objective is to maximize

$$J = E_0 \sum_{t=0}^{\infty} \beta^t \big\{ [d_t - s_{2t}][(1 - L)r_{2t}] - \delta[(1 - L)r_{2t}][(1 - L)r_{1t}]$$

$$- [\delta + \tfrac{1}{2}\theta_2][(1 - L)r_{2t}]^2 - \tfrac{1}{2}\pi_2[1 - \beta][r_{2t}]^2 \big\} \tag{3.3}$$

The second player is modeled as choosing decision rules for both r_{1t} and r_{2t} viewing (3.2) and the stochastic law of motion for S_t as a sequence of linear constraints. To impose the constraints (3.2), we introduce the Lagrangian,

$$J^e = J - E_0 \sum_{t=0}^{\infty} \beta^t m_t \bigg(\sigma_0 [1 - \sigma_1 L] r_{1t} + \delta \left[\frac{(1 - \beta L^{-1})(1 - L)}{(1 - \beta \sigma_1 L^{-1})} \right] r_{2t}$$

$$- \frac{[1 - \beta L^{-1}]}{[1 - \sigma_1 \beta L^{-1}]} [d_t - s_{1t}] \bigg)$$

where m_t is the Lagrange multiplier that is constrained to be in the information set of the player two at time t. Differentiating J^e with respect to r_{1t} and r_{2t} gives the stochastic Euler equations,

$$E_t \big[\delta(1 - \beta L^{-1})(1 - L)r_{2t} + \sigma_0(1 - \sigma_1 \beta L^{-1})m_t \big] = 0 \tag{3.4}$$

$$E_t \bigg\{ \delta[1 - \beta L^{-1}][1 - L]r_{1t} + [(2\delta + \theta_2)(1 - \beta L^{-1})(1 - L)$$

$$+ \pi_2(1 - \beta)]r_{2t} + \delta \left[\frac{(1 - \beta L^{-1})(1 - L)}{(1 - \sigma_1 L)} \right] m_t \bigg\}$$

$$= E_t \big[(1 - \beta L^{-1})(d_t - s_{2t}) \big]$$

for $t = 0, 1, 2, \ldots$, where $m_t = 0$ for negative t, and $r_{1, -1} = r_{2, -1} = 0$.

It is convenient to transform the Lagrange multiplier m_t as follows:[5]

$$m_t^e = \frac{m_t}{(1 - \sigma_1 L)} \tag{3.5}$$

Since m_t is zero for negative values of t, m_{-1}^e is zero. Substituting m_t^e for m_t in (3.4) and (3.5) and stacking the stochastic difference equations (3.1), (3.4), and (3.5) into a system yields

$$E_t \begin{bmatrix} (\theta_1 + \delta)(1 - \beta L^{-1})(1 - L) + \pi_1(1 - \beta) \\ \delta(1 - \beta L^{-1})(1 - L) \\ 0 \end{bmatrix}$$

$$\begin{matrix} \delta(1 - \beta L^{-1})(1 - L) \\ (2\delta + \theta_2)(1 - \beta L^{-1})(1 - L) + \pi_2(1 - \beta) \\ \delta(1 - \beta L^{-1})(1 - L) \end{matrix}$$

$$\begin{matrix} 0 \\ \delta(1 - \beta L^{-1})(1 - L) \\ (\theta_1 + \delta)(1 - \beta L^{-1})(1 - L) + \pi_1(1 - \beta) \end{matrix} \begin{bmatrix} r_{1t} \\ r_{2t} \\ m_t^e \end{bmatrix}$$

$$= E_t \begin{bmatrix} (1 - \beta L^{-1})(d_t - s_{1t}) \\ (1 - \beta L^{-1})(d_t - s_{2t}) \\ 0 \end{bmatrix}$$

or

$$E_t \left[\left(E_1^* \beta L^{-1} + E_0^* + E_1^* L \right) R_t^e \right] = E_t \left[(1 - \beta L^{-1}) S_t^e \right] \tag{3.6}$$

where $R_t^e = [r_{1t}, r_{2t}, m_t^e]'$ and $S_t^e = [(d_t - s_{1t}),(d_t - s_{2t}), 0]'$. This system has the initial condition that R_{-1}^e is zero.

The equilibrium for game E is obtained by solving equation system (3.6) in essentially the same manner as was used in section II, the only difference being the presence of a third equation in the system. As has

---

[5] The variable m_t^e can be interpreted as the Lagrange multiplier associated with the time t stochastic Euler equation for player one.

been demonstrated in Hansen and Sargent (1981), the matrix characteristic function for equation system (3.6) can be factored as follows:

$$E_1^{*\prime} \beta Z^{-1} + E_0^* + E_1^* Z = C^e(\beta Z^{-1})' C^e(Z)$$

where $\det[C^e(Z)]$ is different from zero for $|Z| < \sqrt{\beta}$.[6] The equilibrium stochastic process for R_t^e then satisfies

$$C^e(L)R_t^e = E_t\left\{\left[1 - \beta L^{-1}\right]\left[C^e(\beta L^{-1})'\right]^{-1} S_t^e\right\} \qquad (3.7)$$

The feedforward part of the solution given on the right-hand side of (3.7) is obtained in the same manner as that prescribed in section II.[7]

The solution strategy just outlined for solving game E is a computationally attractive alternative to procedures suggested by Kydland (1977) and Kydland and Prescott (1980). As noted by those authors, the solution to this dominant player game is, in general, not time consistent. In other words, if we restart the game at time period s, where s is positive, the dominant player (player two) will find its decision rules for time s forward but chosen at time zero to be suboptimal. The reason for this is that from the perspective of time s, the constraints (3.2), which link r_{1t} to expected future values of r_{2t}, are not imposed for t less than s. These constraints are ignored because r_{1t} is already determined prior to time s and is therefore treated parametrically when the dominant player evaluates alternative strategies at time s.

The presence of time inconsistency is manifested in solution (3.7) to game E. Notice that (3.7) is a recursive representation of the solution in which R_t^e is expressed in terms of, among other things, R_{t-1}^e. Therefore the solution depends on the initial value, R_{-1}^e, one component of which is m_{-1}^e. For this reason the initial value of m_{-1}^e plays an essential role in the solution. Recall that our derivation of the time-invariant representation (3.7) exploited the requirement that m_{-1}^e is zero. Consider a hypothetical experiment in which the dominant player reoptimizes at time s for some s greater than zero. Then relation (3.7) still gives the ap-

---

[6] The approach in Hansen and Sargent (1981) for factoring the characteristic function for game E requires that

$$\sqrt{\beta}\, E_1^{*\prime} Z^{-1} + E_0^* + \sqrt{\beta}\, E_1^* Z$$

be positive semidefinite for all Z with absolute values of 1. This requirement is satisfied for E_0^* and E_1^* given in (3.6).

[7] See Roberds (1984) for a more extensive discussion of this particular solution.

propriate solution to the time s optimization problem as long as m^e_{s-1} is initialized to zero. However, for the solution calculated from the perspective of time zero, m^e_{s-1} is, in general, not zero. Hence the dominant player has the incentive to alter the sequence of decision rules for a subgame starting at time s as long as m^e_{s-1} is not zero when calculated from the perspective of time period zero.[8]

Solution to Game F

Without some mechanism for requiring the dominant player to maintain the initial sequence of decision rules as the game is played over time, the equilibrium for game E is not viable. For this reason, we consider an alternative game that has a time-consistent solution. The sources of time inconsistency in game E are constraints (3.2). These constraints relate current and past decisions of the competitive player (supplier one) to, among other things, expected future decisions of the dominant player (supplier two). In game F, the second supplier is less dominant in that future decisions are beyond its control at the current time period. In other words, the constraints given in (3.2) link the dominant player's current and past decisions to the nondominant player's current and past decisions, whereas the dominant player's future decisions are viewed as stochastic forcing variables that both players forecast optimally. This different view of constraints (3.2) removes the source of time inconsistency. Another interpretation of game F is that there is a sequence of dominant players, one for each time period. Although the current dominant player cares about the rewards obtained by future dominant players, the current player is unable to control the actions of the future dominant players.

The objective of the second supplier in game F is the same as in game E, but the constraints in (3.2) are viewed differently. The operator $\delta(1 - \beta L^{-1})(1 - L)/(1 - \sigma_1 \beta L^{-1})$ dictates how current, past, and future values of r_{2t} enter into (3.2). This operator can be expressed as

$$\delta \frac{(1 - \beta L^{-1})(1 - L)}{(1 - \sigma_1 \beta L^{-1})} = \delta[(1 + \beta - \sigma_1 \beta) - L] + \frac{\sigma_2 L^{-1}}{(1 - \sigma_1 \beta L^{-1})} \quad (3.8)$$

where $\sigma_2 = \delta[\sigma_1 \beta - (\sigma_1 \beta)^2 - \beta + \beta^2 \sigma_1]$. The first term on the right-hand side of (3.8) is one-sided in nonnegative powers of L, whereas the second

---

[8] In addition to m^e_{-1}, we also assumed that R_{-1} is zero in our analysis. This second assumption is not essential, however. As was noted in footnote 1, nonzero initial values of R_{-1} can be captured by the means of s_{1t} and s_{2t}. In this sense, the presumption that R_{-1} is zero is merely a convenient normalization.

term is one-sided in strictly negative powers of L. For convenience we rewrite the constraints (3.2) as

$$\sigma_0(1-\sigma_1 L)r_{1t} + \delta[(1+\beta-\sigma_1\beta)-L]r_{2t}$$

$$= -E_t\left\{\left[\frac{\sigma_2}{(1-\sigma_1\beta L^{-1})}\right]r^*_{2,t+1} + \left[\frac{(1-\beta L^{-1})}{(1-\sigma_1\beta L^{-1})}\right](d_{1t}-s_{1t})\right\}$$

$$(3.9)$$

where, in equilibrium, $r^*_{2t}=r_{2t}$ for $t=0,1,\dots$. From the perspective of the second player, however, future values of r^*_{2t} are optimally forecast stochastic forcing variables; that is, player two knows the correct equilibrium law of motion for r^*_{2t} but does not exploit the link between r_{2t} and r^*_{2t} when maximizing the objective function.

The equilibrium for game F is obtained by replacing constraint (3.2) by constraint (3.9) for $t=0,1,\dots$. Hence, the Lagrangian for player two is

$$J^f = J - E_0\sum_{t=0}^{\infty}\beta^t m^f_t\{\sigma_0[1-\sigma_1 L]r_{1t}$$

$$+\delta[(1+\beta-\sigma_1\beta)-L]r_{2t}$$

$$+E_t\left\{\left[\frac{\sigma_2}{(1-\sigma_1\beta L^{-1})}\right]r^*_{2,t+1}\right.$$

$$-\left.\left[\frac{(1-\beta L^{-1})}{(1-\sigma_1\beta L^{-1})}\right][d_{1t}-s_{1t}]\right\}$$

where J is given in (3.3). Differentiating J^f with respect to r_{1t} and r_{2t} gives the stochastic Euler equations,

$$E_t[\delta(1-\beta L^{-1})(1-L)r_{2t} + \sigma_0(1-\sigma_1\beta L^{-1})m^f_t]=0 \qquad (3.10)$$

$$E_t\{\delta[1-\beta L^{-1}][1-L]r_{1t} + [(2\delta+\theta_2)(1-\beta L^{-1})(1-L)$$

$$+\pi_2(1-\beta)]r_{2t} + \delta[(1+\beta-\sigma_1\beta)-\beta L^{-1}]m^f_t\}$$

$$= E_t\{[(1-\beta L^{-1})(d_t-s_{2t})]\} \qquad (3.11)$$

for $t=0,1,2,\dots$. A feature of these first-order conditions is that they do not depend on m^f_t for negative t. This fact insures the time consistency of game F.

In equilibrium, r^*_{2t} and r_{2t} are the same so that in solving game F we revert back to using (3.1) instead of (3.9) as an additional stochastic difference equation that must be satisfied in equilibrium. Stacking equations (3.1), (3.10), and (3.11) into a system yields

$$
E_t \begin{bmatrix} (\theta_1 + \delta)(1 - \beta L^{-1})(1 - L) + \pi_1(1 - \beta) \\ \delta(1 - \beta L^{-1})(1 - L) \\ 0 \end{bmatrix}
$$

$$
\begin{bmatrix} \delta(1 - \beta L^{-1})(1 - L) \\ (2\delta + \theta_2)(1 - \beta L^{-1})(1 - L) + \pi_2(1 - \beta) \\ \delta(1 - \beta L^{-1})(1 - L) \end{bmatrix}
$$

$$
\begin{bmatrix} 0 \\ \delta[(1 + \beta - \sigma_1\beta) - \beta L^{-1}] \\ \sigma_0(1 - \sigma_1\beta L^{-1}) \end{bmatrix} \begin{bmatrix} r_{1t} \\ r_{2t} \\ m_t^f \end{bmatrix}
$$

$$
= E_t \begin{bmatrix} (1 - \beta L^{-1})(d_t - s_{1t}) \\ (1 - \beta L^{-1})(d_t - s_{2t}) \\ 0 \end{bmatrix}
$$

or

$$
E_t\big[(F_{-1}L^{-1} + F_0 + F_1 L)R_t^f\big] = E_t\big[(1 - \beta L^{-1})S_t^f\big] \tag{3.12}
$$

where $R_t^f = [r_{1t}, r_{2t}, m_t^f]$ and $S_t^f = S_t^e$. Notice that the last column of F_1 contains all zeros so that lagged values of m_t^f do not enter the difference equations that determine the solution for game F. Hence the only initial conditions for this difference equation system are that $r_{1, -1}$ and $r_{2, -1}$ are zero.

To solve game F, we use a strategy similar to that used in solving games A through E. Define $F(Z)$ to be the characteristic function for game F, given by

$$
F(Z) = F_{-1}Z^{-1} + F_0 + F_1 Z
$$

Unfortunately, because F_{-1} is not equal to βF_1, we cannot use Hansen and Sargent's (1981) results to factor the characteristic function $F(Z)$ for the difference equation (3.12). In appendix B, we show that $\det[F(Z)]$ has five real zeros, two of which are greater than 1 and three of which are between zero and β. In appendix C, we use this information about $\det[F(Z)]$ in conjunction with other properties of $F(Z)$ to show the existence of a one-sided forward operator $M(L^{-1})$ such that

$$
M(L^{-1})F(L) = I - NL \tag{3.13}
$$

where $\det[I - NZ]$ has two zeros, both of which are positive and greater than 1. Recall that the last column of F_1 is zero, which in turn implies that the last column of N is zero also. In appendix C, we show how to calculate N and $M(L^{-1})$ from $F(L)$.

We now calculate the equilibrium for game F. In light of (3.13), the appropriate solution to difference equation system (3.12) is

$$R_t^f = NR_{t-1}^f + E_t\left[(1 - \beta L^{-1})M(L^{-1})S_t^f\right] \tag{3.14}$$

Because the third column of N is zero, solution (3.14) does not feed back on m_{t-1}^f, guaranteeing that the solution is time consistent. Solution (3.14) includes a feedforward part that is the solution to an optimal forecasting problem. The solution to this forecasting problem can be expressed in terms of current and past values of U_t using the representation of $M(Z^{-1})$ given in appendix C and results from Hansen and Sargent (1980). Hence the feedforward part of the solution can be calculated in essentially the same manner as the feedforward part of the solution to the symmetric games.

Comparative Dynamics

Our final task in this section is to compare the limiting behavior of the levels of resource extraction for the nonsymmetric games. In this exercise, the cost parameters of the two players can be distinct, but the forcing variables are trivial. In particular, we assume that $S_t = K^* > 0$ for nonnegative values of t. For sake of comparison, we also consider the symmetric game A, in which both players are competitive. In section II, it was established that for all three symmetric games

$$\lim_{t \to \infty} R_t = (1 - \beta)\pi^{-1}K^* \tag{3.15}$$

At the beginning of this section, we showed that game D could be studied using the analysis of section II, so that (3.15) holds for game D as well.

Conclusions analogous to (3.15) can be obtained for games E and F. Recall that

$$S_t^e = S_t^f = \begin{bmatrix} S_t \\ 0 \end{bmatrix}$$

so that in the special case under consideration here

$$S_t^e = S_t^f = \begin{bmatrix} K^* \\ 0 \end{bmatrix}$$

Also, R_t^e and R_t^f have three components instead of two, where the additional components are the multipliers m_t^e and m_t^f. The limiting values of R_t^e and R_t^f are given by

$$\lim_{t \to \infty} R_t^e = \left[E^*(1) \right]^{-1} \begin{bmatrix} K^* \\ 0 \end{bmatrix}$$

$$= \pi^{-1} \begin{bmatrix} K^* \\ 0 \end{bmatrix}$$

and

$$\lim_{t \to \infty} R_t^f = \left[F(1) \right]^{-1} \begin{bmatrix} K^* \\ 0 \end{bmatrix}$$

$$= \pi^{-1} \begin{bmatrix} K^* \\ 0 \end{bmatrix}$$

where $E^*(Z)$ and $F(Z)$ are the characteristic functions for games E and F. Therefore the ultimate quantities of the resource that are extracted are the same for all of the games considered, both symmetric and nonsymmetric.

To compare how quickly the limiting quantities are approached in the nonsymmetric games, we study the zeros of the determinants of the characteristic functions for the respective games. In appendix A, it is shown that the determinants of the characteristic functions for games A and D have two zeros that are greater than 1 and two zeros that are between zero and β. In appendix B, it is shown that the determinant for the characteristic function for game E has three zeros that are greater than 1 and three zeros that are between zero and β. Also in appendix B, it is shown that the determinant of the characteristic function for game F has two zeros that are greater than 1 and three zeros that are between zero and β.

For all the games, the zeros between zero and β only effect the feedforward parts of the solutions. For the special case in which S_t is equal to K^* for nonnegative t, the feedforward parts of the solutions are constant over time. Therefore, in this case, the zeros that are greater than 1 dictate how fast R_t converges to its limiting value. More precisely, as was argued in section II, the smallest zeros that are greater than 1 dictate the eventual speeds of convergence of R_t to its limiting value. Let Z^a, Z^d, Z^e, and Z^f denote the smallest zeros that are greater than 1 for games A, D, E, and F respectively. In appendix D, it is shown that

$$Z^a > Z^f > Z^d > Z^e \qquad (3.16)$$

This means that the cumulative resource extraction eventually is closest to its limit for game A and furthest away for game E with games F and D in between. In this sense, the resource is depleted more slowly for the dominant-competitive, time-inconsistent game (game E) than for any of the other three games. Furthermore, for any game in which player two is given a strategic advantage, resource extraction is ultimately slowed down for both players relative to the competitive game (game A).

For general specifications of S, the inequalities in (3.16) are not sufficient to order the time paths of resource depletion for the nonsymmetric games. The solution approach suggested in this chapter, however, makes computation of the equilibria for these games straightforward and practical. This solution approach is best viewed as an extension of the approach suggested by Hansen and Sargent (1981) for single-agent rational expectations models and as an alternative to the recursive procedures described by Kydland (1977).

Newbery (1981) has used a solution approach that is substantially different from ours in studying the problem of time inconsistency in dominant-competitive player exhaustible resource games. His analysis compares time paths for prices and extraction rates across games when each player faces constant but possibly distinct marginal costs of extraction. For specifications in which his dominant player model is time inconsistent, however, he does not calculate explicitly the time-consistent solution.

Although the discussion in this section has focused on the interactions of two resource suppliers, our methods can be applied to models in which the dominant player is a government and the competitive player is a representative private agent. In contrast to the specification adopted by Taylor (1979a) and Chow (1981), the government can have a fundamentally dynamic objective function rather than one that depends only on steady-state variances.

IV. ECONOMETRIC IMPLICATIONS

Each of the solutions to the six resource depletion games provides an empirically tractable mapping from the stochastic specification of the forcing variables to the stochastic properties of the endogenous resource depletion quantities and resource prices. This mapping is important because it facilitates estimation of the demand and supply parameters and because it is useful in simulating the impact on endogenous variables of hypothetical interventions in the stochastic specification of the forcing variables and in the specification of the dynamic game.

Estimation of the model requires introducing unobservables into the model in the form of unobserved components to the demand and/or cost shifters, unobserved variables that are useful in forecasting the observable components of the shifters or measurement errors or both.[9] In the absence of these unobservables, the models imply an exact relationship among observed variables (by the econometrician), an implication that would undoubtedly be violated in the observed time series. Once the observed and unobserved forcing processes are specified, one can exploit the mapping from forcing processes to the specified endogenous processes and estimate the parameters by using some method such as maximum likelihood. Hansen and Sargent (1980) describe implications of different specifications of unobservables in linear rational expectations models like those considered here and they suggest some alternative approaches to estimation.[10] Epple and Roberds (in chapter 6) have estimated versions of the models described in this chapter.

As Lucas (1976) and Lucas and Sargent (1981) have emphasized, in simulating the impact of hypothetical interventions either in the processes generating the demand and the supply shifters or in the agents' dynamic games, one must take into account that such interventions will cause resource suppliers to alter their implicit forecasting rules for future prices and for future values of other suppliers' decisions. The rational expectations approach allows explicit predictions about how suppliers' decision rules will change when the economic environment changes. The mappings from the forcing variables to the endogenous variables for the various dynamic games that were deduced earlier make these exercises straightforward and tractable.

V. SIMULATIONS

Simulations for hypothetical cost and demand function parameters serve to illustrate properties of the games discussed in the preceding sections. Parameters in the cost functions are $\theta_1 = .1$, $\theta_2 = .1$, $\pi_1 = .08$, and $\pi_2 = .04$.

---

[9] Obviously, the econometrician is not given complete latitude in specifying unobservables without contaminating the identification of demand and supply parameters. Typically, one has to restrict the dynamic interaction between the observable and unobservable components of the shifters. See Hansen and Sargent (1980).

[10] Sims has emphasized that one should be cautious in studying models like the one presented here using estimation and inference procedures that require the observables be asymptotically stationary. Although our model implies asymptotically stationary prices and quantities whenever the forcing variables are stationary, the asymptotic point of central tendency is one in which there is no incremental exploitation of the resource. Hence, the model seems to be most plausible far away from its asymptotic point of central tendency.

These parameters give player two an obvious cost advantage over player one in that player two's costs increase less rapidly with cumulative output ($\pi_2 < \pi_1$). A real discount rate of 8 percent is assumed. The demand function used in these simulations is

$$P_t = 100 - \left[(1 - L)r_{1t} + (1 - L)r_{2t}\right]$$

Simulations for six market structures are presented in table 5-1. The games correspond to those described in section I. Numerical values for the smallest zero greater than 1 of the determinant of the characteristic function are reported in parentheses for each game. The ordering of period zero prices for these games conforms to the ordering expected in a

TABLE 5-1. PRICES AND EXTRACTION RATES FOR ALTERNATIVE GAMES

Game	Time periods						
	0	5	10	25	50	100	200
A. Competitive ($Z^a = 1.0202$)							
P_t	25.5	32.7	39.1	54.9	72.7	90.0	98.6
$(1 - L)r_{2t}$	45.7	43.5	40.3	30.3	18.4	6.8	0.7
$(1 - L)r_{1t}$	28.8	23.8	20.6	14.7	8.9	3.3	0.4
B. Nash ($Z^b = 1.0139$)							
P_t	46.6	50.5	54.1	63.2	74.3	87.3	96.8
$(1 - L)r_{2t}$	29.4	28.2	27.1	23.3	17.5	9.2	2.3
$(1 - L)r_{1t}$	24.0	21.3	18.9	13.5	8.2	3.6	0.8
C. Collusive ($Z^c = 1.0114$)							
P_t	57.8	60.2	62.3	68.2	76.0	86.4	95.6
$(1 - L)r_{2t}$	26.0	25.8	24.9	21.3	16.1	9.1	2.9
$(1 - L)r_{1t}$	16.2	14.1	12.8	10.5	7.9	4.5	1.5
D. Nash-Competitive ($Z^d = 1.0143$)							
P_t	34.4	42.7	49.2	62.6	75.1	88.0	97.1
$(1 - L)r_{2t}$	19.9	23.1	24.8	24.4	18.7	9.4	2.3
$(1 - L)r_{1t}$	45.7	34.1	26.0	13.0	6.1	2.6	0.6
E. Dominant-Competitive ($Z^e = 1.0133$)							
P_t	31.2	39.5	46.5	61.7	76.0	88.8	97.1
$(1 - L)r_{2t}$	31.2	30.1	28.6	23.6	17.0	8.8	2.4
$(1 - L)r_{1t}$	37.7	30.4	25.0	14.7	7.0	2.4	0.6
F. Dominant-Competitive Time Consistent ($Z^f = 1.0193$)							
P_t	27.8	34.9	41.1	56.0	72.8	89.5	98.5
$(1 - L)r_{2t}$	37.6	38.9	37.7	30.1	18.8	7.2	1.1
$(1 - L)r_{1t}$	34.6	26.2	21.2	13.9	8.4	3.2	0.5

static model with no resource depletion. The period zero price is lowest when both players are competitive and highest when the players collude. The period zero price is lower in the Nash-competitive game (game D) than in the game in which both players adopt Nash strategies (game B) and higher than in the games that feature a dominant player and a competitive fringe (games E and F). The competitive player has a particularly large market share in the early periods in the Nash-competitive game (game D), while the second player produces approximately twice as much as the first player in every time period in the competitive and collusive games (games A and C). The imposition of time consistency on the dominant player has a noticeable but not dramatic impact on the temporal behavior of prices and extraction rates. For instance, player two extracts more in game F in the initial time periods than in game E. Also, the initial prices are lower in game F than in game E.

These simulations indicate that the game the suppliers play can have a substantial impact on the time series of extraction rates and prices. Since these simulations across games use common values of the cost and demand parameters, they do not bear directly on whether there are econometrically identifiable differences among alternative games when such parameters are not specified a priori. In fact, in absence of a prior knowledge of these parameters, it turns out that games A, B, and D are observationally equivalent [see Roberds (1984)].

VI. EXTENSIONS AND CONCLUSIONS

The analysis in this chapter can be extended readily in several dimensions. The particular resource exploitation model can be expanded to include multiple resources whose exploitation costs are interrelated. For instance, Epple (chapter 6) uses a multiple resource version of this model to study the joint exploration of oil and gas. Additional sources of dynamics, such as costs of adjusting extraction or consumption levels or lags in implementing decisions to adjust these levels, can be incorporated into the model. Extending the model in these various directions is only feasible for econometric analyses to the extent that the resulting sources of endogenous dynamics are empirically distinguishable. Undoubtedly, these extensions will confound results on the comparative dynamics of the various games.

The particular solution methods we have used can be applied to other multiple agent environments in which the agents are modeled as solving quadratic optimum problems. Our solutions to the dominant player models should be a useful addition to the arsenal of recursive procedures presently available for such analyses.

APPENDIX A
COMPARATIVE DYNAMICS FOR SYMMETRIC GAMES

In section II we showed that equilibria for three symmetric duopoly games could be calculated by solving a system of linear stochastic difference equations. In this appendix we study the solution to the homogeneous component of that difference equation system. In particular, we consider the solution to

$$H(L)R_t = 0 \tag{A.1}$$

for $t = 0, 1, 2, \ldots$, where

$$H(Z) = \pi + \theta W(Z) \tag{A.2}$$

$$\pi = \begin{bmatrix} \pi_{11} & 0 \\ 0 & \pi_{22} \end{bmatrix} \qquad \theta = \begin{bmatrix} \theta_{11} & \theta_{12} \\ \theta_{12} & \theta_{22} \end{bmatrix}$$

π and θ are positive definite, $\theta_{12} > 0$, and $W(Z) = (1 - Z)(1 - \beta Z^{-1})$. This difference equation system has an initial condition that R_{-1} is given a priori and a terminal condition that

$$\lim_{t \to \infty} \sqrt{\beta^t}\, R(t) = 0$$

Each of the three symmetric games corresponds to distinct values for elements of the matrix θ.

Two additional functions are closely related to the function H. Let

$$H^*(W) = \pi + \theta W$$

and

$$P(W) = (\pi_{11} + \theta_{11}W)(\pi_{22} + \theta_{22}W) - (\theta_{12})^2 W^2 \tag{A.3}$$

Notice that $H^*[W(Z)] = H(Z)$ and $P[W(Z)] = \det[H(Z)]$. Without loss of generality, suppose that

$$\frac{\pi_{11}}{\theta_{11}} < \frac{\pi_{22}}{\theta_{22}}$$

From (A.3), it follows that $P(0)$ is positive and $P(-\pi_{11}/\theta_{22})$ is negative, so P has a zero in the interval $(-\pi_{11}/\theta_{11}, 0)$. This zero, which we denote

W_1, is the largest of two zeros because the graph of P opens up. Evaluating H^* at W_1 yields

$$H^*(W_1) = \begin{bmatrix} \alpha_1 & -\alpha_2 \\ -\alpha_2 & \alpha_2^2/\alpha_1 \end{bmatrix}$$

where $\alpha_1 = \pi_{11} + \theta_{11}W_1 > 0$ and $\alpha_2 = -\theta_{12}W_1 > 0$. Hence the equation

$$H^*(W_1)\mu_1 = 0 \tag{A.4}$$

implies that $\mu_1 = \tau_1[\alpha_2 \quad \alpha_1]'$ for some τ_1.

Let $W_2 < W_1$ be the smallest zero of the function P. From (A.3) and the fact that θ is positive definite, it follows that $P(-\pi_{22}/\theta_{22})$ is negative and, for sufficiently negative values of W, $P(W)$ is positive. Therefore, W_2 is less than $-\pi_{22}/\theta_{22}$. Evaluating H^* at W_2 gives

$$H^*(W_2) = \begin{bmatrix} -\alpha_3 & -\alpha_4 \\ -\alpha_4 & -\alpha_4^2/\alpha_3 \end{bmatrix}$$

where $\alpha_3 = -(\pi_{11} + \theta_{11}W_2) > 0$ and $\alpha_4 = -\theta_{12}W_2 > 0$. Hence the equation

$$H^*(W_2)\mu_2 = 0 \tag{A.5}$$

implies that $\mu_2 = \tau_2[\alpha_4 \quad -\alpha_3]'$ for some τ_2.

Next, we use the calculations performed above to study the solution to difference equation (A.1). The function W is zero at $Z = 1$ and is strictly decreasing for Z greater than or equal to 1.
Let

$$W(Z_1) = W_1 \quad \text{for } Z_1 > 1 \tag{A.6}$$

and

$$W(Z_2) = W_2 \quad \text{for } Z_2 > 1 \tag{A.7}$$

Since W_1 is greater than W_2, it follows from the properties of the function W that Z_1 is less than Z_2. In light of (A.4) through (A.7), the solution to (A.1) is given by

$$R_t = \begin{bmatrix} \alpha_2 \\ \alpha_1 \end{bmatrix}\tau_1(Z_1)^{-t} + \begin{bmatrix} \alpha_4 \\ -\alpha_3 \end{bmatrix}\tau_2(Z_2)^{-t} \tag{A.8}$$

where τ_1 and τ_2 are determined by the given initial value of R_{-1}. Because Z_1 is less than Z_2, the behavior of the solution (A.8) ultimately is dominated by the term

$$\begin{bmatrix} \alpha_2 \\ \alpha_1 \end{bmatrix} \tau_1(Z_1)^{-t}$$

In the remainder of this appendix, we compare the values of Z_1 for different specifications of the symmetric games. Superscript letters denote the values of parameters for the corresponding games. We begin by comparing the values of W_1 for each of the games and then use the properties of the function W to compare the values of Z_1.

Game A vs. Game B

Note that $\theta_{12}^a = \theta_{12}^b$, $\theta_{11}^a < \theta_{11}^b$, and $\theta_{22}^a < \theta_{22}^b$. These relations imply that $-\pi_{11}/\theta_{11}^a < -\pi_{11}/\theta_{11}^b$. Recall that W_1^b is in the interval $(-\pi_{11}/\theta_{11}^b, 0)$. In this same interval,

$$P^b(W) - P^a(W) = \left(\pi_{11} + \theta_{11}^b W \right)\left(\pi_{22}^b + \theta_{22}^b W \right)$$
$$- \left(\pi_{11} + \theta_{11}^a W \right)\left(\pi_{22} + \theta_{22}^a W \right) < 0$$

It follows that W_1^a is less than W_1^b.

Game B vs. Game C

Note that $\theta_{12}^c > \theta_{12}^b$, $\theta_{11}^c = \theta_{11}^b$, and $\theta_{22}^c = \theta_{22}^b$. These relations imply that, in the interval $(-\pi_{11}/\theta_{11}^b, 0)$,

$$P^c(W) - P^b(W) = -\left(\theta_{12}^c W \right)^2 - \left(\theta_{12}^b W \right)^2 < 0$$

It follows that W_1^c is greater than W_1^b.

Combining the inequality comparisons across games, we have that $W_1^a < W_1^b < W_1^c < 0$. To complete our discussion, we must order the values of Z_1 for the different games. Since the function W is strictly decreasing for Z greater than or equal to 1, $Z_1^a > Z_1^b > Z_1^c$.

APPENDIX B
CHARACTERISTIC FUNCTION FOR GAME F

The location of the zeros of the determinant of the characteristic function for game F is important in showing that this game has a solution and in applying the algorithm given in appendix C to calculate this solution. In studying game F it is convenient to study game E simultaneously, especially because some of our comparative dynamic results described in section III and justified in appendix D rely on a comparison of the zeros of the determinants of the characteristic functions for the respective games.

In section III, we showed that the characteristic function for game E is given by

$$E(Z) = \begin{bmatrix} \theta_1 + \delta & \delta & 0 \\ \delta & 2\delta + \theta_2 & \delta \\ 0 & \delta & \theta_1 + \delta \end{bmatrix} W(Z) + \begin{bmatrix} \pi_1 & 0 & 0 \\ 0 & \pi_2 & 0 \\ 0 & 0 & \pi_1 \end{bmatrix} (1 - \beta)$$

and the characteristic function for game F is given by

$$F(Z) = \begin{bmatrix} E_{11}(Z) & E_{21}(Z) & 0 \\ E_{12}(Z) & E_{22}(Z) & \left[\delta W(Z) - Z\sigma_1 \delta W(\sigma_1^{-1})\right]/(1 - \sigma_1 Z) \\ E_{13}(Z) & E_{23}(Z) & \sigma_0(1 - \sigma_1 \beta Z^{-1}) \end{bmatrix}$$

where $W(Z) = (1 - \beta Z^{-1})(1 - Z)$, $E_{ij}(Z)$ is the ijth element of $E(Z)$, and σ_0 and σ_1 are as defined in section III. Consider now an alternative matrix function $G(Z)$ that is related to $F(Z)$ via the formula,

$$G(Z) = F(Z) \begin{bmatrix} 1 & 0 & 0 \\ 0 & 1 & 0 \\ 0 & 0 & (1 - \sigma_1 Z) \end{bmatrix} \tag{B.1}$$

Then $\det[G(Z)] = (1 - \sigma_1 Z)\det[F(Z)]$. Notice that the functions G and E have identical elements except in the $(2, 3)$ position. Hence, we have the convenient relation that

$$\det[G(Z)] = \det[E(Z)] + E_{11}(Z)[\delta W(Z)][Z\sigma_1 \delta W(\sigma_1^{-1})] \tag{B.2}$$

Next, we consider $\det[E(Z)]$. Notice that $E_{11}(Z) = E_{33}(Z)$. Hence

$$\det[E(Z)] = E_{11}(Z)\det[H^e(Z)] \tag{B.3}$$

where $H^e(Z) = \pi + \theta^e W(Z)$ and

$$\theta^e = \begin{bmatrix} \theta_1 + \delta & \sqrt{2}\,\delta \\ \sqrt{2}\,\delta & \theta_2 + 2\delta \end{bmatrix}$$

The function $E_{11}(Z)$ has zeros at σ_1^{-1} and $\beta\sigma_1$, and the matrix function $H^e(Z)$ is a special case of the matrix function $H(Z)$ studied in appendix A. Therefore, $\det[E(Z)]$ has three zeros between zero and β and three zeros greater than 1.

We can now exploit relations (B.1) and (B.2) and our knowledge about $H^e(Z)$ to infer information about the zeros of $\det[G(Z)]$. Combining (B.2) and (B.3), we have that

$$\det[G(Z)] = E_{11}(Z)G_1(Z) \tag{B.4}$$

where

$$G_1(Z) = \det[H^e(Z)] + \delta^2\sigma_1 W(\sigma_1^{-1})ZW(Z) \tag{B.5}$$

The function $G_1(Z)$ has four zeros because $Z^2G_1(Z)$ is a fourth-order polynomial that does not have a zero at zero.

In order to locate the zeros of $G_1(Z)$, we will show that

$$G_1(\beta) > 0, \quad G_1(1) > 0 \tag{B.6}$$

$$G_1(\sigma_1^{-1}) < 0, \quad G_1(\beta\sigma_1) < 0 \tag{B.7}$$

and

$$\lim_{r \downarrow 0} G_1(r) = +\infty, \quad \lim_{r \to +\infty} G_1(r) = +\infty \tag{B.8}$$

Once these relations are established, it follows that G_1 has zeros in each of the following four intervals:

$$(0, \beta\sigma_1), \ (\beta\sigma_1, \beta), \ (1, \sigma_1^{-1}), \ (\sigma_1^{-1}, +\infty) \tag{B.9}$$

We begin by establishing the inequalities in (B.6). Recall from appendix A that $W(\beta)$ and $W(1)$ are both zero, and

$$\det[H^e(Z)] = P^e[W(Z)]$$

where P^e is a special case of the function P. Because $P^e(0)$ is positive, $\det[H^e(1)]$ and $\det[H^e(\beta)]$ are both positive. The relations in (B.6) then follow from (B.5).

Next, we consider the inequalities in (B.7). Evaluating W at σ_1^{-1} and $\beta\sigma_1$, we obtain

$$W(\sigma_1^{-1}) = W(\beta\sigma_1)$$

Furthermore,

$$P^e\big[W(\sigma_1^{-1})\big] = -2\big[\delta W(\sigma_1^{-1})\big]^2$$

Therefore, from (B.5), it follows that

$$G_1(\sigma_1^{-1}) = -\big[\delta W(\sigma_1^{-1})\big]^2 < 0$$

and

$$G_1(\beta\sigma_1) = -2\big[\delta W(\sigma_1^{-1})\big]^2 + \beta\big[\sigma_1\delta W(\sigma_1^{-1})\big]^2 < 0$$

which establishes (B.7).

Finally, in verifying relations (B.8), the following facts are useful:

$$\lim_{r \downarrow 0}\det\big[H^e(r)\big] = \lim_{r \downarrow 0}\big\{\big[(\theta_1 + \delta)(\theta_2 + 2\delta)\big] - 2\delta^2\big\}\beta^2 r^{-2} = +\infty$$

$$\lim_{r \to +\infty}\det\big[H^e(r)\big] = \lim_{r \to +\infty}\big\{(\theta_1 + \delta)(\theta_2 + 2\delta)\big] - 2\delta^2\big\}r^2 = +\infty$$

$W(\sigma_1^{-1})$ is negative, and

$$\lim_{r \to +\infty}W(r) = -\lim_{r \to +\infty}r = -\infty$$

These observations, in conjunction with (B.5), imply the limits in (B.8).

We have now established that G_1 has zeros in the intervals given in (B.9). This property of G_1 and relations (B.1) and (B.4) imply that $F(Z)$ has one zero at $\beta\sigma_1$ and has four other zeros in the intervals given in (B.9). Therefore $F(Z)$ has three zeros between zero and β and two zeros greater than 1.

APPENDIX C
FACTORING A NONSYMMETRIC
CHARACTERISTIC FUNCTION

Whittle's (1963) procedure for factoring a spectral density matrix can be extended to obtain a procedure for factoring the nonsymmetric characteristic function for the dominant-competitive time-consistent game (game F). The characteristic function for game F can be written,

$$F(Z) = F_{-1}Z^{-1} + F_0 + F_1 Z$$

We showed in appendix B that $\det[F(Z)]$ has five zeros. One is in the interval $(1, \sigma_1^{-1})$ and is denoted Z_1, one is in the interval $(\sigma_1^{-1}, +\infty)$ and is denoted Z_2, and three are between zero and β and are denoted Z_3, Z_4, and Z_5. Also, the third column of the matrix F_1 is zero. Our goal in this section is to show that there exists a rational function $M(Z)$ with poles at Z_3^{-1}, Z_4^{-1}, and Z_5^{-1} such that

$$M(Z^{-1})F(Z) = I - NZ \tag{C.1}$$

where the third column of the matrix N is zero and $\det[I - NZ]$ is zero at Z_1 and Z_2. Relation (C.1) is used in section four to solve game F.

First, we obtain a partial fractions decomposition of $F(Z)^{-1}$. For convenience, we consider a second-order matrix polynomial $F^*(Z)$ that is closely related to $F(Z)$. In particular,

$$F^*(Z) = F_1 + F_0 Z + F_{\,1} Z^2$$
$$= ZF(Z^{-1}) \tag{C.2}$$

Since $\det[F(Z)]$ has five distinct zeros that are strictly positive, $\det[F^*(Z)]$ has six distinct zeros, five that are the reciprocals of the zeros of $\det[F(Z)]$ and one that is zero. The inverse of $F^*(Z)$ can be represented as

$$[F^*(Z)]^{-1} = \frac{\text{adj}[F^*(Z)]}{\det[F^*(Z)]}$$

Hence $[F^*(Z)]^{-1}$ has a matrix partial fractions decomposition

$$[F^*(Z)]^{-1} = V_1(Z - Z_1^{-1})^{-1} + V_2(Z - Z_2^{-1})^{-1}$$
$$+ \cdots + V_5(Z - Z_5^{-1})^{-1} + V_6 Z^{-1} \tag{C.3}$$

The partial fractions decomposition given in (C.3) has several important properties. For instance,

$$F^*(Z_j^{-1})V_j = 0 \tag{C.4}$$

for $j = 1, 2, \ldots, 5$, and

$$F^*(0)V_6 = 0$$

Whiteman (1983) shows that $V_1, V_2, \ldots, V_6$ are rank one matrices and that $F^*(0)$ has rank two (see Theorem 2 and its corollary on pages 105 and

106). Since $F^*(0)$ is F_1 and the third column of F_1 is zero, the matrix V_6 has all zero elements except in the third row, which has at least one nonzero element.

The partial fractions decomposition of $[F^*(Z)]^{-1}$ is useful in obtaining a partial fractions decomposition of $F(Z)^{-1}$. For instance, relations (C.2) and (C.3) imply that

$$F(Z)^{-1} = V_1\left(1 - Z_1^{-1}Z\right)^{-1} + V_2\left(1 - Z_2^{-1}Z\right)^{-1} + V_6$$
$$- V_3 Z_3 Z^{-1}\left(1 - Z_3 Z^{-1}\right)^{-1} - V_4 Z_4 Z^{-1}\left(1 - Z_4 Z^{-1}\right)^{-1}$$
$$- V_5 Z_5 Z^{-1}\left(1 - Z_5 Z^{-1}\right)^{-1} \tag{C.5}$$

Next, we calculate the matrix N used in (C.1). Postmultiplying (C.1) by $F(Z)^{-1}$ gives

$$M(Z^{-1}) = F(Z)^{-1} - ZNF(Z)^{-1} \tag{C.6}$$

where $M(Z^{-1})$ has one-sided Laurent series expansion in nonpositive powers of Z in the region $\beta < |Z| < 1$. For (C.6) to be true, it follows from (C.5) that

$$N\left[V_1\left(1 - Z_1^{-1}Z\right)^{-1}\right] + V_2\left[\left(1 - Z_2^{-1}Z\right)^{-1} + V_6\right]$$
$$= V_1 Z_1^{-1}\left(1 - Z_1^{-1}Z\right)^{-1} + V_2 Z_2^{-1}\left(1 - Z_2^{-1}Z\right)^{-1}$$

Therefore, a function $M(Z^{-1})$ and a matrix N exist satisfying (C.1) as long as there exists a matrix N satisfying

$$NV_1 = V_1(Z_1)^{-1}$$
$$NV_1 = V_1(Z_1)^{-1}$$
$$NV_6 = 0 \tag{C.7}$$

Given that a matrix N exists satisfying relations (C.7), the columns of the rank one matrices V_1, V_2, and V_6 are eigenvectors of N with corresponding eigenvalues $(Z_1)^{-1}$, $(Z_2)^{-1}$, and zero. Hence $\det[I - NZ]$ is zero at Z_1 and Z_2. To verify the existence of such a matrix N, it is sufficient to show that the nondegenerate columns of V_1, V_2, and V_6 are linearly independent. Let $f_j = (f_{j1}, f_{j2}, f_{j3})'$ denote a nondegenerate column of V_j. We have already shown that f_{61} and f_{62} are zero. Below, we show that the signs of f_{11} and f_{12} are the same while the signs of f_{21} and f_{22} are different. It will then follow that the only real numbers w_1, w_2, and w_6 for which $w_1 f_1 + w_2 f_2 + w_6 f_6 = 0$ are $w_1 = w_2 = w_6 = 0$. This in turn will imply that f_1, f_2, and f_6 are linearly independent.

To show that the signs of f_{11} and f_{12} are the same while the signs of f_{21} and f_{22} are different, recall that the first and third rows of $F(Z)$ are given by

$$F^1(Z) = \left[\sigma_0(1 - \sigma_1 \beta Z^{-1})(1 - \sigma_1 Z) \quad \delta W(Z_1) \quad 0 \right]$$
$$F^3(Z) = \left[0 \quad \delta W(Z) \quad \sigma_0(1 - \sigma_1 \beta Z^{-1}) \right]$$

In light of (C.2) and (C.4), it follows that

$$F^1(Z_1) f_1 = 0 \tag{C.8}$$

$$F^3(Z_1) f_1 = 0 \tag{C.9}$$

$$F^1(Z_2) f_2 = 0 \tag{C.10}$$

$$F^3(Z_2) f_2 = 0 \tag{C.11}$$

The third elements of $F^3(Z_1)$ and $F^3(Z_2)$ are different from zero. Therefore (C.9) implies that f_{11} and f_{12} cannot both be zero, and (C.11) implies that f_{21} and f_{22} cannot both be zero. Because Z_1 is between 1 and σ_1^{-1}, the first element of $F^1(Z_1)$ is positive while the second element is negative. In order for (C.8) to hold, the signs of f_{11} and f_{12} must be the same. Since Z_2 is greater than σ_1^{-1}, the first two elements of $F^1(Z_2)$ are negative. In order for (C.10) to hold, the signs of f_{21} and f_{22} must be different. Hence f_1, f_2, and f_6 are indeed linearly independent.

We have now verified that there exists a matrix N that satisfies (C.7). To calculate this matrix, (C.7) may be stated as

$$N[f_1, f_2, f_6] = [f_1, f_2, f_6] \begin{bmatrix} Z_1^{-1} & 0 & 0 \\ 0 & Z_2^{-1} & 0 \\ 0 & 0 & 0 \end{bmatrix} \tag{C.12}$$

The matrix $[f_1, \quad f_2, \quad f_6]$ is invertible because its columns are linearly independent. Solving (C.12) for N, we obtain

$$N = [f_1, f_2, f_6] \begin{bmatrix} Z_1^{-1} & 0 & 0 \\ 0 & Z_2^{-1} & 0 \\ 0 & 0 & 0 \end{bmatrix} [f_1, f_2, f_6]^{-1}$$

Our final task in this appendix is to calculate $M(Z^{-1})$. Substituting (C.5) into (C.6) and using relations (C.7), it follows that

$$M(Z^{-1}) = Z_3\left(NV_3 - Z^{-1}V_3\right)\left(1 - Z_3Z^{-1}\right)^{-1}$$
$$+ Z_4\left(NV_4 - Z^{-1}V_4\right)\left(1 - Z_4Z^{-1}\right)^{-1}$$
$$+ Z_5\left(NV_5 - Z^{-1}V_5\right)\left(1 - Z_5Z^{-1}\right)^{-1} + V_1 + V_2 + V_6$$

APPENDIX D
COMPARATIVE DYNAMICS FOR
NONSYMMETRIC GAMES

In this appendix we establish the comparative dynamics results described in section III. More precisely, we compare the smallest zeros that are greater than 1 for games A, D, E, and F. We denote these zeros Z^a, Z^d, Z^e, and Z^f, respectively. Our comparison of these zeros across the different nonsymmetric games is analogous to the comparison we made in appendix A across symmetric games. In appendix A, we showed that these zeros dominate asymptotically the behavior of the solution to the homogeneous component of stochastic difference equations for the respective games. The results in this section build heavily on results in appendixes A and B.

The characteristic functions for games A and D are special cases of the characteristic function H studied in appendix A. In particular, these characteristic functions are given by

$$H^a(Z) = \theta^a W(Z) + \pi$$
$$H^d(Z) = \theta^d W(Z) + \pi$$

where

$$\theta^a = \begin{bmatrix} \theta_1 & 0 \\ 0 & \theta_2 \end{bmatrix} + \begin{bmatrix} \delta & \delta \\ \delta & \delta \end{bmatrix}$$

$$\theta^d = \begin{bmatrix} \theta_1 & 0 \\ 0 & \theta_2 \end{bmatrix} + \begin{bmatrix} \delta & \delta \\ \delta & 2\delta \end{bmatrix}$$

and $W(Z)$ is defined in appendix A. From the analysis in appendix A, it follows that

$$P^a\left[W\left(\sigma_1^{-1}\right)\right] = P^d\left[W\left(\sigma_1^{-1}\right)\right] = -\delta^2\left[W\left(\sigma_1^{-1}\right)\right]^2$$

Because $P(0)$ is positive for all games,

$$W\left(\sigma_1^{-1}\right) < W(Z^a) < 0$$

and

$$W\left(\sigma_1^{-1}\right) < W(Z^e) < 0 \qquad\qquad\qquad\qquad\text{(D.1)}$$

The properties of the function W imply that

$$Z^a < \sigma_1^{-1}$$

and

$$Z^d < \sigma_1^{-1} \qquad\qquad\qquad\qquad\text{(D.2)}$$

From relation (B.3) and the fact that H^e is a special case of the function H given in appendix A, it follows that

$$\det\left[H^e(1)\right] > 0$$

and

$$Z^e < \sigma_1^{-1} \qquad\qquad\qquad\qquad\text{(D.3)}$$

Additional inequalities will also be used in this appendix. To obtain these inequalities, define a function W^* to be

$$W^*(Z) = \left(1 - \beta Z^{-1}\right)\left(Z^{-1} - 1\right) = W(Z)/Z$$

This function is strictly increasing for real numbers greater than 1. In addition,

$$W^*(Z^a) = \frac{W(Z^a)}{Z^a}$$

$$W^*(Z^d) = \frac{W(Z^d)}{Z^d}$$

$$W^*\left(\sigma_1^{-1}\right) = \sigma_1 W\left(\sigma_1^{-1}\right)$$

Hence inequalities (D.2) and (D.3) imply that

$$0 > \sigma_1 W(\sigma_1^{-1}) > \frac{W(Z^a)}{Z^a} > 0$$

and

$$0 > \sigma_1 W(\sigma_1^{-1}) > \frac{W(Z^d)}{Z^d} > 0 \tag{D.4}$$

Game A vs. Game F

We first compare Z^a with Z^f. In making this comparison, we will show that

$$G_1(Z^a) < 0 \tag{D.5}$$

where G_1 is defined in (B.5). Because $G_1(1)$ is positive, it will then follow from the analysis in appendix B that Z^f is less than Z^a. To verify (D.5), we note that

$$\det[H^e(Z)] = \det[H^a(Z)] + \delta W(Z)[(\theta_1 + \delta)W(Z) + \pi_1(1 - \beta)] - \delta^2 W(Z)^2 \tag{D.6}$$

By definition, $\det[H^a(Z^a)]$ is zero. Hence evaluating both sides of (D.6) at Z^a gives

$$\det[H^e(Z^a)] = \delta W(Z^a)[(\theta_1 + \delta)W(Z^a) + \pi_1(1 - \beta)] - \delta^2 W(Z^a)^2 \tag{D.7}$$

Inequality (D.4) implies that

$$\delta^2 \sigma_1 Z^a W(\sigma_1^{-1}) > \delta^2 W(Z^a) \tag{D.8}$$

From (D.1), we know that $W(Z^a)$ is negative. Therefore, multiplying both sides of (D.8) by $W(Z^a)$ yields the inequality,

$$\delta^2 \sigma_1 Z^a W(\sigma_1^{-1}) W(Z^a) < \delta^2 W(Z^a)^2 \tag{D.9}$$

Hence (D.7), (D.9), and the definition of G_1 given in (B.5) guarantee that

$$G_1(Z^a) < \delta W(Z^a)[(\theta_1 + \delta)W(Z^a) + \pi_2(1 - \beta)] \tag{D.10}$$

It turns out that the right-hand side of (D.10) is negative. This claim follows from the facts that

$$(\theta_1 + \delta)W(Z^a) + \pi_2(1 - \beta) > (\theta_1 + \delta)W(\sigma_1^{-1}) + \pi_2(1 - \beta) = 0$$

and $W(Z^a)$ is negative. Thus the inequality in (D.5) is verified.

Game D vs. Game E

Next, we compare Z^d and Z^e. From the analysis in appendix B, we know that $\det[H^e(Z)]$ has only one zero in the interval $(1, \sigma_1^{-1})$. The functions $\det[H^e(Z)]$ and $\det[H^d(Z)]$ are related via

$$\det[H^e(Z)] = \det[H^d(Z)] - \delta^2 W(Z)^2 \tag{D.11}$$

Therefore

$$\det[H^e(Z^d)] < 0$$

In light of (D.3), it follows that $Z^e < Z^d$

Game D vs. Game F

Finally, we compare Z^d and Z^f. We will make this comparison by first showing that

$$G_1(Z^d) > 0 \tag{D.12}$$

The conclusion that $Z^d < Z^f$ follows from the fact that Z^f is the only zero of G_1 in the interval $(1, \sigma_1^{-1})$. To establish (D.12), we note that (B.5) and (D.11) imply that

$$G_1(Z^d) = -\delta^2 W(Z^d)^2 + \delta^2 \sigma_1 Z^d W(\sigma_1^{-1}) W(Z^d)$$

$$= \delta^2 W(Z^d) Z^d \left[\sigma_1 W(\sigma_1^{-1}) - \frac{W(Z^d)}{Z^d} \right] \tag{D.13}$$

Because $W(Z^d)$ is negative, relations (D.13) and (D.4) imply (D.12).

Combining the results obtained in this appendix, we have shown that $Z^a > Z^f > Z^d > Z^e$.

REFERENCES

Chow, G. C. 1981. *Econometric Analysis by Control Methods* (New York, John Wiley & Sons).

Hansen, L. P., and T. J. Sargent. 1980. "Formulating and Estimating Dynamic Linear Rational Expectations Models," *Journal of Economic Dynamics and Control* vol. 2, no. 1, pp. 7–46.

———. 1981. "Linear Rational Expectations Models for Dynamically Interrelated Variables," in R. E. Lucas, Jr., and T. J. Sargent, eds., *Rational Expectations and Econometric Practice*, vol. 1 (Minneapolis, Minn., University of Minnesota Press) pp. 127–156.

Jagannathan, R. 1981. "Equivalence of Open-loop and Closed-loop Equilibrium in Discrete Dynamic Dominant Player Games When There Is Continuum of Competitive Agents." Working paper (Pittsburgh, Pa., Carnegie-Mellon University).

Kydland, F. E. 1975. "Noncooperative and Dominant Player Solutions in Discrete Dynamic Games," *International Economic Review* vol. 16, no. 2, pp. 321–325.

———. 1977. "Equilibrium Solutions in Dynamic Dominant-Player Models," *Journal of Economic Theory* vol. 15, no. 2, pp. 307–324.

———, and E. C. Prescott. 1977. "Rules Rather Than Discretion: The Inconsistency of Optimal Plans," *Journal of Political Economy* vol. 85, no. 3, pp. 473–491.

———. 1980. "Dynamic Optimal Taxation, Rational Expectations and Optimal Control," *Journal of Economic Dynamics and Control* vol. 2, no. 1, pp. 79–91.

Lucas, R. E., Jr. 1976. "Econometric Policy Evaluation; A Critique," in K. Brunner and A. Meltzer, eds., *The Phillips Curve and Labor Markets*, Carnegie-Rochester Conferences on Public Policy, vol. 1 (Amsterdam, North-Holland).

———, and E. C. Prescott. 1971. "Investment Under Uncertainty," *Econometrica* vol. 39, pp. 659–681.

———, and T. J. Sargent, eds. 1981. "Introduction," *Rational Expectations and Econometric Practice* (Minneapolis, Minn., University of Minnesota Press).

Newbery, D. M. G. 1981. "Oil Prices, Cartels, and the Problem of Dynamic Inconsistency," *The Economic Journal* vol. 91, pp. 617–646.

Reinganum, J. F., and N. L. Stokey. 1983. "The Period of Commitment in Dynamic Games," CMSESM discussion paper, no. 508RR (Evanston, Ill., Northwestern University, March).

Roberds, W. 1984. "Essays on the Econometric Applications of Dynamic Game Models." Unpublished Ph.D. dissertation (Pittsburgh, Pa., Carnegie-Mellon University).

Salant, S. 1976. "Exhaustible Resources and Industrial Structure: A Nash-Cournot Approach to the World Oil Market," *Journal of Political Economy* vol. 84, no. 5, pp. 1079–1093.

Sargent, T. J. 1979. *Macroeconomic Theory* (New York, Academic Press).

Stiglitz, J. 1976. "Monopoly and the Rate of Extraction of Exhaustive Resources," *The American Economic Review* vol. 66, no. 4, pp. 655–661.

Sweeney, J. 1977. "Economics of Depletable Resources: Market Forces and Intertemporal Bias," *Review of Economic Studies* vol. 44, no. 1, pp. 125–141.

Taylor, J. B. 1979a. "Estimation and Control of Macroeconomic Model with Rational Expectations," *Econometrica* vol. 47, no. 5, pp. 1267–1287.

———. 1979b. "An Econometric Business Cycle Model with Rational Expectations," unpublished manuscript.

Whiteman, C. H. 1983. *Linear Rational Expectations Models: A User's Guide* (Minneapolis, Minn., University of Minnesota Press).

Whittle, P. 1963. *Prediction and Regulation by Linear Least-Square Methods* (Princeton, N.J., Van Nostrand-Reinhold).

6

The Econometrics of Exhaustible Resource Supply: A Theory and an Application

Dennis Epple

A great deal of attention has been devoted to the analysis of theoretical models of optimal resource depletion.[1] This outpouring of theoretical work, however, has had limited effect on empirical models of the supply of exhaustible resources. The objectives of the present analysis are (1) to develop a model in which the supply of exhaustible resources is rigorously derived from a theoretical model of optimal resource depletion, and (2) to apply that framework to study oil and natural gas supply in the United States.

Petroleum supply in the United States has been the subject of several previous econometric studies (Fisher, 1964; Erickson and Spann, 1971; Khazzoom, 1971; American Gas Association, 1973; MacAvoy and Pindyck, 1973, 1975; Epple, 1975). These models all share a common deficiency: they do not fully capture the intertemporal dynamics of resource exhaustion. Furthermore, in most cases, the models that are estimated are not derived from a characterization of the resource extraction problem being solved by the producer. Instead, the equations that are estimated are derived from intuitive arguments about the forces determining supply. In those cases in which an explicit statement of the producers' objective function is used to derive the econometric

Dennis Epple is Professor of Economics, Carnegie-Mellon University.
[1] See, for example, Dasgupta and Heal (1979).

equations, producers are assumed to solve a static optimization problem; that is, producers ignore the effects of their actions at a given date on the costs of future extraction.[2] This failure to capture the intertemporal dynamics of producers' decisions is characteristic not only of econometric models of oil and natural gas supply but also of econometric models of all exhaustible resources.

A second class of models used to study exploitation of U.S. petroleum resources is process models (see, for example, Electric Power Research Institute, 1978; Kim and Thompson, 1978). In this class of models, supply in each period is determined by the solution of an intertemporal optimization problem intended to capture the producer's decision-making problem. Although process models provide an elegant treatment of the intertemporal dynamics of resource exhaustion, they are typically not subjected to the discipline of validation against historical data. Often, such validation is not feasible because the models contain more parameters than can be econometrically identified with available data. In addition, these models often lack an adequate representation of short-run adjustment costs. As a result, users of these models frequently must insert ad hoc constraints to prohibit dramatic output changes during short time periods. Not uncommonly these constraints are a major determinant of the output predictions of the models, particularly during the short to intermediate run.

The model developed in this chapter reflects an attempt to combine the attractive features of both the econometric and process approaches. The analysis begins with the specification of an objective function of the resource extractor. That objective is assumed to be maximization of the expected present value of revenues net of extraction costs. Solution of this maximization problem yields equations that characterize the producer's optimal plan for extracting the resources. Thus these equations embody the optimality properties of solutions derived from process models. The parameters of these equations are estimated econometrically, thereby providing a complete integration of the optimization and estimation problems.

Additional features of this model that are not normally embodied in either econometric or process models of exhaustible resources are (1) explicit treatment of uncertainty about future prices and extraction costs, and (2) explicit treatment of producers' expectations about future prices and extraction costs.[3] The equations characterizing producers' formation

---

[2] The model developed by Epple (1975) and parts of the American Gas Association (1973) and MacAvoy and Pindyck (1975) models are derived from an explicit statement of the problem producers are assumed to solve.

[3] In large measure, those desirable features are achieved by adapting the framework developed by Hansen and Sargent (1980, 1981) for the study of exhaustible resource supply.

of expectations about prices and costs, coupled with the equations characterizing the optimal extraction paths of the resources, constitute the econometric model.

I. THEORETICAL FRAMEWORK

The econometric equations estimated in this chapter are derived from a dynamic, stochastic optimization model of resource depletion in which producers choose extraction rates that maximize the expected discounted net present value of the resources.[4] Suppliers are assumed to be uncertain about future prices of the resources and future extraction costs. These sources of uncertainty give rise to disturbance terms in the econometric equations.

Let y_t be a vector of resources, measured in terms of cumulative exploitation as of time t. Thus $y_t - y_{t-1} = \Delta y_t$ denotes the additional resource exploitation occurring during time period t. Let the resource exploitation cost at time t be given by

$$\Delta y_t' \theta \Delta y_t + \Delta y_t' \pi y_t + \Delta y_t' c_t + \Delta y_t' \phi \tag{1.1}$$

where ϕ is a column vector with the same dimension as y_t, θ and π are matrices conformable with y_t, θ is symmetric, and $(1 + \beta)\theta + \pi$ is positive definite. The technology shock vector c_t is of the same dimension as Δy_t and is observed by the supplier but not by the econometrician. It turns out that c_t will give rise to disturbance terms in the regression equations that will be derived.

The novel feature of this cost specification is the quadratic term

$$\Delta y_t' \pi y_t$$

The appearance of this term in the exploitation cost expression means that marginal exploitation costs increase as the amounts of the resources extracted increase.

The owner of the resources is assumed to maximize the discounted present value of the resources. The objective function for this maximization problem is given by

$$E_t \sum_{j=0}^{\infty} \beta^j \left\{ \Delta y_{t+j}' q_{t+j} - \Delta y_{t+j}' \theta \Delta y_{t+j} - \Delta y_{t+j}' \pi y_{t+j} - \Delta y_{t+j}' c_{t+j} - \Delta y_{t+j}' \phi \right\} \tag{1.2}$$

---

[4] The model presented in this section was developed jointly with Lars Hansen, who provided the derivation of the decision rules for the model.

where E_t denotes the expectation operator conditioned on information available to the supplier at time period t, q_t is the vector of prices of the resources, and β is the discount rate.

In order to derive the decision rules that maximize (1.2), the generating equations for q_t and c_t must be specified. The supplier is assumed to use these generating equations at date t to forecast future prices and extraction costs. Thus the specification of these generating equations will provide the information necessary to derive expressions for the expected value at date t of variables relevant to the supplier's decision. The supplier is also assumed to have information at date t about current and past values of variables in the generating equations and past values of the cumulative extraction vector. The generating equations are assumed to be linear so that the decision rules will be linear in a subset of the variables known by the supplier at date t.

Let q_t be a subvector of x_t. The vector x_t contains all variables the producer uses to predict future prices. It is assumed in the derivation that follows that the cumulative exploitation vector y_t is not included in x_t. Thus the derivation will characterize the behavior of a supplier whose own output has negligible impact on prices. It will be assumed that x_t has an autoregressive representation

$$\zeta(L)x_t = s_t^x \tag{1.3}$$

where

$$\zeta(L) = I - \zeta_1 L - \zeta_2 L^2 - \cdots - \zeta_r L^r$$

L is the lag operator and

$$E_{t-1}(s_t^x) = 0$$

As noted previously, current and past x's are contained in the supplier's information set.

Similarly, let c_t be a subvector of e_t, where e_t can be represented as[5]

$$\gamma(L)e_t = s_t^e \tag{1.4}$$

where

$$\gamma(L) = I - \gamma_1 L - \cdots - \gamma_r L^r$$

---

[5] It is assumed that the polynomials $\zeta(Z)$ and $\gamma(Z)$ have their roots outside $|Z| \geq \sqrt{\beta}$ to insure that the optimization problem is well defined. This allows for q_t and c_t to be nonstationary and to grow through time. The notion that the resource price grows at the discount rate is explicitly ruled out, however.

and

$$E_{t-1}(s_t^e) = 0$$

The vector e_t contains variables the producer uses to predict future technology shocks c_t. Thus at date t, the producer knows current and past values of e_t. The e_t are assumed not to be observed by the econometrician, however.

The decision rules that maximize (1.2), given (1.3) and (1.4), are derived by using the methods developed by Hansen and Sargent (1980).[6] These decision rules are

$$y_t = \frac{1}{\sqrt{\beta}}\psi_1 y_{t-1} + \psi_0^{-1}\sum_{m=1}^{k}\sigma_m\sum_{j=0}^{\infty}\rho_m^j E_t(q_{t+j} - c_{t+j})$$

$$- (1-\beta)\psi_0^{-1}(I - \sqrt{\beta}\psi_1')^{-1}\phi + \psi_0^{-1}\mu(q_t - c_t) \qquad (1.5)$$

The parameters in this set of decision rules are determined by the parameters of the objective function (1.2) and the equations of motion for the prices and stochastic shocks (1.3 and 1.4) by the following relationships:

$$\psi_0 + \psi_1'\psi_0\psi_1 = 2(1+\beta)\theta + \pi + \pi' \qquad (1.6)$$

$$\psi_1'\psi_0 = \sqrt{\beta}(2\theta + \pi) \qquad (1.7)$$

where ψ_0 and ψ_1 are real and ψ_0 is symmetric and positive definite, and by the following matrix partial fractions decomposition:

$$(1 - \beta Z^{-1})(I - \psi_1'\sqrt{\beta}Z^{-1})^{-1} = \mu + \frac{\sigma_1}{1 - \rho_1 Z^{-1}} + \cdots + \frac{\sigma_k}{1 - \rho_k Z^{-1}}$$

$$(1.8)$$

To complete the decision rules, it is necessary to obtain explicit solutions for the prediction problems,

$$\sum_{j=0}^{\infty}\rho_m^j E_t q_{t+j}$$

$$\sum_{j=0}^{\infty}\rho_m^j E_t c_{t+j} \qquad (1.9)$$

---

[6] This discrete time calculus of variations approach is discussed in some detail in Sargent (1979). Details of the derivation of the decision rules are presented in appendix D. Decision rules for the single-resource care are studied in Epple and Hansen (1981).

Using prediction formulas derived in Hansen and Sargent (1980) and using equations (1.3) and (1.4), it can be shown that

$$\sum_{j=0}^{\infty} \rho_m^j E_t q_{t+j} = U\zeta(\rho_m)^{-1} \left[I + \sum_{j=1}^{r-1} \left(\sum_{n=j+1}^{r} \rho_m^{n-j} \zeta_n \right) L^j \right] x_t \qquad (1.10)$$

and

$$\sum_{j=0}^{\infty} \rho_m^j E_t c_{t+j} = U\gamma(\rho_m)^{-1} \left[I + \sum_{j=1}^{r-1} \left(\sum_{n=j+1}^{r} \rho_m^{n-j} \gamma_n \right) L^j \right] e_t \qquad (1.11)$$

where U is a matrix with k rows and is of the form $U = [I \ 0]$.

Substitution of equations (1.10) and (1.11) into (1.5) yields an expression for the decision rules in terms of variables in the supplier's information set. The above result demonstrates that the parameters of the decision rules depend both on the parameters of the objective function (1.2) and on parameters of the generating equations for x_t and c_t (1.3 and 1.4). If the parameters in the generating equations are altered, the impact on the decision rules can be explicitly determined. This distinction proves to be quite important for the empirical analysis in section III.

The fact that e_t and hence c_t are unobservable to the econometrician introduces a disturbance term into the expression for the decision rules for y_t. Also, the decision rules are linear in the variables and time invariant. These properties are desirable from the standpoint of econometric estimation.

Although the decision rules are linear in the variables, in general they are relatively complex functions of the underlying parameters. This should not obscure the fact that the right-hand-side variables in the decision rules include current and lagged prices and disturbances and lagged values of the decision variables. This may be illustrated by the special case in which prices follow a random walk, the shocks are serially uncorrelated, and other variables known to the supplier are not correlated with the technology shocks (that is, $e_t = c_t$). In this case, the decision rules (1.5) become

$$y_t = \left(\frac{\psi_1}{\sqrt{\beta}} \right) y_{t-1} + (1 - \beta)\psi_0^{-1}(I - \sqrt{\beta}\,\psi_1')^{-1}(q_t - \phi) - \psi_0^{-1} c_t \qquad (1.12)$$

In general, the number of lagged values of prices appearing in the decision rules is one less than the number of lagged values appearing in the generating equations. The same is true for the number of lagged values of the technology shocks that appear. The reason for the appearance of these variables, as indicated by (1.10) and (1.11), is that they are part of the information producers use in forecasting future prices and technology shocks. In contrast, as a consequence of the cost function specification (1.1), only one lagged value of the cumulative exploitation vector appears in the decision rules. Additional lags of the cumulative exploitation vector would appear in the decision rules only if additional lagged values of the exploitation vector were introduced into the exploitation cost function. Such additional lags might be motivated, for example, by terms introduced to capture costs of adjusting the rate of output from period to period.

The model presented in this section is essentially a prototype that could be tailored to study a variety of resource exploitation problems. An important feature of this model is the assumption that the price-generating equations do not depend on the output of the supplier being studied. It will be argued in section III that this model is appropriate for the study of oil and natural gas supply in the United States, and empirical evidence supporting this claim will be presented. Hansen, Epple, and Roberds (chapter 5 in this volume) provide a derivation of econometric equations appropriate to the study of a single resource when suppliers are noncompetitive or when aggregate data are used to study the behavior of competitive suppliers.

II. MODELING OIL AND NATURAL GAS DISCOVERIES

The model introduced in section I may now be cast in a form suitable for modeling oil and natural gas discoveries in the United States. Several issues must be confronted in applying this model. First, although resource owners know with reasonable certainty the amounts of the resource discovered each year, econometricians do not. Hence amounts discovered per year must be inferred from data on reserves and production. Second, the market for undeveloped reservoirs, to the extent that one exists, is not one for which price data are available. Thus the value of a newly discovered reservoir must be inferred from data on wellhead prices, development costs, and production costs. Finally, this framework provides no explicit treatment of taxes, so taxes that affect various stages of oil and natural gas supply must be introduced into the framework.

To address these issues, we present a simple characterization of the petroleum supply process, from exploration through production at the wellhead. By adopting simple, and yet reasonable, mechanical rules to characterize the development and production processes, we obtain a tractable model for studying oil and natural gas discoveries.

The petroleum supply process is customarily and fruitfully subdivided into three components: exploration, development, and production. Exploratory drilling at some date τ results in the discovery of new oil and natural gas reservoirs. The amount discovered in year τ is denoted $\Delta y_{i,\tau}$, where subscript i indicates either oil ($i = 1$) or natural gas ($i = 2$). Because the amounts discovered are unobserved, the $\Delta y_{i,\tau}$ will be estimated as latent variables by using the structure outlined next.

After a reservoir is discovered, exploitation of the reservoir begins. As developmental drilling proceeds in the years following discovery, reserves are added. The amount of reserves added at date t in a reservoir discovered at date τ is denoted $\Delta a_{i,t,\tau}$, where i again denotes either oil or gas. Published estimates of "proved reserve" additions of oil and natural gas by reservoir vintage are available and are used in estimating the model. Proved reserves are defined as the amount of oil (or natural gas) "which geological and engineering data demonstrate with reasonable certainty to be recoverable in future years under existing economic and operating conditions." Essentially, proved reserves are an estimate of the amount of oil (or natural gas) that will be produced from wells in place at a particular date. The third stage of the process, production, is the gradual withdrawal of oil or gas from a reservoir.

Production at date $t + k$ from reserves $\Delta a_{i,t,\tau}$ added at date t is assumed to be

$$(1 - \varepsilon_i)\varepsilon_i^k \Delta a_{i,t,\tau} \tag{2.1}$$

This specification implies that a constant fraction $(1 - \varepsilon_i)$ of remaining reserves is produced each period. The constant of proportionality may differ for oil and gas.

Also assumed is that reserve additions at date t from a reservoir discovered at date τ are:

$$\Delta a_{i,t,\tau} = \xi_i \gamma_{1,i}^{t-\tau} \Delta y_{i,\tau} \qquad t > \tau \tag{2.2}$$

where $\Delta a_{i,t,\tau} = a_{i,t,\tau} - a_{i,t-1,\tau}$. The initial condition, $a_{i,\tau,\tau} = \alpha_i \Delta y_{i,\tau}$ captures reserves added during the discovery year. For convenience, write (2.2) in the following equivalent form:

$$a_{i,t,\tau} = \gamma_{1,i} a_{i,t-1,\tau} + \gamma_{0,i} \Delta y_{i,\tau} \qquad t > \tau \tag{2.2'}$$

The parameters in (2.2) and (2.2') are related by

$$\xi_i = \left(\alpha_i - \frac{\gamma_{0,i}}{1 - \gamma_{1,i}} \right)\left(1 - \frac{1}{\gamma_{1,i}} \right) \tag{2.3}$$

Equation (2.2) indicates that reserve additions decline geometrically after the discovery date. The latent variables $\Delta y_{i,\tau}$ are a measure of relative size of a discovery in the sense that a doubling of $\Delta y_{i,\tau}$ would result in a doubling of proved reserves and production each date after discovery. These latent variables and the other parameters in (2.2') are estimated by using a time series $(t > \tau)$ for each vintage for several vintages. The $\Delta y_{i,\tau}$ are the quantity variables in the exploration model.

In equations (2.1) and (2.2), variables over which the producer, in fact, has some degree of control are specified as being determined by mechanical processes. In practice, the rate at which reserves are added in a newly discovered reservoir is determined in part by the rate of exploratory drilling in the years after a discovery. The producer also has control, subject to technological constraints, over the rate at which production from reserves occurs.[7] Adoption of (2.1) and (2.2) is based on the presumption that, from the standpoint of a firm contemplating exploration for oil or natural gas, those equations together provide a reasonably accurate characterization of the time path of production that the exploration firm expects from a discovery. The investigation of models possibly using the generic framework of section I, in which production and development are determined endogenously, is an interesting problem for future research. It should also be noted that (2.1) and (2.2) imply that development and production patterns are the same for reservoirs regardless of vintage. In particular, ε_i, α_i, $\gamma_{0,i}$, and $\gamma_{1,i}$ differ for oil and gas, but, as the absence of time subscripts indicates, they do not vary either with date of discovery or date of exploitation.

The price of a discovery is the expected present value of revenues net of production and development costs and taxes generated by the discovery. As will be shown presently, development costs can conveniently be combined with exploration costs. Therefore an expression is developed for the expected present value of after-tax revenues net of after-tax production costs. By substituting (2.2) into (2.1) and dividing by $\Delta y_{i,\tau}$, an expression is obtained for production at any date $t + k$ from a reservoir of unit size discovered at date τ. Making this substitution, multiplying by net-of-tax price less net-of-tax unit production costs, and discounting the resulting income stream to the date of discovery yields

$$q_{i,\tau} = E_\tau \left[\sum_{t=\tau+1}^{\infty} \xi_i \gamma_{1,i}^{t-\tau} \beta^{t-\tau} \sum_{k=0}^{\infty} (1-\varepsilon_i) \varepsilon_i^k \beta^k \left(P_{i,t+k} T_{r,i} - c_{p,i} T_{p,i} \right) \right.$$
$$\left. + \alpha_i \sum_{k=0}^{\infty} (1-\varepsilon_i) \varepsilon_i^k \beta^k \left(P_{i,\tau+k} T_{r,i} - c_{p,i} T_{p,i} \right) \right] \qquad (2.4)$$

---

[7] Epple (1975) contains a discussion of factors that influence development and production decisions.

In this expression, $P_{i,t+k}$ is the wellhead price of resource i at date $t + k$. Unit production cost $c_{p,i}$ is assumed to be constant in real terms. $T_{r,i}$ is a tax variable denoting the proportion of revenues not paid in taxes, and $T_{p,i}$ is a tax variable denoting the proportion of production costs not deductible for tax purposes. Derivation of all tax variables is detailed in appendix A. Values for $c_{p,i}$ and tax rates are estimated in appendix B.

Define the following expression in the lag operator:

$$\omega_i(L^{-1}) = (1 - \varepsilon_i)(1 - \beta\varepsilon_i L^{-1})^{-1}\left[\xi_i(1 - \beta\gamma_{1,i}L^{-1})^{-1} + \alpha_i - \xi_i\right]$$

$$(2.5)$$

Using this expression, (2.4) may be written more compactly as

$$q_{i,\tau} = T_{r,i}E_\tau\omega_i(L^{-1})P_{i,\tau} - \omega_i(1)c_{p,i}T_{p,i} \qquad (2.6)$$

As this notation suggests, $q_{i,\tau}$ plays a role in the exploration model analogous to that price plays in the generic model of section I.

Expression (2.4) implicitly assumes that oil or gas is sold on the spot market as it is produced. For oil, this is a reasonably accurate characterization, but for natural gas, it is not. Gas has historically been committed to sale under long-term contract. Hence the conditions of long-term contracts prevailing at the date of sale determine the relevant price for natural gas. In the empirical analysis, it is assumed that the price prevailing during the date of discovery is the relevant contract price for the life of a field. In essence, this implies that $P_{i,\tau}$ should replace $P_{i,t+k}$ when (2.4) is applied to gas ($i = 2$), which in turn implies that $\omega(L^{-1})$ should be replaced by $\omega(1)$ in the first expression on the right-hand side of (2.4) for $i = 2$. The implications of this assumption will be discussed more fully when the empirical results are presented.

It is assumed that the unit cost of development (that is, the cost per unit of reserves added) is constant for reservoirs of a given vintage. This unit cost is assumed to increase with cumulative discoveries, however, and hence to increase from vintage to vintage. The assumption that unit cost is constant for a given vintage allows using a simple expression for the present value of development costs for a given vintage. The assumption that unit development costs increase from vintage to vintage captures the fact that new reservoirs are typically in deeper, less accessible locations than old reservoirs and hence are more costly to develop.

Let $\mu'_i + c'_{d,i}y_{\tau-1,i}$ be the unit cost of development for reservoirs discovered at date τ. Here $y_{\tau-1,i} = \sum_{s=\tau_0}^{t-1}\Delta y_{s,i}$ is cumulative discoveries through date $\tau - 1$, and μ'_i and $c'_{d,i}$ are parameters. Using this expression and (2.2), the present after-tax value at date τ of development costs for reservoirs discovered at date τ is

$$\left(\mu_i' + c_{d,i}' y_{\tau-1,i}\right) T_{d,i} \sum_{t=\tau}^{\infty} \beta^{t-\tau} \Delta a_{t,\tau,i} = \mu_i \Delta y_{\tau,i} + c_{d,i} \Delta y_{\tau,i} y_{\tau-1,i} \quad (2.7)$$

where

$$\mu_i = \mu_i' \delta_i T_{d,i}$$

$$c_{d,i} = c_{d,i}' \delta_i T_{d,i}$$

$$\delta_i = \frac{\xi_i \beta \gamma_{1,i}}{1 - \beta \gamma_{1,i}} + \alpha_i - \xi_i$$

In (2.7), $T_{d,i}$ is the proportion of development costs not deductible for tax purposes. Parameters μ_i' and $c_{d,i}'$ are estimated in appendix B.

For convenience, the discussion of the exploration model uses the following matrices and vectors:

$$\Delta y_\tau = \begin{vmatrix} \Delta y_{\tau,1} \\ \Delta y_{\tau,2} \end{vmatrix}, \qquad y_\tau = \begin{vmatrix} y_{\tau,1} \\ y_{\tau,2} \end{vmatrix}, \qquad q_\tau = \begin{vmatrix} q_{\tau,1} \\ q_{\tau,2} \end{vmatrix}, \qquad \mu = \begin{vmatrix} \mu_1 \\ \mu_2 \end{vmatrix},$$

$$c_d = \begin{vmatrix} c_{d,1} & 0 \\ 0 & c_{d,2} \end{vmatrix} \qquad\qquad\qquad\qquad (2.8)$$

The exploration cost function is assumed to be of the form given in (1.1). Given the specification of development costs, the sum of exploration and development costs, net of taxes, can be combined in the form of (1.1)

$$T_x \left[\Delta y_\tau' \theta \Delta y_\tau + \Delta y_\tau' \pi y_\tau + \Delta y_\tau' c_\tau + \Delta y_\tau' \phi + (1/T_x) \Delta y_\tau' (\mu + c_d y_{\tau-1}) \right]$$
$$= \Delta y_\tau' \theta^* \Delta y_\tau + \Delta y_\tau' \pi^* y_\tau + \Delta y_\tau' \phi^* + \Delta y_\tau' c_\tau \qquad (2.9)$$

where

$$\phi^* = T_x \phi + \mu$$

$$\theta^* = T_x \theta - c_d$$

$$\pi^* = T_x \pi + c_d$$

The nine parameters in ϕ, θ, and π characterize the exploration cost function and are the main focus of the empirical analysis. T_x is the proportion of exploration costs that cannot be deducted for tax purposes.

Using the "prices" defined in (2.6) and the cost function defined in (2.9), the objective function of the oil and gas exploration firm is as

shown in (1.2). To obtain decision rules in a form analogous to (1.5), it is necessary to take account of the way in which q_τ is defined in (2.6). Wellhead prices $P_{i,t}$ are assumed to be a subvector of x_t defined in (1.3). Therefore the partial fractions decomposition (1.8) must be modified to reflect the fact that the $P_{i,t}$ determine the path of $q_{i,\tau}$.
Let

$$\Omega(L^{-1}) = \begin{vmatrix} \omega_1(L^{-1}) & 0 \\ 0 & \omega_2(1) \end{vmatrix}, \quad T_r = \begin{vmatrix} T_{r,1} & 0 \\ 0 & T_{r,2} \end{vmatrix} \tag{2.10}$$

where $\omega_i(L^{-1})$ is as defined in (2.5). The appearance of $\omega_2(1)$ in the lower right-hand corner of $\Omega(L^{-1})$ is a result of the assumption that natural gas is sold under long-term contract. Replace the partial fractions decomposition (1.8) with the following partial fractions decomposition:

$$(1 - \beta Z^{-1})T_r\Omega(Z)\left(I - \psi_1'\sqrt{\beta}\,Z^{-1}\right)^{-1} = \hat{\mu} + \frac{\hat{\sigma}_1}{1 - \rho_1 Z^{-1}} + \frac{\hat{\sigma}_2}{1 - \rho_2 Z^{-1}}$$

$$+ \frac{\hat{\sigma}_3}{1 - \rho_3 Z^{-1}} + \frac{\hat{\sigma}_4}{1 - \rho_4 Z^{-1}}$$

$$\tag{2.11}$$

where ρ_1 and ρ_2 are determined as before, $\rho_3 = \beta\varepsilon_1$, and $\rho_4 = \beta\gamma_{1,1}$. With this partial fractions decomposition, the decision rule (1.5) and prediction formulas (1.10) and (1.11) are applicable, with $\hat{\mu}$ replacing μ and $\hat{\sigma}_m$ replacing σ_m and with an upper bound of 4 on the summation indexed by m in (1.5).

Before turning to the empirical results, it is appropriate to highlight the assumptions in the preceding derivation that it would be desirable to relax. First, it would be desirable to have development and production determined endogenously rather than treating them as determined by the mechanical rules in (2.1) and (2.2). This would surely be a significant research effort in its own right.

Second, even accepting (2.1) and (2.2) as mechanical rules, explicitly including stochastic elements in those equations and taking those stochastic elements into account in the derivation of equations (2.6), (2.7), and (2.9) would be desirable. This is not entirely straightforward because an additive shock in (2.2) would introduce an additive shock multiplying $y_{\tau-1,i}$ in (2.7), which would be carried forward into (2.9). This additional shock is not encompassed by the generic specification in section I. Possibly, a modification of the treatment of development costs would circumvent this difficulty.

Third, in the model developed in this section, resource owners are assumed to know the amount discovered at the date of discovery. Although resource owners' estimates of amounts discovered are generally agreed to be more accurate than published ultimate recovery estimates, particularly in the early years after a discovery, resource owners do not know the amounts discovered with certainty. Developmental drilling serves both to define the size of a newly discovered reservoir and to install wells to be used in production. If feasible, a useful modification of the model would be to permit resource owners to be uncertain about the size of reservoir they have discovered.

Finally, and perhaps most importantly, the way this model introduces random shocks into the exploration process is not a complete characterization of the way uncertainty enters in practice. In this model, firms make a decision about the amount to be discovered knowing the cost of discovering that amount. Costs of future discoveries are uncertain due to the shock c_τ in (2.9). In practice, firms choose a drilling plan. Both the cost of executing the drilling plan and the amounts that will be discovered by executing that plan are uncertain. Accommodating these sources of uncertainty would require modifying the model in section I by introducing a stochastic production function in which amounts discovered are a function of drilling effort and random shocks; in addition, the model would need a stochastic cost function for drilling. An ideal assumption would be that firms know past but not current values of these shocks at the time they make their decisions. Whether such modifications can be introduced that preserve the resource depletion and certainty-equivalence features of the model and deliver a tractable econometric specification is a question for further research.

III. EMPIRICAL RESULTS

In principle, simultaneous estimation of all of the model's parameters is possible but would be prohibitively expensive because of the highly nonlinear nature of the model and the large number of parameters. Hence separate estimation of subsets of parameters is essential. Estimation of many of the parameters (for example, the $c_{p,i}$ in (2.4) and the tax parameters) is straightforward and of subsidiary interest; derivation and estimation of such parameters are detailed in appendixes A and B. Of central interest is estimation of the cost function parameters ϕ, θ, and π embedded in the decision rules for exploration. Because of the unique features of the petroleum exploration process, amounts discovered are latent variables in (2.2′). Therefore, estimation of (2.2′) is necessary before proceeding to estimate the price-generating equations and decision rules for exploration.

As emphasized in section I, estimates of the parameters of the price-generating equations (1.3) are required in order to identify the cost function parameters. The price-generating equations are estimated separately. Their parameters are fixed at their estimated values, and the cost function parameters are estimated from the decision rules.

The results from estimating the price-generating equations confirm the a priori expectation that the price-generating regime changed in 1973 at the time of the oil embargo. The model permits explicit treatment of such unanticipated regime changes. Unfortunately, however, relatively few observations are available for the postembargo period. Therefore results from estimating the decision rules are first presented for the preembargo period, followed by a discussion of methods of using these decision rules in conjunction with ultimate recovery forecasts from such sources as the U.S. Geological Survey. Finally, we present results from estimating the decision rules combining data for before and after the embargo. Appendix C contains complete documentation of data sources, units of measurement, and treatment of taxes.

Latent Discovery Variables

A time series of observations on cumulative reserve additions in oil and natural gas reservoirs by vintage is available from the American Petroleum Institute and the American Gas Association.[8] Specifically, these organizations published estimates of $a_{i,t,\tau}$ for $t\varepsilon$ (1966, 1979), $\tau\varepsilon$ (1920, t) and $i = (1, 2)$. The subset of these observations for reservoirs discovered in the period $\tau\varepsilon$ (1947, 1979) is used to estimate the latent discovery variables.

Estimation of the latent discovery variables using these data is possible because of the structure that (2.2′) puts on the development process. The amount discovered in a given year $\Delta y_{i,\tau}$ is a scale variable that shifts the development path up or down. The shape of the development path, which is determined by $\gamma_{0,i}$ and $\gamma_{1,i}$, is the same for all vintages, however.

The following equations are estimated separately for oil and natural gas:

$$a_{i,t,\tau} = \begin{cases} \gamma_{1,i}a_{i,t-1,\tau} + \gamma_{0,i}\Delta y_{i,\tau} + \eta_{i,t,\tau} & t > \tau \\ \alpha_i\Delta y_{1,\tau} + \eta_{i,t,\tau} & t = \tau \end{cases} \tag{3.1}$$

---

[8] These data are available in American Petroleum Institute, "Reserves of Crude Oil...." Unfortunately, publication of the data series was discontinued in 1980.

The error terms $\eta_{i,t,\tau}$ are assumed to have constant variance and to be serially and contemporaneously uncorrelated.[9] The parameters of these equations are estimated by nonlinear least squares.[10] The results are presented in tables 6-1 and 6-2 for oil and natural gas, respectively. Because the latent variables are determined only up to a constant of proportionality, they are normalized by setting the 1947 values of the latent variables equal to 1. Hence estimates of the amounts discovered in subsequent years are proportions of the amounts discovered in 1947. These results indicate a decline in new oil and gas discoveries in recent years. The higher standard errors for recent years are to be expected because fewer observations are available. The absence of a standard error for 1979 is due to the fact that only one observation is available for that vintage. The estimated values of $\Delta y_{i,\tau}$ in tables 6-1 and 6-2 are the quantity variables for the exploration model.

Price-Generating Equations

As explained in section I, the decision rules were derived under the assumption that past values of the cumulative exploitation vector do not enter the price-generating equations; that is, they do not Granger-cause prices. The reasons for expecting this specification to be appropriate in studying oil and natural gas discoveries in the United States are as follows. First, prior to the formation of OPEC, the price of oil in the United States was effectively fixed by the joint efforts of producing states and the U.S. government. Through prorationing restrictions, the producing states limited domestic production of oil. Imports were limited by the oil import quota. In combination, the quota and prorationing maintained a price for oil in the U.S. market that was substantially above the world market price. Since 1973, the price of oil in the United States has been determined by federal regulations and, increasingly, by the world market. Thus before the formation of OPEC, domestic regulatory policy effectively short-circuited the response of the domestic price of oil to changes in domestic discoveries and production. Subsequent to the embargo,

---

[9] This disturbance is not explicitly incorporated in the optimization problem of the firm engaged in oil and gas exploration, though to do so would be desirable.

[10] These parameter estimates and those reported in table 6-7 were obtained using the nonlinear estimation package developed at Princeton University by Goldfeld and Quandt. That package includes, among others, the conjugate gradient method developed by Powell, the Davidon-Fletcher-Powell algorithm, and the quadratic hill-climbing algorithm developed by Goldfeld and Quandt. Convergence by all three of those algorithms was achieved for the parameter values reported in this chapter. See Goldfeld and Quandt (1971) for an explanation of these algorithms. Linear regression results in tables 6-3 and 6-4 were obtained using TSP. Significance levels reported in table 6-5 and the decompositions reported in table 6-6 were computed using RATS.

TABLE 6-1.   OIL DEVELOPMENT MODEL

Coefficient	Estimate	Standard error	t-Statistic
$\gamma_{0,1}$	0.371	0.023	16.05
$\gamma_{1,1}$	0.763	0.013	54.54
α_1	0.247	0.023	10.34
1947	1.000	—	—
1948	2.245	0.058	38.15
1949	2.125	0.056	37.66
1950	1.698	0.047	36.05
1951	1.084	0.035	30.77
1952	0.835	0.031	26.77
1953	1.381	0.040	33.89
1954	1.379	0.040	33.86
1955	0.977	0.033	29.28
1956	1.216	0.037	32.10
1957	1.294	0.039	32.89
1958	0.726	0.029	24.53
1959	0.472	0.026	17.91
1960	0.609	0.028	21.67
1961	0.305	0.024	12.26
1962	0.638	0.028	22.46
1963	0.301	0.024	12.10
1964	0.559	0.027	20.34
1965	0.447	0.026	16.80
1966	0.340	0.025	13.47
1967	0.503	0.028	17.89
1968	0.676	0.032	21.08
1969	0.425	0.029	14.44
1970	0.524	0.032	16.24
1971	0.415	0.032	12.74
1972	0.232	0.032	7.15
1973	0.434	0.037	11.62
1974	0.305	0.038	7.87
1975	0.348	0.043	8.09
1976	0.237	0.047	4.98
1977	0.430	0.059	7.22
1978	0.204	0.072	2.82
1979	0.302	—	—

$R^2_{\Delta a}{}^* = .56$
$R^2_a = .99$
$N = 351$

$^*R^2_{\Delta a}$ is the proportion of variance in reserve additions explained by the model, while R^2_a is the variance in cumulative additions explained by the model.

TABLE 6-2. NATURAL GAS DEVELOPMENT MODEL

Coefficient	Estimate	Standard error	t-Statistic
$\gamma_{0,2}$	3.83	0.360	10.63
$\gamma_{1,2}$	0.70	0.25	27.14
α_2	4.05	0.375	10.78
1947	1.000	—	—
1948	0.667	0.049	13.37
1949	1.920	0.090	21.31
1950	1.077	0.061	17.65
1951	0.847	0.054	15.57
1952	1.283	0.067	18.98
1953	0.993	0.058	16.97
1954	1.234	0.066	18.70
1955	0.796	0.053	15.00
1956	1.503	0.075	19.99
1957	1.322	0.069	19.08
1958	1.509	0.075	20.00
1959	0.685	0.051	13.39
1960	0.968	0.057	16.74
1961	0.802	0.053	15.07
1962	0.893	0.055	15.99
1963	0.942	0.057	16.52
1964	0.696	0.050	13.71
1965	0.673	0.050	13.45
1966	0.643	0.049	13.11
1967	0.473	0.046	10.20
1968	0.481	0.048	10.00
1969	0.526	0.050	10.33
1970	0.391	0.050	7.76
1971	0.625	0.058	10.78
1972	0.613	0.060	10.09
1973	0.747	0.068	10.98
1974	0.535	0.067	7.98
1975	0.670	0.075	8.87
1976	0.479	0.078	6.07
1977	0.541	0.091	5.91
1978	0.453	0.107	4.21
1979	0.687	—	—

$R^2_{\Delta a}{}^* = .35$
$R^2_a = .988$
$N = 351$

*See note to table 6-1.

domestic production does not appear to have played a major role in determining either domestic oil price control policy or the world price of oil.

As in the case of oil, natural gas price regulations have prevented price from adjusting in response to changes in domestic discoveries or production. Although the price of natural gas was not regulated prior to 1956, during that period, as during the period of regulation up to the time of the major oil price increases, there was little price movement. Therefore, in the interest of limiting the number of separate price regimes used in estimating the decision rules, the period prior to 1956 is not treated as a separate regime from the period following 1956.

Different vintages of natural gas have been subjected to different price ceilings throughout the period of natural gas price regulation. Since the introduction of federal price controls on oil in 1973, oil prices have also differed by vintage. Thus choosing price series for oil and gas is difficult. For periods when federal price regulations were in force, the price for new (upper-tier) oil and the average price on new natural gas sold under interstate contracts were used. The appropriateness of these price series will be discussed further in the context of the empirical results.

As expected, the results in table 6-3 confirm that two oil price regimes are appropriate, one for the years prior to the formation of the OPEC cartel in 1973 and one for the years following formation of the cartel. The first equation presents the mean oil price for the entire period. In equation 2 in the table, the mean is assumed to be different for the years subsequent to formation of the OPEC cartel than for the prior years. This simple regression explains 97 percent of the variance in the oil price series. The standard error of the price forecast is 24 cents (per barrel) in equation 2 as compared to $1.27 in equation 1. A regression for the entire period (equation 11), which has a constant, two lagged oil prices and two lagged gas prices, does not fit as well as equation 2.

It is of interest to compare more complex price equations for the two subperiods with the same equation for the entire period. Unfortunately, such a comparison requires that observations be deleted during the transition from one period to the next, and the second subperiod already contains few observations. Equations 5 and 6 of table 6-3 contain one such comparison. A constant and one lagged oil price are fitted to the entire period in equation 5 and separately for each subperiod in equation 6. Separate equations for the two subperiods perform slightly better than a single equation for the entire period, although the gain from separate treatment of the two subperiods is not as pronounced as the gain of equation 2 over equation 1. The reason is that the observation for 1974 must be deleted for this comparison; with this observation deleted, the single equation for the entire period performs reasonably well. When the

TABLE 6-3. OIL PRICE EQUATIONS

Equation	Period	Constant	Oil prices		Gas prices		R^2	SE
			$P_{1,-1}$	$P_{1,-2}$	$P_{2,-1}$	$P_{2,-2}$		
1	1949–79	3.643						1.273
		(15.92)						
2a	1949–73	3.040						.167
		(91.0)						
2b	1974–79	6.155					.965	.457 / .243
		(33.00)						
3	1949–79		1.0					
								.556
4a	1949–73		1.0					.181
								/ .247
4b	1975–79		1.0					.461
5	1949–73	.187	.946				.962	.24
	1975–79	(1.39)	(26.51)					
6a	1949–73	1.930	.367				.085	.163
		(2.54)	(1.46)					
6b	1975–79	2.420	.593				.968 / .29	.487 / .226
		(7.27)	(1.11)					
7	1949–73	.360	.817	.071			.968	.190
	1976–79	(3.12)	(5.20)	(.47)				
8	1949–79	.281	.944				.812	.561
		(.88)	(11.20)					
9	1949–73	2.276	.457	−.206			.12	.164
		(2.69)	(1.69)	(.94)				
10	1949–73	1.23	.910	−.364	2.615	−1.095	.979	.161
	1976–79	(3.76)	(6.61)	(1.97)	(2.00)	(1.10)		
11	1949–79	3.049	1.168	−1.422	11.065	−6.764	.940	.334
		(6.88)	(10.51)	(7.40)	(5.73)	(4.29)		

1974 observation is restored, the performance of the single equation is substantially worse (compare equations 5 and 8). More evidence of the importance of deleting observations at the transition point is provided by equations 9 and 11. Equation 9 differs from 11 only in that two observations are dropped; yet the standard error of the regression in 9 is half of that in 11. The events of the time, the importance of the observations at the transition point, and the comparison between equations 2 and 11 all suggest that the oil price-generating process changed between 1973 and 1974.

The usefulness of gas prices as an aid in forecasting oil prices was evaluated. As the comparison of equations 7 and 10 of table 6-3 indicates, gas prices make a modest contribution to the prediction of oil prices over the sample period.

Modeling prices as a random walk results in considerable computational savings when estimating the decision rules. Therefore the random walk model is used as a baseline in estimating the decision rules. The performance of the random walk model of oil prices over the relevant periods is summarized in equations 3 and 4 of table 6-3. Comparing the standard errors, the random walk model equation 4 performs almost as well as the other equations in the table.

Table 6-4 contains the same equations as table 6-3, with the roles of oil and gas prices interchanged and with one additional equation. Here, in contrast to oil, the price regimes show very little evidence of being different for the two subperiods. For example, a single regression for the entire period (equation 11) performs much better than the simple scheme

TABLE 6-4.   GAS PRICE EQUATIONS

Equation	Period	Constant	Oil prices $P_{1,-1}$	$P_{1,-2}$	Gas prices $P_{2,-1}$	$P_{2,-2}$	R^2	SE
1	1949–79	.295 (6.15)						.267
2a	1949–73	.178 (15.96)					.823	.056 ⎱ .11
2b	1974–79	.782 (7.78)						.246 ⎰
3	1949–79				1.0			.065
4a	1949–73				1.0			.026 ⎱ .067
4b	1975–79				1.0			.132 ⎰
5	1949–73 1975–79	−.009 (.50)			1.075 (22.09)	.945		.064
6a	1949–73	−.0114 (.65)			1.138 (11.18)	.84	.988	.022 ⎱ .031
6b	1975–79	.456 (4.66)			.546 (4.40)	.86		.065 ⎰
7	1949–73 1976–79	.018 (2.10)			1.742 (17.25)	−.816 (6.92)	.987	.032
8	1949–79	.008 (.48)			1.073 (22.40)		.94	.063
9	1949–73	−.0093 (.53)			1.500 (5.02)	−.393 (1.28)	.855	.022
10	1949–73 1976–79	−0.15 (.28)	.059 (2.39)	−.048 (1.43)	1.615 (6.82)	−.702 (3.90)	.990	.029
11	1949–79	.110 (2.61)	.081 (7.59)	−.030 (1.68)	1.194 (6.45)	−.400 (2.62)	.987	.032
12	1949–79	.018 (1.19)			1.598 (9.11)	−.630 (3.08)	.959	.059

in which the mean price differs between the two periods (equation 2). A comparison of equation 5 to equation 8 and equation 10 to equation 11 indicates that deleting observations at the transition between the two subperiods is much less important for gas than for oil, although the omission of 1974 does lead to some reduction in the standard error of the regression. Also, oil prices appear to contribute substantially to the prediction of gas prices, as the comparison of 11 and 12 indicates. The random walk model performs well prior to 1973, as indicated by 4a, but not well compared to 6b after 1973.

The finding that oil prices help predict natural gas prices is not surprising. Fuel oil, the price of which moves closely with the price of crude oil, is a major substitute for natural gas. Prior to the imposition of natural gas regulation, the price of oil may have been a major factor influencing the price of natural gas. In the early 1970s, the severity of the natural gas shortage induced by the price regulations provoked a reevaluation of those policies. The dramatic jump in the price of oil in 1973 increased the demand for natural gas and contributed to changes in regulatory policy that permitted gas prices to rise.

Additional evidence on the role of past prices in predicting future prices is presented in tables 6-5 and 6-6. Those tables also contain evidence bearing on the assumption that past discoveries were not a major determinant of prices over the sample period. Table 6-5 presents marginal significance levels of lagged explanatory variables in the price generating equations. A given equation in the bottom half of the table was estimated with the same explanatory variables as the corresponding equation in the top half but with the price of natural gas as the dependent variable rather than the price of oil. A given equation also includes the same number of lagged values of each explanatory variable. Thus, for example, the marginal significance level of the two lagged natural gas prices in explaining oil prices, equation 2 in the top half of table 6-5, is .225.

The marginal significance levels of lagged prices in table 6-5 provide further evidence to support the results in tables 6-3 and 6-4. Of greater interest in table 6-5 is the evidence concerning the role of past discoveries in predicting oil and natural gas prices.[11] For the period 1949–1973, the

---

[11] Because the theoretical model implies that the series for oil and natural gas discoveries will be nonstationary, those variables were first regressed against a time trend and a squared time trend. The residuals from those regressions, denoted $\Delta \tilde{y}_1$ and $\Delta \tilde{y}_2$, were then used as explanatory variables for the regressions reported in table 6-5. Significance levels for $\Delta \tilde{y}_1$ and $\Delta \tilde{y}_2$ of comparable magnitude to those reported in table 6-5 were obtained when a trend and a squared trend were included as regressors with the unadjusted discovery data. Comparable significance levels were also obtained for the 1949–79 period when the dummy variables for 1974 and 1975 were deleted.

TABLE 6-5. MARGINAL SIGNIFICANCE LEVELS OF LAGGED VARIABLES IN PRICE REGRESSIONS

Equation	Dates	Number of lags	Lagged regressors				R^2	SE
			P_1	P_2	$\Delta\hat{y}_1$	$\Delta\hat{y}_2$		
			Dependent variable: Oil price (P_1)					
1a	1949–73	1	.100	.238			142	.161
2a	1949–73	2	.158	.225			246	.159
3a	1949–73	2	.880	.196	.157		452	.151
4a*	1949–79	2	$.2 \times 10^{-6}$	.007		.229	987	.161
5a*	1949–79	2	$.2 \times 10^{-5}$	.027	.341	.320	989	.161
			Dependent variable: Natural gas price (P_2)					
1b	1949–73	1	.218	$.3 \times 10^{-9}$		.854	022	
2b	1949–73	2	.320	$.5 \times 10^{-8}$		.871	022	
3b	1949–73	2	.243	$.4 \times 10^{-7}$	.528	.274	902	.021
4b	1949–79	2	.069	$.1 \times 10^{-9}$		.990	029	
5b	1949–79	2	.010	$.8 \times 10^{-9}$	.046	.244	993	.026

*To facilitate comparison of these results to those in tables 6-3 and 6-4, two dummy variables were included for these regressions. One takes the value 1 in 1974 and zero otherwise. The other takes the value 1 in 1975 and zero otherwise. Thus, equation 4 of this table corresponds to equations 10 of tables 6-3 and 6-4.

TABLE 6-6. DECOMPOSITION OF VARIANCE OF FORE-CAST ERRORS FOR PRICES

Step	P_1	P_2	$\Delta \tilde{y}_1$	$\Delta \tilde{y}_2$
Percent of variance of k-step-ahead forecast error in P_1 explained by:				
1	100.00	0.00	0.00	0.00
2	93.18	4.60	0.25	1.95
3	76.73	17.65	4.48	1.12
4	61.87	29.56	7.84	0.71
5	53.31	37.92	8.02	0.73
6	48.07	43.76	7.23	0.92
7	43.99	48.15	6.49	1.34
8	40.44	51.59	6.04	1.90
9	37.44	54.25	5.73	2.57
10	35.03	56.22	5.46	3.26
11	33.15	57.65	5.22	3.96
12	31.69	58.63	5.01	4.64
13	30.58	59.25	4.86	5.29
14	29.80	59.56	4.74	5.87
15	29.34	59.61	4.67	6.36
16	29.17	59.43	4.64	6.74
17	29.26	59.11	4.65	6.96
18	29.53	58.74	4.68	7.03
19	29.89	58.39	4.73	6.97
20	30.24	58.16	4.78	6.80
Percent of variance of k-step-ahead forecast error in P_2 explained by:				
1	22.08	77.91	0.00	0.00
2	35.17	61.92	2.88	0.01
3	36.97	59.32	3.33	0.36
4	35.68	59.69	3.82	0.79
5	33.45	60.93	4.17	1.43
6	31.29	62.27	4.30	2.12
7	29.42	63.44	4.25	2.86
8	27.82	64.41	4.13	3.62
9	26.42	65.18	3.99	4.38
10	25.21	65.77	3.86	5.14
11	24.21	66.16	3.74	5.87
12	23.43	66.36	3.64	6.54
13	22.92	66.36	3.57	7.14
14	22.68	66.16	3.53	7.61
15	22.72	65.80	3.52	7.93
16	23.02	65.33	3.56	8.07
17	23.51	64.81	3.63	8.04
18	24.08	64.33	3.72	7.85
19	24.63	63.97	3.81	7.58
20	25.06	63.75	3.89	7.28

significance levels for $\Delta \tilde{y}_1$ and $\Delta \tilde{y}_2$ in equations 3 of table 6-5 indicate that those variables do not make a significant contribution to prediction of prices. This is also true for the period 1949–1979 for oil prices, as equation 5a of table 6-5 indicates. For natural gas prices for the 1949–1979 period, equation 5b indicates that natural gas discoveries do not make a significant contribution to predicting natural gas prices, but oil discoveries do. The significance level of oil discoveries in 5b is much lower, however, than the significance levels for lagged oil and natural gas prices. Thus the overall evidence in table 6-5 is that lagged discoveries do not make an important contribution to predicting prices.

Further evidence in support of this conclusion is provided in table 6-6. The proportion of the k-step-ahead forecast error variance explained by discoveries is small for both oil and natural gas prices. Several alternative orthogonalizations of the errors in the moving average representation used to decompose the forecast variance were tried. For those orthogonalizations, as for the one reported in table 6-6, discoveries make a small contribution to the explanation of prices.[12] Thus the evidence in tables 6-5 and 6-6 is consistent with the assumption that lagged discoveries do not help predict (Granger-cause) prices.

Decision Rules with One Price Regime

For the years prior to the formation of the OPEC cartel in 1973, oil and natural gas prices in the United States exhibited very little movement, as is evident in equations 2a in tables 6-3 and 6-4. Thus producers' predictions of future prices during that period were presumably relatively accurate. A random walk model or a model that predicted a constant price would have been quite accurate for both oil and natural gas. The formation of the OPEC cartel and its viability were largely unexpected and can reasonably be characterized as an unexpected change in the regime generating oil prices. Very little concrete evidence exists, however, from which to select generating equations to characterize producers' price expectations in the years immediately following the formation of the OPEC cartel. Although certain of the results in tables 6-3 and 6-4 are used to estimate the decision rules after 1973, five observations provide

---

[12] The innovations for oil and natural gas prices in the vector autoregression in equation 5 of table 6-5 display a relatively high correlation (.48), but the remaining correlations among the innovations are relatively small. The relative proportion of the forecast variances explained by oil and natural gas prices varies considerably depending on the orthogonalization used in the moving average prepresentation. Interestingly, and somewhat surprisingly in the light of the significance tests, the proportion of the forecast error variance explained by natural gas prices is relatively high for other orthogonalizations, as it is for that reported in table 6-6. Lagged discoveries explained a small proportion of the forecast error of prices in all orthogonalizations that were investigated.

scant basis for characterizing the formation of price expectations during such a turbulent period. Therefore results from estimating the decision rules for the preembargo period will be presented first, followed by results from both periods combined.

Before results from estimation of the decision rules are presented, a clarification of the treatment of taxes in the decision rules is necessary. In deriving the decision rules in section II, the tax parameters ($T_{r,i}$, $T_{p,i}$, $T_{d,i}$, and $T_{x,i}$) were treated as constants. This implies that producers behave as if they believe the tax parameters prevailing at a given date will continue in the future. Thus any change in tax parameters that occurs is unanticipated, and producers believe the change will be permanent. A more desirable characterization would be to assume that producers attempt to predict tax rate changes.

The characterization that tax changes are unexpected is used in order to retain the certainty-equivalence properties exploited in the derivation of the decision rules in section I. The derivation in section II embeds the tax parameters in the decision rules. Given the assumptions about producer expectations concerning taxes, the tax parameters appearing in the decision rules for a particular year should be the tax parameters prevailing during that year. Hence, in estimating the model, any tax changes that occur during the sample period are captured by changing values of the tax parameters appearing in the decision rules. Although this approach does not capture producers' expectations of tax rate changes, it does capture the effects of permanent taxes in a theoretically attractive way. As detailed in appendix A, the model incorporates tax rules that permit differential tax treatment of costs incurred at various stages of the petroleum supply process, and it incorporates the oil depletion allowance and state severance taxes. The model thus permits an extensive treatment of the effects of permanent taxes on ultimate recovery and the rate of discovery; that is, the path of exploitation under the observed tax regime can be compared to a hypothetical path in which one or more tax rates are assumed to have been permanently set at a different level.

Results from estimation of the decision rules for the period 1948 through 1972 are reported in column (1) of table 6-7.[13] These are

---

[13]A real discount rate of 8 percent was used for all of the results shown in the table. Experiments with other rates suggest that the fit of the model is relatively insensitive to choice of discount rate. Parameters are estimated by the method of maximum likelihood. Standard error estimates for these and subsequent parameter estimates were calculated numerically. In all instances, the resulting t-statistics were large (> 3.5); in many instances, they were implausibly large. Therefore these numerically computed standard errors are not reported here. Computation of analytic derivatives for the likelihood function is not feasible for the model presented here. The likelihood ratio statistic is used for tests discussed in the text.

TABLE 6-7. EXPLORATION COST PARAMETERS AND DECISION RULE PARAMETERS

Parameter	(1)	(2)	(3)	(4)	(5)	(6)
ϕ_1	−2.743	−.592	−.973	−3.09	.044	−1339.
ϕ_2	−6.025	−.476	−2.800	−1.14	0	−14.58
θ_{11}	.137	1.214	.121	.505	.085	130.1
θ_{12}	.355	.032	.109	0	−.003	.221
θ_{22}	.977	.317	.619	.241	.233	3.060
π_{11}	.209	0	.134	.182	.118	51.37
π_{12}	−.064	0	−.044	0	−.065	−.001
π_{21}	−.023	0	−.007	0	−.024	.0
π_{22}	.208	0	.096	.043	.029	.402
$\psi_{0,11}$	.297	1.352	.227	.707	.171	188.3
$\psi_{0,12}$	.382	.035	.110	0	−.031	.251
$\psi_{0,22}$	1.254	.345	.765	.300	.271	3.78
$\psi_{1,11}$	.775	.953	.824	.884	.810	.888
$\psi_{1,12}$	.107	.001	.061	0	.076	.0
$\psi_{1,21}$	.041	.001	.004	0	−.048	.004
$\psi_{1,22}$	.881	.934	.908	.896	.933	.922
$R^2_{\Delta y_1}$	.86	.23	.84	.82	.84	.83
$R^2_{\Delta y_2}$	.51	−.29	.50	.50	.47	.47
LnL^2	2.645	−23.06	+.464	−.977	.005	.952
N	25	25	25	25	25	32

estimates of the parameters in equation (1.5) with prices and quantities as defined in section II. For these and the remaining estimates in table 6-7, the shocks c_t to the cost function in equation (1.1) are assumed to be contemporaneously correlated but serially uncorrelated. These estimates were obtained with random walk price-generating equations for both oil and natural gas. As indicated in section I, the decision rules take the form in equation (1.12), in which prices follow a random walk. Estimated parameter values for the decision rules during this time period are not sensitive to the choice of price forecasting equations. This is not surprising, because there was little price variability during this period, and the random walk provides a very good fit to the price data.

The reduced-form coefficients ψ_0 and ψ_1 are also presented in table 6-7. These parameters vary by year because of changes in tax rates. The values reported in the table are computed with the tax rates that prevailed in 1972.

The fit of the decision rules with the parameters in column (1) of table 6-7 is quite good, as indicated by the R^2 statistics. Furthermore, the coefficient estimates, except for the ϕ parameters, conform to the predictions of the theoretical model; the cost function in equation (1.1) is assumed to have positive values for the ϕ_i. The implications of negative estimates for the ϕ_i will be addressed within the context of an evaluation of the extent to which the model provides a satisfactory characterization of the supply of oil and natural gas discoveries.

One of the main reasons for developing a model of exhaustible resources is to measure the magnitude and significance of resource depletion. This can be done by imposing restrictions on the parameters of the model that imply no resource depletion and testing whether those restrictions significantly reduce the fit of the model. Another measure of depletion is obtained by determining the amount of the resource remaining to be discovered.

If the resources were nondepletable, all terms in the matrix π would be zero. To provide an indication of the significance of resource depletion, the model was reestimated with all elements of π set equal to zero.[14] The resulting estimates are reported in column (2) of table 6-7. These restrictions dramatically reduce the fit of the model as indicated by the R^2 statistics. A likelihood ratio test of these restrictions results in a chi-square statistic of 51.4, which, with four degrees of freedom, implies rejection of the restrictions at a significance level far below 1 percent.[15] Thus, this test confirms what the results in tables 6-1 and 6-2 would lead one to expect. Oil and natural gas resources in the United States are subject to a relatively rapid rate of depletion.

In 1982, the U.S. Geological Survey (USGS) published estimates of undiscovered recoverable oil and natural gas resources in the United States.[16] The USGS estimated that 63.5 billion barrels of oil and 497 trillion cubic feet of natural gas remained to be discovered at the end of 1979. It is of interest to compare the predictions of our model to these estimates.

In our model, the amounts discovered each period are latent variables normalized to 1 in 1947. For purposes of comparison with other estimates, these latent variables can be converted into conventional units by use of the development model, equation (2.2′). Estimates reported in

---

[14]A reviewer noted that to test the hypothesis of no depletion, one should also set $c_{d,i}$ in equation (3.7) equal to zero. This is correct. The model encompasses two aspects of depletion. The matrix π captures the aspect of depletion associated with increasing costs of finding reservoirs, while $c'_{d,i}$ captures the aspect of depletion reflected in increasing costs of exploiting reservoirs that are found. Only the hypothesis $\pi = 0$ is tested in column (2) of table 6-7. The significance of the $c'_{d,i}$ is reported in appendix B.

[15]The likelihood ratio statistics reported in the text may be larger than the values that would be obtained if all parameters were permitted to vary when constraints are imposed. The contrast in results between columns (1) and (2) of table 6-7 is sufficiently great, however, that the significance of the resource depletion phenomenon is in little doubt.

[16]"U.S. Geological Survey Circular 860." These are mean estimates for the lower 48 states—the geographic region for which the model is estimated.

tables 6-1 and 6-2 imply that $[\gamma_{0,1}/(1 - \gamma_{1,1})] = 1.565$ billion barrels of oil are recovered per unit of oil discovered and $[\gamma_{0,2}/(1 - \gamma_{1,2})] = 12.767$ trillion cubic feet of natural gas are recovered per unit of natural gas discovered. These conversion factors will be used to convert predicted future discoveries from the model into units of ultimately recoverable oil and gas reserves.

Predicted ultimate recovery can be obtained from the decision rules. Let expected ultimate recovery of the resource vector, given information available at date t, be denoted $y_{t,\infty}$, where

$$y_{t,\infty} = \lim_{k \to \infty} E_t y_{t+k}$$

and let $q_{t,\infty}$ be the vector of backstop prices expected, given information available at date t,

$$q_{t,\infty} = \lim_{k \to \infty} E_t q_{t+k}$$

Assume that

$$c_t = 0 \quad \text{and} \quad E_t c_{t+k} = 0 \quad \forall k$$

Then it follows from equation (1.5) that

$$y_{t,\infty} = \pi^{-1}(q_{t,\infty} - \phi) \tag{3.2}$$

As equation (3.2) indicates, predictions of ultimate recovery from the model depend on assumed backstop prices. Thus, to compare the predictions of the model to USGS predictions, prices must be specified for which the USGS predictions are expected to be valid. The USGS makes no explicit use of prices in its estimates. Rather it states that it is "... assumed that undiscovered resources of oil and gas will be recoverable under conditions represented by a continuation of price-cost relationships and trends that prevailed at the time of the assessment (1980)."[17] This could be interpreted to mean that the estimates are based on prices prevailing at the time the assessment was made, or it could be interpreted to mean that the estimates are based on prices expected to prevail in the future.

At prices approximating currently observed values—$30 per barrel (BBL) for oil and $3 per thousand cubic feet (MCF) for natural gas—the parameters in column (1) of table 6-7 imply that 45 billion barrels of oil

---

[17] Circular 860, p. 7.

and 312 trillion cubic feet of natural gas remained to be discovered in 1980. These amounts are 71 percent and 63 percent, respectively, of the USGS estimates of undiscovered oil and natural gas resources. With 50 percent higher prices, the column (1) parameters imply that 74 billion barrels of oil and 481 trillion cubic feet of natural gas remain to be discovered—respectively, 17 percent above and 3 percent below the USGS estimates of resources remaining to be discovered in 1980.

More formal comparisons of the ultimate recovery predictions of the model to predictions made by others can be accomplished by first solving equation (3.2) for ϕ and restating the resulting expression in terms of tax- and cost-adjusted parameters and prices to obtain

$$\phi^* = q_{t,\infty} - \pi^* y_{t,\infty} \tag{3.3}$$

The two restrictions in (3.3) can be imposed in estimating the decision rules. These restrictions assure that the parameter values obtained by estimating the decision rules will yield the ultimate recovery predictions $y_{t,\infty}$ when the backstop prices are $q_{t,\infty}$. Thus, to test whether the ultimate recovery predictions of others are significantly different from those implied by the model, the model can be estimated with $y_{t,\infty}$ in the restrictions in (3.3) set equal to the estimates made by others.

The estimates in column (3) of table 6-7 were obtained with the restrictions in (3.3), using 1979 tax rates, the ultimate recovery estimates of the USGS, and prices of \$30/BBL of oil and \$3/MCF of natural gas. A likelihood ratio test of these restrictions yields a chi-square statistic of 4.36 with two degrees of freedom. Thus, at the above prices, these restrictions would be rejected at a significance level of roughly 15 percent. When the USGS estimates of ultimate recovery are imposed on the model at prices of \$45/BBL and \$4.5/MCF,[18] an estimated likelihood function value of 2.08 is obtained. Thus, at these prices, imposition of the USGS ultimate recovery restrictions does not markedly reduce the fit of the model.

Another way of relating the ultimate recovery predictions of the USGS to those of the model in this paper is to ask what backstop prices would make predicted ultimate recovery from the model equal to the USGS predictions. This question can be answered by solving equation (3.3) for $q_{t,\infty}$ and using the result and equation (2.6) to solve for $P_{i,\infty}$, $i = 1, 2$. At backstop prices of \$38/BBL of oil and \$4.75/MCF of natural gas, the model with parameters from column (1) of table 6-7 gives ultimate recovery predictions equal to those of the USGS.

---

[18] These prices are above those currently prevailing, but they are below at least some estimates of backstop prices. See, for example, Energy Modeling Forum 6 (1982).

The model, then, implies that U.S. oil and natural gas resources are depletable. Moreover, the model's predictions of ultimate recovery are of the same order of magnitude as USGS estimates within ranges of prices that presumably reflect economic conditions assumed by the USGS.

Another issue of interest regarding oil and natural gas discoveries is the issue of "directionality," that is, the extent to which oil and natural gas discoveries are interdependent.[19] Our model allows for directionality by permitting the off-diagonal elements of θ and π to be nonzero. To provide an indication of the interdependence between oil and natural gas discoveries, the model was reestimated with the off-diagonal elements of the matrices θ and π set equal to zero. These restrictions imply that the dependence, if any, between oil and natural gas discoveries arises only because of covariance between the residuals of the two equations. The results are reported in column (4) of table 6-7. A likelihood ratio test of these restrictions leads to rejection at the 5 percent significance level. Thus considerable evidence exists of interdependence between oil and natural gas discoveries.

It is of interest to note the magnitude of the elements of the matrix ψ_1 for the parameter estimates in column (4) of table 6-7. (Recall that the values of these parameters are computed using the tax rates prevailing in 1972). The off-diagonal elements are zero because of the restrictions on the θ and π matrices. Without depletion, the diagonal elements of the matrix would be equal to .962 ($= \sqrt{\beta}$). Thus, in this special case, the diagonal elements of the matrix ψ_1 provide an indication of the relative rates of depletion of the two resources.

The model appears to fit the data reasonably well. It gives ultimate recovery predictions that are of the right order of magnitude, and it can be used to test questions concerning resource depletion and interdependence of costs of resource exploitation. In addition, the model can be used to forecast future discoveries using the estimated decision rules, future reserve additions by using the discovery predictions and the development equation (2.2), and future production by using predicted reserve additions and the equations for production (2.1). Such forecasts can be generated with alternative assumptions about the equation that generates prices, which allows investigation of the implications of alternative future price regimes.

In one respect, however, the model's estimates are not satisfactory—the negative estimates of ϕ_i in column (1) of table 6-7. One way to assess the importance of the negative ϕ_i is to impose the restrictions that the ϕ_i be non-negative and then reestimate the model. The results of this exercise are reported in column (5) of table 6-7. When ϕ_2 is set equal to zero, the

---

[19]See, for example, Erickson and Spann (1971).

estimate of ϕ_1 is positive. A likelihood ratio test of this restriction yields a chi-square statistic of 5.28 with one degree of freedom, which implies rejection at the 5 percent level of significance. Thus requiring the ϕ_i to be non-negative substantially reduces the fit of the model.

A second way to assess the importance of the negative ϕ_i is to substitute the parameter estimates from column (1) of table 6-7 into the cost function, equation (2.9). When this is done, costs are found to be negative. Predicted costs are increasing through time, and they are near zero at the end of the sample period. By this measure, the negative ϕ_i are not negligible in magnitude as compared to other elements of the cost function.

A third way to assess the implications of the negative ϕ_i is to compute implied ultimate recovery of the resources when the ϕ_i are required to be non-negative. The parameter estimates in column (5) of table 6-7 were used to compute ultimate recovery with oil and natural gas prices of \$30/BBL and \$3/MCF, respectively. The resulting estimates of un-discovered resources are 129 billion barrels of oil and 1,439 trillion cubic feet of natural gas. These values are too high to be considered credible. Thus, when the ϕ_i are constrained to be non-negative, the model yields unreasonable ultimate recovery predictions.

The role of the negative ϕ_i can be understood intuitively by consider-ing the parameter estimates in conjunction with equation (3.2). Note that the diagonal elements of the π matrix in column (1) of table 6-7 are larger than the corresponding elements in column (5), while the off-diago-nal elements are roughly the same. The ϕ_i in column (1) are negative, while in column (5) they are positive. Equation (3.2) implies that a simultaneous increase in $-\phi$ and the diagonal elements of π reduces the sensitivity of ultimate recovery to changes in price. Thus the estimates in column (1) result in a lower sensitivity of ultimate recovery to changes in price than do the estimates in column (5).

By the same logic, the estimates in column (1) imply a lower sensitivity of changes in discoveries to changes in price than do the estimates in column (5). To see this, consider the second expression on the right-hand side of equation (1.12). An increase in $-\phi$ and a decrease in the magnitude of the elements of the matrix multiplying $(q_t - \phi)$ results in a decrease in the sensitivity of the expression to changes in q_t. The estimates in column (1) differ from the estimates in column (5) in precisely this fashion. Thus the negative ϕ_i are associated with a lower sensitivity of both ultimate recovery and changes in the rate of dis-coveries to changes in prices.

Clearly the negative ϕ_i contribute importantly to the relatively favor-able empirical performance of the model. This implies that the theoretical model provides an imperfect characterization of the exploitation of oil and natural gas resources. It appears that the model's quadratic cost function does not permit a sufficiently rapid increase in costs with increases in cumulative exploitation. With non-negative ϕ_i, the model implies too great a sensitivity of ultimate recovery and changes in the rate of discoveries to changes in prices. A formulation in which costs increase more rapidly with cumulative exploitation than the quadratic cost function of equation (1.1) permits would presumably generate decision rules that display less sensitivity to price.

The nature of the problem is illustrated in figure 6-1, in which, for simplicity, extraction of a single resource is considered. Suppose the curve OB depicts actual ultimate recovery as a function of backstop price. The model implies that ultimate recovery is a linear function of backstop prices (equation 3.2). If actual prices for the resource fall in the interval from q^1 to q^2, then estimation of the model might yield values of ϕ and π that correspond to the line CD in figure 6-1. This line closely

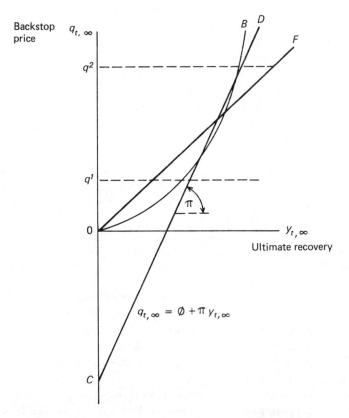

Figure 6-1.   Resource price and recovery relationships

approximates the curve OB in the range of observed prices, and it has a negative intercept ($\phi < 0$). If ϕ were forced to be non-negative, then estimation of the model might yield values of ϕ and π that correspond to line OF in figure 6-1. This line poorly approximates the true relationship of ultimate recovery to price, and it implies that ultimate recovery is more sensitive to price than it actually is. If ϕ is permitted to be negative, the estimated model may well provide a satisfactory approximation to the true relationship of ultimate recovery and price within the relevant price range.

Decision Rules with Two Price Regimes

The investigation of price-generating regimes confirmed that the regime for oil prices changed at the time of the oil embargo in 1973. The framework presented in section I permits estimation of decision rule parameters when more than one price regime exists. The difficulty in applying this framework is determining an appropriate characterization of producers' formation of oil price expectations in the postembargo period.

A diverse and changing set of regulations has been imposed on domestic oil and natural gas prices since the oil price increases of 1973. Federal price restrictions were initially imposed on "old" oil—oil discovered before 1973. The price of new oil—oil discovered after 1973—was initially unregulated, then subsequently brought under price controls. Various proposals for taxing domestic oil production were discussed for some time before the "windfall profits tax" was imposed. Thus retroactive imposition of price controls and taxes on domestic oil were a subject of continual debate after 1973, and both eventually occurred. The continual threat of some form of price controls surely affected producers' expectations of future prices during this period.

Natural gas has been subject to price regulation since 1956. The natural gas price used in this chapter is the average price of gas sold under new interstate contracts. For the years after 1973, that average is far in excess of the regulated ceiling price on new contracts. This suggests that much of the new gas sold during those years was sold under "emergency" authorization, which permitted the actual price of gas to exceed the ceiling price. Probably, emergency authorization could be obtained for only limited quantities of natural gas. Producers may simply have chosen to withhold gas from sale—as was widely alleged—rather than sell it at the regulated ceiling price. Thus the price used here may not reflect the price available for marginal sales during the years since 1973. Debate during this period was between advocates of deregulation and advocates of tougher price regulations, and as with oil prices, this surely affected producers' expectations of future prices.

Another important feature of natural gas price regulation is the "grandfathering" of prices by date of initial contract. An increase in the ceiling price on new contracts has typically not resulted in a corresponding increase in prices on contracts signed in previous years. In effect, gas prices have been fixed in nominal terms at the price prevailing at the date of initial sale. With this type of price regulation, an increase in the expected rate of inflation reduces the expected present value of a natural gas discovery. This can best be understood by reference to equation (2.4) (equivalently, 2.6). In the presence of inflation, a fixed nominal price will result in a declining real price. Thus, the more rapid the expected rate of inflation, the lower will be the expected value of net revenues generated in equation (2.4). The treatment of natural gas prices in section II implicitly assumes that real prices are fixed under long-term contract. To the extent that producers do not expect regulation to permit prices on old contracts to rise with inflation, this treatment overstates the value of new discoveries in a period of rising inflation.

Given the distinctions after 1973 between old and new oil, producers possibly expected that a regulatory strategy of grandfathering prices might eventually be adopted for oil as well. In that case, a falling real price may be appropriate for evaluating (2.6) for oil for the years following 1973.[20]

A final factor influencing producers' price expectations in the years after 1973 was the uncertain viability of the OPEC cartel. Predictions that the cartel would collapse were commonplace in the period following the price increase in 1973. Although those predictions are heard with decreasing frequency, they were taken quite seriously for some time—and the possibility of OPEC collapse still exists. Furthermore, in 1973, estimates of the real cost of producing synthetic fuels, such as oil from shale, were much lower than current estimates. Thus oil producers may well have expected that the probability was high that world oil prices would eventually drop substantially from the levels observed in the years immediately following the formation of the cartel.

For all of these reasons, probably none of the price equations presented in tables 6-3 and 6-4 adequately capture producers' price expectations for the years immediately following 1973. In fact, producers quite likely expected that the real prices at which they would be able to sell newly discovered oil or gas in the future would be substantially less than

---

[20] To explore the potential of this factor, the model was estimated using nominal discount rates to evaluate equation (1.5). Although the parameter estimates improved somewhat, this factor alone is not sufficient to account for the unsatisfactory parameter estimates discussed below.

the prices actually observed during 1973 through 1979. Hence these expected prices would have been substantially less than prices forecast by the equations in tables 6-3 and 6-4. Gas producers probably could not sell all that they would like to have sold at the average new contract prices observed during the period from 1973 through 1979.

The complex set of factors influencing price expectations in the post-1973 period and the limited set of observations available make adequate capture of expectation formation by regressions based on observed price data impossible. Thus the analysis that follows must necessarily be exploratory in nature.

When the parameters in column (1) of table 6-7 are applied to the entire sample with prices following a random walk, the fit is extremely poor ($LnL = -32.4$, $R_1^2 = .19$, $R_2^2 = .10$). This poor fit can only be attributable to a very poor fit to observations for 1973 through 1979. With these parameters, predicted discoveries are much larger than actual discoveries during those five years.

When the decision rules were estimated for the entire sample period with prices following a random walk, the estimates in column (6) of table 6-7 were obtained. The fit of the equations, as measured by the R^2 statistics, is almost as good as the fit obtained in column (1) of table 6-5 for the preembargo period. The parameter estimates are substantially different, however, and their implications for ultimate recovery are unsatisfactory. They imply that 2 billion barrels of oil and 229 trillion cubic feet of natural gas remained to be discovered from 1980 onward at prices of \$30/BBL and \$3/MCF for oil and natural gas, respectively. This estimate for natural gas is somewhat pessimistic, while the estimate for oil is not credible.

Qualitatively similar results were obtained by using other price forecasting regimes from tables 6-3 and 6-4. Extensive testing of the model with alternative price forecasting equations did not markedly improve the fit of the equations or substantially alter the parameter values.

To study further the role of price expectations in the postembargo period, hypothetical expected-price paths were investigated to determine whether decision rules based on lower expected real prices could potentially account for the post-1973 discovery data. Hypothetical price paths of the following form were studied:

$$P_{i,t} = a_i + b_i P_{i,t-1} \qquad a_i > 0, \, 0 < b_i < 1 \tag{3.4}$$

Essentially, this equation assumes that producers believed that the price would rise to a "backstop" of $P_{i,\infty} = a_i/(1 - b_i)$ at a rate of $(1 - b_i)$ percent of the difference ($P_{i,\infty} - P_{i,t-1}$). Price paths for the years 1973 through 1979 that would have been observed if (3.4) had prevailed without error from 1972 onward were generated. Discoveries predicted by the decision rules were then determined assuming that producers behaved as if the prices so generated were the prevailing prices and that future prices would be generated by the same equations. This behavior might have been motivated by the producers' belief that in the years from 1973 through 1979 prices would increase gradually from the values observed in 1972 to backstop values determined by the cost of the next cheapest technologies. Each year during 1973 through 1979, producers observed actual prices after reaching their decisions about exploration for that year. When actual prices departed from the expected path, the producers believed those departures to be temporary and did not modify their expectations about the future price path.

The following price-generating parameters were used in equation (3.4):

$$a_1 = .33 \qquad b_1 = .945$$
$$a_2 = .0275 \qquad b_2 = .945$$

These parameters imply backstop prices in current dollars of $18/BBL for oil and $1.50/MCF for natural gas. This oil price is roughly the prevailing price on new oil in 1979. This natural gas price is less than the actual average new contract price in 1979, but it is greater than the regulated price on new contracts before passage of the Natural Gas Policy Act.

The fit of the model for the period 1948 to 1979 was evaluated with the parameters in column (1) of table 6-7. A random walk in prices was assumed for 1948 through 1972 and the described hypothetical price regime was assumed for 1973 through 1979. The fit with these parameters and the hypothetical price regime ($LnL = 8.35$, $R_1^2 = .87$, $R_2^2 = .54$) is better than the fit of the model in column (6) of table 6-7. Thus, with this hypothetical price regime, the cost function parameters estimated with data for the years prior to 1973 fit quite well for the years after 1973.

Thus producers may have expected prices well below prices actually realized after 1972, and the results with the hypothetical price regime demonstrate that the data are consistent with this hypothesis. Because the hypothetical price regime is not based on data on actual price expectations during this period, however, these results cannot be considered a test of the hypothesis.

Discussion

The empirical analysis in this section potentially could be improved in several ways. For example, in estimating the decision rules for exploration, the shocks to the cost function were assumed to be serially uncorrelated; reestimation of the model relaxing this assumption would be useful. In estimating the development equations (3.1), the error terms were assumed to be serially and contemporaneously uncorrelated and to have constant variance; exploring the consequences of relaxing these assumptions would also be useful, as would exploring the feasibility of joint estimation of the decision rules, the price-generating equations, and the development equations. Joint estimation could most usefully be done in the context of a derivation of the producers' decision rules that takes explicit account of the presence of stochastic shocks to (2.2'), perhaps in the additive form explored in (3.1). Whether or not this change in the derivation of the decision rules is made, joint estimation would entail estimating roughly 100 parameters in a highly nonlinear model—an undertaking that would be very costly but, perhaps, feasible. Finally, exploring the addition of adjustment cost terms in the cost function (1.1) would be of interest. This change would enable the model to accommodate a greater range of potential responses to shocks in prices or costs.

IV. CONCLUSIONS

In this chapter, we have developed and applied a framework for econometric modeling of exhaustible resource supply. The econometric equations are derived as the optimal extraction plans of resource owners maximizing the present value of their resources in the presence of uncertainty about future prices and extraction costs.

Although the signs of two of the estimated parameters do not conform to the a priori restrictions of the theoretical model, the signs of the remaining parameters do conform and, in all other respects, the fit of the model to the data is quite good. The ability to estimate the decision rules for different price regimes proved to be particularly useful. With this feature, price regimes with expected prices below prices actually realized proved capable of explaining the data on discoveries for the period after 1972.

The two incorrect parameter signs apparently result from the restrictions on functional form embodied in the theoretical structure. The theoretical model specifies extraction costs as a quadratic function of current and cumulative extraction. For oil and natural gas resources in the United States, costs may simply be increasing more rapidly than the quadratic function can accommodate.

A modeling framework in which ultimate recovery could be permitted to vary nonlinearly with expected backstop prices would clearly be desirable. At the present time, no framework is available that provides this feature and, at the same time, permits formal derivation of estimable decision rules as the optimal extraction plans of producers maximizing the expected net present value of their resources under uncertainty. The current alternatives are to use a framework of the form employed here or to use econometric equations not explicitly derived from a model of producer behavior. The latter leaves the econometrician with limited information by which to judge the equations being estimated.

The theoretical model plays an important role in interpreting the empirical results. Because of the information the model provides, the strategy used here appears to be superior to other currently available econometric approaches to modeling exhaustible resource supply. The development of a framework that places weaker a priori restrictions on the extraction cost function remains an important agenda item for future research.

APPENDIX A
OIL AND GAS TAX PROVISIONS

Several tax provisions affect oil and natural gas production.[21] Since 1926, oil and natural gas producers have been permitted to deduct from tax obligations a depletion allowance equal to a specified percentage of the value of oil or natural gas produced. The original depletion allowance of 27.5 percent was reduced to 22 percent in 1969. In 1975, the law was changed to prohibit major integrated firms from using the depletion allowance. Small, independent firms were permitted to continue using the allowance, but no more than 2,000 barrels a day qualified for the allowance. This limit was gradually reduced to 1,000 barrels in 1980, and the depletion allowance rate has been gradually reduced to 15 percent in 1984.

In addition to the depletion allowance, during the sample period, oil-producing firms were permitted to deduct intangible costs (of non-salvageable items, including labor, power, fuel, and the like) for drilling and equipping productive wells and all exploration costs for dry holes, except geological and geophysical expenditures resulting in the acquisition or retention of properties.

As an alternative to percentage depletion, the producer has always had the option of cost depletion of all items not expensed. This entails deducting a proportion of costs equal to the amount of oil or gas sold during the year as a proportion of the total amount estimated to remain in the property at the beginning of the year. Cost depletion ceases when all costs have been deducted. Although this option was less attractive

---

[21] Epple (1975), pp. 73–80, provides additional details pertaining to tax treatment of oil and natural gas.

than percentage depletion prior to 1975, it is the only option for firms no longer permitted to use percentage depletion.

The equations for calculating tax deductions applicable to exploration, development, and production use the following notation:

m_1 = proportion of exploratory footage drilled in dry wells

$1 - m_1$ = proportion of exploratory footage in successful wells

m_2 = proportion of development footage in dry wells

$1 - m_2$ = proportion of development footage in successful wells

m_3 = proportion of drilling expenses in successful wells that are tangible

$1 - m_3$ = proportion of drilling expenses that are intangible

m_4 = proportion of exploration expenditure for drilling

m_5 = proportion of exploration expenditure for geological expenditures and scouting

$1 - m_4 - m_5$ = proportion of exploration expenditures for overhead

m_6 = proportion of development expenditures for drilling

m_7 = proportion of development expenditures for lease equipment

$1 - m_6 - m_7$ = proportion of development expenditures for improved recovery and overhead

μ_e = proportion of exploration expenses that are expensed as incurred for tax purposes

μ_d = proportion of development expenses that are expensed as incurred

s_e = proportion of exploration expenses that are capitalized and depreciated for tax purposes

$1 - \mu_d$ = proportion of development expenditures that are capitalized and depreciated for tax purposes

$1 - \mu_e - s_e$ = proportion of exploration expenditures that cannot be depreciated if percentage depletion is being used

ρ = present value for tax purposes of depreciable cost at the date costs are incurred[22]

u_f = U.S. government corporate profit tax rate

u_v = state ad valorem tax rate

u_p = state production tax rate

u_d = depletion allowance rate

---

[22] With sum-of-years-digits depreciation and no investment tax credit,

$$\rho = \frac{2}{rN}\left[1 - \frac{1}{rN}(1 - e^{-rN})\right]$$

where N is the depreciation period and r is the discount rate. (See Raviv and Zemel, 1977.) A ρ value of .735 is used throughout. This is consistent with $r = .08$ and $N = 12.5$ or with $r = .10$ and $N = 10$.

For calculating tax deductions, the proportions m_1 through m_7 are assumed to be constant. Exploration costs that may be expensed are overhead $(1 - m_4 - m_5)$; intangible drilling costs for successful wells $[m_4(1 - m_1)(1 - m_3)]$; dry hole costs $(m_1 m_4)$; and geological, geophysical, and scouting expenses for unproductive property $(m_1 m_5)$. The proportion of the last category of expenses devoted to unproductive property is assumed equal to the proportion of exploratory footage that is dry (m_1). Summing these items, the expensible proportion of exploration costs is

$$\mu_e = 1 - (1 - m_1)(m_3 m_4 + m_5) \tag{A.1}$$

Tangible exploratory drilling costs must be capitalized and depreciated. Hence,

$$s_e = (1 - m_1) m_3 m_4 \tag{A.2}$$

Geological, geophysical, and scouting expenses for successful wells cannot be deducted if percentage depletion is being taken. Hence,

$$1 - \mu_e - s_e = (1 - m_1) m_5 \tag{A.3}$$

Development costs that may be expensed as incurred are overhead costs and expenditures for improved recovery $(1 - m_6 - m_7)$, intangible costs for successful development wells $[m_6(1 - m_2)(1 - m_3)]$, and dry hole drilling costs $(m_2 m_6)$. Summing these items gives expensible development costs.

$$\mu_d = 1 - (1 - m_2) m_3 m_6 - m_7 \tag{A.4}$$

The remaining development costs for lease equipment (m_7) and tangible costs of successful wells $[(1 - m_2) m_3 m_6]$ may be capitalized and deducted.

$$1 - \mu_d = (1 - m_2) m_3 m_6 + m_7 \tag{A.5}$$

The 1975 changes in the tax laws will be reflected by setting δ equal to zero for 1975 on. It will be assumed that geological, geophysical, and scouting expenses for successful wells are capitalized and depreciated beginning in 1975. All items in equations (A.2) and (A.3) are then combined, and from 1975 on

$$s_e = (1 - m_1)(m_3 m_4 + m_5) \qquad\qquad\qquad (A.3')$$

This representation of the tax changes ignores the continuing availability of the depletion allowance to independent firms. Independent firms contribute a small amount to total domestic production, and they are permitted to use the allowance for relatively small amounts of production, so ignoring the allowance entirely after 1975 introduces little error. No changes need to be made in deductions for development or production costs.

The tax variables used in sections II and III can now be written as

$$T_r = 1 - u_v - u_f(1 - u_v - u_d) \qquad\qquad\qquad (A.6)$$

$$T_p = 1 - u_f \qquad\qquad\qquad (A.7)$$

$$T_d = 1 - u_f[\mu_d + \rho(1 - \mu_d)] \qquad\qquad\qquad (A.8)$$

$$T_x = 1 - u_f(\mu_e + \rho s_e) \qquad\qquad\qquad (A.9)$$

The producer pays a proportion u_v of revenues in state taxes and pays a federal tax rate u_f on revenues after deducting state taxes and the oil depletion allowance u_d. The remainder is T_r as shown in (A.6). Production costs are expensed as incurred, and the proportion not deducted is simply $1 - u_f$, as shown in (A.7). Equations (A.8) and (A.9) give the proportion of development and exploration costs not deducted, with differential weighting of expensed and capitalized items.

Estimates of the parameters in these expressions are presented in appendix B.

APPENDIX B
ESTIMATION OF COST AND TAX PARAMETERS

Exploration, development, and production cost data used to estimate these cost and tax parameters are from the American Petroleum Institute *Joint Association Survey of Industry Drilling Costs* (JAS). Real unit production costs for crude oil and natural gas are assumed to be constant over time. Cost data are from the entry entitled "Producing Costs" in table I, section II of the JAS for the years 1955, 1956, and 1959 through 1974. These cost figures were deflated to 1967 dollars by the wholesale price index and then regressed against annual crude oil and natural gas production with the following result:

$$\text{Producing Costs} = \frac{.401}{(.031)} \text{ (Oil Production)}$$

$$+ \frac{.0408}{(.005)} \text{ (Natural Gas Production)}$$

$$R_2 = .97, \; D = W = 1.95, \text{ Obs.} = 18$$

This regression indicates that oil production costs are 40 cents/BBL and natural gas production costs are 4 cents/MCF in 1967 dollars. A constant term introduced in the above equations is not statistically significant. The residuals do not display a trend as is evident from the Durbin-Watson statistic. Thus, this regression appears to strongly support the assumption of constant real unit production costs.

Real unit costs for development are assumed to be a linear function of cumulative discoveries; that is, the cost per unit of reserve additions for a given reservoir is assumed constant, but more recently discovered reservoirs are assumed to be more costly to develop than reservoirs discovered in the past. Oil development costs per barrel are assumed to be ten times the development cost per cubic foot of natural gas. This ratio was chosen to be same as the ratio estimated for production costs. Cost data are from the JAS for 1955, 1956, and 1959 through 1974. Costs of improved recovery were deducted from reported development costs to obtain the numerator of the left-hand side. Oil and gas reserve additions are the sum of discoveries, revisions, and extensions, as reported by the American Petroleum Institute with Alaska excluded. Cumulative oil and gas discoveries are values estimated in the text. The development cost parameters were estimated from the following regression:

$$\frac{\text{Development Costs}}{10 \times \text{Oil Reserve Additions} + \text{Gas Reserve Additions}}$$

$$= \frac{.0155}{(.012)} + \frac{.002}{(.0006)} \left(\frac{\text{Cum. Oil Discoveries} + \text{Cum. Gas Discoveries}}{2} \right)$$

$$R^2 = .428, \; D = W = 1.05, \text{ Obs.} = 18$$

These coefficient estimates indicate that in 1946 development costs (in 1967 dollars) were 1.5 cents/MCF of natural gas. By 1974, costs had increased to approximately $1.5 + .2(20)$, or 5.5 cents/MCF. For oil, the comparable figures for 1946 and 1974 are 15.5 cents/BBL and 55 cents/BBL.

Next, the state production and ad valorem tax rates were estimated using JAS data. Production taxes as a percent of revenue were found to be rising over time, while ad valorem taxes as a percent of revenue were declining. It thus appears that production tax rates were being increased more rapidly than oil prices and ad valorem tax rates were being reduced. Total taxes were found to be roughly a constant fraction of revenue, however. Thus, the production tax rate is taken to be zero and the mean and standard error of the ad valorem tax rate for 1955, 1956, and 1959 through 1974 are found to be

$$\frac{\text{Production} + \text{Ad Valorem Taxes}}{\text{Revenue}} = \frac{.05631}{(.00036)}$$

The standard error of the parameter estimate is only .00036. Thus total state taxes have behaved like a sales tax at the rate of 5.631 percent, with little variation from year to year and no apparent trend.

The next step in the analysis was to estimate the parameters required for computing tax deductions.

The proportion of exploratory footage drilled in successful wells, $1 - m_1$, was obtained by calculating the mean of the ratio,

$$\frac{\text{Total Exploratory Footage in Producing Wells}}{\text{Total Exploratory Footage}} = \frac{.2158}{(.004)}$$

Data for this calculation were obtained from the June issues of the *Bulletin of the American Association of Petroleum Geologists* (AAPG) for 1945 through 1975.

The proportion of development footage in successful wells, $1 - m_2$, was similarly estimated.

$$\frac{\text{Total Development Footage in Successful Wells}}{\text{Total Development Footage}} = \frac{.7533}{(.004)}$$

The data are for the period 1966 through 1975 and are taken from the June issues of the AAPG *Bulletin*.

Parameters m_3 through m_7 were estimated using cost data from section III of the JAS.

The proportions of drilling expenses in successful oil and gas wells that are tangible expenses, m_3, were obtained from the following:

$$\frac{\text{Intangible Drilling Expenses for Successful Oil Wells}}{\text{Total Drilling Expenses for Successful Oil Wells}} = \frac{.6998}{(.003)}$$

$$\frac{\text{Intangible Drilling Expenses for Successful Gas Wells}}{\text{Total Drilling Expenses for Successful Gas Wells}} = \frac{.7361}{(.003)}$$

Data for these calculations are for the years 1959 through 1964, the only years for which JAS reported such data.

The remaining parameters were estimated using JAS data for 1967 through 1975. The format for reporting costs was changed in 1967, so data for prior years were not used.

Total exploration expenditures were computed by combining expenditures for drilling and equipping exploratory wells, contributions toward test wells, geological and geophysical expenditures, land leasing and scouting costs, and direct and indirect overhead. The proportion of exploration expenditures for drilling, m_4, was then estimated from

$$\frac{\text{Exploration Expenditures for Drilling \& Equipping Wells}}{\text{Total Exploration Expenditures}} = \frac{.5296}{(.011)}$$

and the proportion of exploration expenditures for geological expenditures and scouting, m_5, was estimated from

$$\frac{\text{Geological, Geophysical, Land Leasing \& Scouting Costs}}{\text{Total Exploration Costs}} = \frac{.2639}{(.0075)}$$

Total development costs were computed by combining expenditures for drilling and equipping development wells, lease equipment costs, and expenses for improved recovery, and direct and indirect overhead. The proportion of development expenditure for drilling, m_6, was then computed from

$$\frac{\text{Development Expenditures for Drilling \& Equipping Wells}}{\text{Total Development Expenditures}} = \frac{.6014}{(.004)}$$

and the proportion of development expenditures for lease equipment, m_7, was computed from

$$\frac{\text{Expenditures for Lease Equipment}}{\text{Total Development Expenditures}} = \frac{.1629}{(.005)}$$

The proportion of reserves produced each period was estimated by taking the ratio of production in a representative year (1970) to reserves at the end of the previous year (1969). This yielded a value of $\varepsilon_1 = .888$ and $\varepsilon_2 = .924$.

The complete set of parameter and standard error estimates is summarized in table B-1.

TABLE B-1.   COST AND TAX PARAMETERS, CRUDE OIL
AND NATURAL GAS PRODUCTION

Parameter	Estimated value	Standard error
$c_{p,1}$	.401	.031
$c_{p,2}$	.0408	.005
μ'_1	.155	.012
μ'_2	.0155	.12
$c'_{d,1}$	.02	.006
$c'_{d,2}$	.002	.0006
u_v	.05631	.036
u_p	0	—
m_1	.7842	.004
m_2	.2467	.004
$m_{3,1}$	.6998	.003
$m_{3,2}$	.7361	.003
$m_{3,1+2}$	.7112	.003
m_4	.5296	.011
m_5	.2639	.0075
m_6	.6014	.004
m_7	.1629	.005
ε_1	.888	—
ε_2	.924	—

APPENDIX C
DATA

Estimates of ultimate recovery by year of discovery for oil and natural gas ($a_{i,t,\tau}$) are taken from "Reserves of Crude Oil, Natural Gas Liquids and Natural Gas in the United States and Canada," published annually by the American Petroleum Institute. These data are presented in tables C-1 and C-2.

The average price of oil is used for the years prior to 1973. For years after 1973, the price of new or upper tier oil is used. These data are obtained from *Petroleum Facts and Figures*, published by the American Petroleum Institute, and the *Monthly Energy Review*, published by the U.S. Department of Energy.

The average prices on new contracts for natural gas for 1947 through 1976 were obtained from Foster Associates, Washington, D.C. These can also be assembled from the Office of Coal Research and Federal Power Commission publications listed in the references for this chapter. Data from Foster Associates were not available for 1977 through 1979, but new contract prices are reported for selected states in the *Monthly Energy Review* beginning in 1975. In addition, data prepared by Foster Associates (Federal Power Commission, docket no. RM77-13, appendix M, schedule 1) detail the amounts of natural gas committed for new interstate contract sales in 1976 from South Louisiana, the Texas Gulf Coast, and selected other areas. Together, South Louisiana and the Texas Gulf Coast produced most (89 percent) of the gas committed to new interstate contract sales in 1976. Average new contract prices for 1977 through 1979 were computed by weighting the prices reported for Texas and Louisiana in the *Monthly Energy Review* for those years by .838 and .162 respectively. These fractions are the proportions South Louisiana and the Texas Gulf Coast contributed to their combined total in 1976.

All prices and costs were converted to 1967 dollars by the wholesale price index for all commodities. The real prices for oil and natural gas are presented as P_1 and P_2, respectively, in table C-3. The corporate profits tax rate u_f and the oil depletion allowance rate u_d are taken from Pechman (1977). These are also reported in table C-3.

TABLE C-1.   ULTIMATE RECOVERY ESTIMATES FOR OIL
(IN BILLIONS OF BARRELS)

Date of Discovery	Date of Estimate					
	1979	1978	1977	1976	1975	1974
1947	1,610,088	1,569,950	1,561,494	1,628,160	1,617,418	1,589,755
1948	3,428,826	3,463,620	3,509,702	3,482,095	3,399,531	3,448,467
1949	3,453,185	3,425,747	3,384,584	3,366,324	3,318,199	3,237,370
1950	2,814,225	2,742,861	2,721,301	2,675,727	2,657,727	2,646,994
1951	1,746,185	1,733,548	1,716,768	1,700,002	1,691,170	1,686,751
1952	1,317,003	1,305,393	1,308,134	1,290,719	1,281,207	1,276,734
1953	2,178,612	2,155,211	2,122,830	2,128,112	2,113,059	2,099,617
1954	2,162,627	2,148,544	2,137,865	2,114,059	2,078,399	2,064,469
1955	1,545,259	1,524,844	1,519,221	1,519,314	1,495,904	1,494,552
1956	1,941,343	1,923,458	1,891,402	1,883,357	1,858,625	1,872,021
1957	2,077,305	2,062,730	2,049,013	2,018,157	1,997,419	1,970,320
1958	1,181,188	1,174,559	1,173,397	1,163,927	1,140,988	1,125,569
1959	754,060	740,835	736,098	727,697	721,425	724,553
1960	1,022,576	1,005,062	973,897	945,287	937,583	923,252
1961	505,984	498,103	496,984	487.062	477,915	474,812
1962	974,043	962,187	961,306	954,282	948,046	1,004,586
1963	497,114	475,096	464,493	448,882	443,767	446,920
1964	857,083	848.054	848,214	848,296	842,189	858,416
1965	772,074	721,243	701,832	681,265	700,347	633,743
1966	513,367	502,826	496,244	492,989	479,092	470,876
1967	707,100	700,716	685,905	670,740	681,427	686,538
1968	981,918	967,261	959,034	946,885	915,944	868,901
1969	599,209	577,728	568,882	555,881	541,713	564,968
1970	734,637	706,396	695,534	673,816	674,359	681,189
1971	605,807	595,627	551,316	529,627	482,607	363,107
1972	322,046	313,327	278,842	244,734	192,237	206,975
1973	579,082	513,009	477,472	441,469	320,932	243,573
1974	391,331	351,363	300,498	194,645	135,903	65,684
1975	384,196	344,584	304,877	207,118	108,599	
1976	239,457	172,881	116,901	44,267		
1977	364,972	136,542	68,020			
1978	115,716	63,341				
1979	74,622					

Source: American Petroleum Institute, et al., "Reserves of Crude Oil, Natural Gas Liquids, and Natural Gas in the United States and Canada," vol. 21–34 (Washington, D.C., American Petroleum Institute).

			Date of Estimate				
1973	1972	1971	1970	1969	1968	1967	1966
1,527,065	1,492,011	1,452,179	1,438,974	1,481,509	1,470,925	1,486,815	1,454,593
3,433,431	3,403,783	3,408,859	3,307,859	3,325,351	3,300,879	3,213,266	2,888,528
3,152,467	3,079,560	3,034,841	2,982,393	2,919,553	2,894,844	2,827,358	2,725,528
2,624,824	2,592,129	2,570,248	2,565,372	2,522,132	2,489,585	2,492,968	2,631,658
1,634,059	1,630,523	1,612,157	1,630,002	1,622,072	1,551,598	1,545,257	1,544,196
1,375,397	1,386,929	1,346,288	1,355,773	1,356,189	1,414,773	1,400,858	1,423,703
2,100,769	2,099,629	2,164,503	2,130,909	2,115,978	2,083,300	2,011,744	1,957,977
2,140,631	2,143,163	2,123,601	2,084,831	2,026,300	2,031,959	1,949,457	1,859,373
1,505,680	1,487,405	1,525,169	1,508,148	1,459,667	1,457,648	1,438,583	1,392,031
1,838,253	1,794,826	1,736,637	1,702,787	1,658,438	1,552,461	1,468,027	1,407,179
1,947,851	1,856,249	1,856,414	1,838,601	1,715,090	1,658,208	1,609,033	1,523,760
1,113,317	1,040,927	1,027,373	971,967	917,685	903,030	906,895	871,013
707,637	705,810	692,922	685,078	689,744	690,825	667,459	627,778
897,056	874,472	813,516	801,414	730,445	731,534	695,053	683,255
465,827	467,156	463,890	458,753	416,995	420,588	410,942	444,326
1,005,624	970,856	924,054	912,782	900,711	826,832	746,197	679,264
437,343	436,272	425,439	418,834	420,134	385,499	371,891	343,723
832,748	814,525	798,150	791,624	776,518	645,909	567,575	513,275
612,160	525,857	486,767	478,752	461,666	443,042	357,937	285,350
463,608	467,818	470,748	445,777	352,382	249,065	167,784	84,022
689,013	716,134	622,971	586,755	501,770	360,281	134,372	
861,499	778,768	721,587	608,264	466,218	191,607		
456,077	444,699	426,693	343,616	92,198			
494,468	464,462	341,600	120,357				
273,516	196,215	85,456					
154,710	86,015						
111,280							

TABLE C-2.   ULTIMATE RECOVERY ESTIMATES FOR NATURAL GAS
(IN TRILLIONS OF CUBIC FEET)

Date of Discovery	Date of Estimate					
	1979	1978	1977	1976	1975	1974
1947	14,337,647	12,979,673	12,765,764	13,054,860	12,708,216	12,417,567
1948	8,416,682	8,410,519	8,430,609	8,176,057	8,381,543	8,403,273
1949	25,625,500	25,205,289	24,746,630	24,897,203	24,968,458	25,351,789
1950	14,193,910	14,094,975	14,122,230	13,921,647	13,929,949	13,851,944
1951	11,319,417	11,271,837	11,014,262	10,922,641	11,248,758	11,339,593
1952	16,822,046	16,717,494	16,629,005	16,838,771	16,449,493	16,258,325
1953	12,588,592	12,453,573	12,540,181	12,782,631	13,132,693	13,125,585
1954	16,169,013	16,145,862	16,192,194	16,332,820	16,253,507	15,802,741
1955	10,298,538	10,151,902	9,951,958	10,108,782	10,236,403	10,164,398
1956	19,979,492	19,643,476	19,083,918	18,858,820	18,766,510	18,997,824
1957	15,817,629	15,610,694	15,584,664	15,633,960	15,686,792	15,749,890
1958	19,980,475	19,858,278	20,089,234	20,368,651	20,191,575	18,492,754
1959	7,660,585	7,539,562	7,571,507	7,739,018	7,627,083	7,769,428
1960	12,870,841	12,525,595	11,947,037	12,091,299	12,019,920	11,842,113
1961	9,788,063	9,667,604	9,655,450	9,762,013	10,514,303	10,494,449
1962	11,074,726	11,069,304	10,982,744	10,926,967	11,151,961	10,988,579
1963	12,825,159	12,554,403	12,313,881	12,478,194	12,476,818	12,243,003
1964	9,545,178	9,313,717	9,090,252	8,402,249	8,061,328	8,123,929
1965	8,608,562	8,087,609	8,088,284	8,355,145	7,666,379	7,376,777
1966	8,239,194	7,880,757	7,794,982	6,198,510	7,389,481	6,991,846
1967	5,159,472	5,048,732	4,926,977	5,048,948	4,973,587	5,017,506
1968	6,311,176	6,223,586	6,019,698	6,206,124	6,037,307	5,834,331
1969	6,670,703	6,255,893	6,158,143	6,136,287	6,116,858	6,017,316
1970	4,646,240	4,285,527	4,227,514	4,211,663	5,428,572	4,058,503
1971	8,289,342	7,953,648	7,702,304	7,395,203	5,503,267	6,017,167
1972	7,969,434	7,565,324	7,097,693	6,606,453	5,540,950	4,705,247
1973	9,443,785	8,670,847	8,086,043	6,931,887	6,511,443	4,061,146
1974	6,394,057	5,601,174	5,026,580	4,325,977	3,091,973	2,276,442
1975	6,875,831	6,540,000	6,479,530	4,991,885	2,587,754	
1976	4,725,740	4,293,588	3,441,096	1,532,109		
1977	4,609,073	3,648,774	2,203,195			
1978	3,044,679	1,804,628				
1979	2,784,884					

Source: American Petroleum Institute, et al., "Reserves of Crude Oil, Natural Gas Liquids, and Natural Gas in the United States and Canada," vol. 21–34 (Washington, D.C., American Petroleum Institute).

Date of Estimate							
1973	1972	1971	1970	1969	1968	1967	1966
12,457,125	12,214,051	12,271,296	12,119,219	12,053,135	12,137,052	11,902,909	12,593,244
8,769,172	8,739,125	9,085,270	8,915,363	8,563,604	8,427,025	8,458,758	8,173,067
25,729,868	23,116,149	23,484,457	23,678,546	24,509,214	24,093,592	23,868,120	24,539,868
13,697,015	13,274,547	13,091,607	12,891,955	12,978,109	13,256,360	13,368,006	12,551,183
11,310,025	10,088,409	10,252,462	10,421,429	10,404,136	10,363,062	10,483,068	10,671,486
16,303,492	16,125,888	15,761,484	15,703,547	15,756,762	15,790,826	15,481,234	14,991,166
13,182,265	12,905,824	12,654,837	12,767,457	12,284,356	11,940,252	11,722,230	11,583,432
15,115,524	15,116,461	15,470,887	15,091,202	14,580,113	14,476,788	13,991,734	13,585,827
10,220,833	10,075,126	9,804,420	9,498,734	9,237,465	9,677,144	9,217,343	8,293,071
18,811,247	18,010,595	17,779,382	18,145,360	17,157,954	17,539,817	17,449,978	15,008,738
15,999,157	21,730,294	19,923,167	19,973,971	19,059,456	18,753,247	17,782,438	18,219,971
18,969,395	18,296,590	17,997,182	17,944,839	16,736,845	16,599,493	14,913,952	14,719,059
7,629,879	8,710,854	11,707,519	12,169,409	12,680,086	14,285,133	11,984,127	12,006,069
11,754,462	12,352,293	12,436,737	12,791,058	13,599,210	12,974,897	12,854,345	12,770,013
10,926,098	11,769,196	11,569,259	9,977,157	8,748,756	9,082,727	8,327,472	8,056,680
10,919,920	11,340,476	11,172,766	10,946,526	10,736,069	10,017,755	8,835,564	7,048,683
12,196,260	12,283,714	11,823,638	11,067,355	10,826,100	10,734,038	10,858,960	11,447,214
7,970,273	8,794,843	8,505,728	8,023,964	7,764,677	7,124,274	6,950,364	5,716,302
7,443,021	8,742,139	8,640,992	8,913,527	8,670,438	8,883,143	8,167,425	6,381,673
7,253,212	7,826,824	7,240,342	7,426,372	6,849,612	6,285,749	5,707,939	3,886,831
5,480,215	6,342,116	5,710,665	5,770,774	5,346,125	4,751,805	3,537,669	
6,107,466	5,126,675	4,759,982	3,443,783	2,320,935	1,612,970		
5,722,693	5,740,406	4,627,881	3,705,622	2,100,399			
3,428,813	3,605,405	3,315,419	2,423,709				
4,741,409	4,274,897	1,725,436					
3,571,912	1,902,536						
2,185,088							

TABLE C-3. REAL WELLHEAD PRICES AND TAX RATES

Date	Price (1967$)		Corporate profits tax rate	Oil depletion allowance rate
	P_1 ($/BBL)	P_2 ($/MCF)	u_f	u_d
1947	2.520	0.068	0.380	0.275
1948	3.140	0.072	0.380	0.275
1949	3.230	0.084	0.380	0.275
1950	3.070	0.103	0.420	0.275
1951	2.780	0.097	0.507	0.275
1952	2.860	0.114	0.520	0.275
1953	3.070	0.152	0.520	0.275
1954	3.170	0.134	0.520	0.275
1955	3.150	0.164	0.520	0.275
1956	3.080	0.163	0.520	0.275
1957	3.310	0.181	0.520	0.275
1958	3.180	0.197	0.520	0.275
1959	3.060	0.194	0.520	0.275
1960	3.030	0.192	0.520	0.275
1961	3.060	0.189	0.520	0.275
1962	3.060	0.185	0.520	0.275
1963	3.060	0.180	0.520	0.275
1964	3.040	0.171	0.500	0.275
1965	2.960	0.180	0.480	0.275
1966	2.890	0.174	0.480	0.275
1967	2.920	0.184	0.480	0.275
1968	2.870	0.186	0.480	0.275
1969	2.900	0.184	0.480	0.275
1970	2.880	0.201	0.480	0.220
1971	2.980	0.228	0.480	0.220
1972	2.850	0.269	0.480	0.220
1973	3.540	0.363	0.480	0.220
1974	6.330	0.366	0.480	0.220
1975	6.880	0.607	0.480	0.000
1976	6.390	0.846	0.480	0.000
1977	5.780	0.980	0.480	0.000
1978	5.810	0.961	0.480	0.000
1979	5.740	0.936	0.480	0.000

Sources: See appendix C text.

APPENDIX D
DERIVATION OF DECISION RULES

The following stochastic Euler equations arise from the optimization of objective function (1.2).[23]

$$q_{t+j} - \beta E_{t+j} q_{t+j+1} - c_{t+j} + \beta E_{t+j} c_{t+j+1} - \phi + \beta \phi$$
$$- (2\theta + \pi + \pi') \Delta y_{t+j} + \beta (2\theta + \pi + \pi') E_{t+j} \Delta y_{t+j+1}$$
$$- \pi y_{t+j-1} + \beta \pi y_{t+j} - \beta \pi' E_{t+j} \Delta y_{t+j+1} = 0 \qquad j = 0, 1, \ldots$$

Rearranging terms,

$$- \beta (2\theta + \pi) E_{t+j} y_{t+j+1} + (2\theta + 2\beta\theta + \pi + \pi') y_{t+j} - (2\theta + \pi') y_{t+j-1}$$
$$= (q_{t+j} - \beta E_{t+j} q_{t+j+1} - c_{t+j} + \beta E_{t+j} c_{t+j+1} - \phi + \beta \phi) \qquad \text{(D.1)}$$

Also associated with the maximization of (1.2) is the terminal or transversality condition, which requires

$$\lim_{\tau \to \infty} E_t \beta^\tau \{ q_{t+\tau} - c_{t+\tau} - \phi - (2\theta + \pi + \pi') \Delta y_{t+\tau} - \pi y_{t+\tau-1} \} = 0 \quad \text{(D.2)}$$

The solution to the difference equation (D.1) that satisfies the transversality condition (D.2) provides an expression for the decision rule for the owner of the exhaustible resources.

Deriving the solution to (D.1) that satisfies (D.2) first requires factoring the following characteristic polynomial in Z that is obtained from the left-hand side of (D.1):

$$p(Z) = -\beta (2\theta + \pi) Z^{-1} + 2(1 + \beta)\theta + \pi + \pi' - (2\theta + \pi') Z$$

With the substitution $Z = \sqrt{\beta} \, W$, this expression can be rewritten as

$$-2\sqrt{\beta} \, \theta W^{-1} + 2(1 + \beta)\theta - 2\sqrt{\beta} \, \theta W - \sqrt{\beta} \, \pi W^{-1} + \pi + \pi' - \sqrt{\beta} \, \pi' W$$
$$= 2(I - \sqrt{\beta} \, W^{-1})\theta (I - \sqrt{\beta} \, W) - \sqrt{\beta} \, \pi W^{-1} + \pi + \pi' - \sqrt{\beta} \, \pi' W$$

Because θ and π are both positive definite, there exist real matrices ψ_0

---

and ψ_1 such that

$$\left(I - \psi_1' W^{-1}\right)\psi_0\left(I - \psi_1 W\right) = 2\left(I - \sqrt{\beta}\, W^{-1}\right)\theta\left(I - \sqrt{\beta}\, W\right)$$
$$- \sqrt{\beta}\,\pi W^{-1} + \pi + \pi' - \sqrt{\beta}\,\pi' W$$

where $\det(I - \psi_1 W)$ has all its roots outside the unit circle.[24] Here ψ_0 is symmetric and positive definite, and

$$\psi_0 + \psi_1'\psi_0\psi_1 = 2(1 + \beta)\theta + \pi + \pi'$$
$$\psi_1'\psi_0 = \sqrt{\beta}\,(2\theta + \pi)$$

The substitution $W = (1/\sqrt{\beta})Z$ yields the desired factorization,

$$\left(I - \psi_1'\sqrt{\beta}\, Z^{-1}\right)\psi_0\left[I - \psi_1(1/\sqrt{\beta})Z\right] = p(Z) \tag{D.3}$$

Using the factorization of the characteristic polynomial obtained in (D.3), equation (D.1) can be rewritten as

$$\left[I - \left(\psi_1/\sqrt{\beta}\right)L\right]y_t = \psi_0^{-1}E_t\left(I - \sqrt{\beta}\,\psi_1'L^{-1}\right)^{-1}$$
$$\times\left[(1 - \beta L^{-1})q_t - (1 - \beta L^{-1})c_t\right]$$
$$- (1 - \beta)\psi_0^{-1}\left(I - \sqrt{\beta}\,\psi_1'\right)^{-1}\phi \tag{D.4}$$

where

$$E_t L^{-j}q_t \equiv E_t q_{t+j}$$

and

$$E_t L^{-j}c_t \equiv E_t c_{t+j}$$

Rewriting the expression on the right-hand side of (D.4) in terms of current and past values of the variables requires factoring

$$\det\left(I - \psi_1'\sqrt{\beta}\, Z^{-1}\right) = \left(1 - \rho_1 Z^{-1}\right)\left(1 - \rho_2 Z^{-1}\right)\cdots\left(1 - \rho_k Z^{-1}\right)$$

where k is the dimensionality of the y_t vector and $|\rho_m| < \sqrt{\beta}$ for $m = 1, \ldots, k$. Thus the matrix partial fractions decomposition of

---

[24] Linear prediction theory can be used to verify the existence of such a factorization. It can be shown that $(1 - \sqrt{\beta}\, W^{-1}\theta)(1 - \sqrt{\beta}\, W)$ and $\pi W^{-1} + \pi + \pi' - \sqrt{\beta}\,\pi' W$ are covariance-generating functions for first-order moving average processes. If the processes are orthogonal, the sum of these terms is the covariance-generating function for the vector process obtained by adding the two stochastic processes together. That this resulting covariance-generating function can be factored as described in the text is a standard result from linear prediction theory (see, for example, Rozanov, 1967).

$(1 - \beta Z^{-1})(I - \psi_1'\sqrt{\beta}\, Z^{-1})^{-1}$ can be written

$$\mu + \frac{\sigma_1}{1 - \rho_1 Z^{-1}} + \cdots + \frac{\sigma_k}{1 - \rho_k Z^{-1}}$$

Substitution of this result into (D.4) yields Equation (1.5) of the text.

APPENDIX E
SPECIFICATION OF THE LIKELIHOOD FUNCTION

This appendix details the derivation of the likelihood function used in estimating the decision rules in section III. The nine parameters being estimated are the two elements of the vector ϕ, the three elements of the symmetric matrix θ, and the four elements of the matrix π (see equation 2.9).

The logarithm of the concentrated likelihood function is

$$\text{Ln } L = -T(1 + \text{Ln } 2\pi) - \frac{T}{2}\text{Ln }|\Sigma| \tag{E.1}$$

where Σ is the two-dimensional estimated covariance matrix, and T is the number of observations. Index date $t = 1$ corresponds to 1948. The two-dimensional residual vector used to calculate the covariance matrix is obtained from the following vector equation:

$$\varepsilon_t = y_t - \frac{1}{\rho\beta}\psi_1 y_{t-1} - \psi_0^{-1}\sum_{m=1}^{4}\hat{\sigma}_m\sum_{j=0}^{\infty}\rho_m^j E_t q_{t+j}$$

$$+ (1 - \beta)\psi_0^{-1}\left(I - \sqrt{\beta}\,\psi_1'\right)^{-1}\phi^* - \psi_0^{-1}\hat{\mu}q_t \tag{E.2}$$

To calculate the elements of (E.2), first calculate the elements of the vector μ and the diagonal matrix c_d defined in (2.8) for date t using equations (2.7), (A.8), and (A.4). Use parameter values in tables 6-1, 6-2, and B.1 and data for the u_f series in table C-3. Calculate T_x for date t using (A.9), (A.1), and (A.2) or (A.3'). Next, use equation (2.9) to calculate Φ^*, θ^*, and π^*. Use the procedure detailed in Hansen and Sargent (1981), appendix C, to calculate ψ_0 and ψ_1 of the factorization of equation (D.3) of appendix D, where ψ_0 and ψ_1 satisfy

$$\psi_0 + \psi_1'\psi_0\psi_1 = 2(1 + \beta)\theta^* + \pi^* + \pi^{*'}$$

$$\psi_1'\psi_0 = \sqrt{\beta}\,(2\theta^* + \pi^*)$$

Calculate the elements of the diagonal matrix T_r defined in (2.10) for date t using equation (A.6), the value of u_v from table B-1, and data for the

u_f and u_d series from table C-3. Compute $\hat{\mu}, \hat{\sigma}_i, \rho_i$ using the partial fractions decomposition in equation (2.11). For this computation, note that $\Omega(L^{-1})$ is defined in equation (2.10) and that the elements of $\Omega(L^{-1})$ are defined in (2.5). Note also that the coefficients in (2.5) can be determined by use of (2.3) and parameter estimates reported in tables 6-1 and 6-2. Next evaluate the infinite sums in equation (E.2) using the following prediction formula:

$$\sum_{j=0}^{\infty} \rho_m^j E_t q_{t+j} = \xi(\rho_m)^{-1} \left[I + \sum_{j=1}^{r-1} \left(\sum_{n=j+1}^{r} \rho_m^{n-j} \zeta_n L^j \right) \right] x_t \qquad \text{(E.3)}$$

In (E.3), the ρ_i are from the partial fractions decomposition in equation (2.11), the ξ_i are defined in equation (1.3) and estimated in tables 6-3 and 6-4, and x_t is a two-dimensional vector containing the well-head prices of crude oil and natural gas. These price series are reported in table C-3. Next, evaluate equation (E.2), recalling that

$$y_{\tau,i} = \sum_{s=\tau_0}^{\tau} \Delta y_{\tau,i}$$

and that the $\Delta y_{\tau,i}$ are reported in tables 6-1 and 6-2. Compute the covariance matrix for the likelihood function (E.1) from

$$\Sigma = \sum_{t=1}^{T} \frac{\varepsilon_t \varepsilon_t'}{T} \qquad \text{(E.4)}$$

This concludes the specification of the likelihood function.

REFERENCES

American Gas Association. 1973. *Total Energy Resources Analysis (TERA) System Description* (Arlington, Va., May).

American Petroleum Institute. American Gas Association and Canadian Petroleum Association Annual. "Reserves of Crude Oil, Natural Gas Liquids and Natural Gas in the United States and Canada." (Washington, D.C., annual.)

———. *Joint Association Survey of Industry Drilling Costs* (Washington, D.C., various years).

———. 1969. *Petroleum Facts and Figures* (Washington, D.C.).

Dasgupta, P., and G. M. Heal. 1979. *Economic Theory and Exhaustible Resources* (Cambridge, Mass., Cambridge Press).

Dolton, et al. "Estimates of Undiscovered Recoverable Oil and Gas Resources in the United States," Circular 860 (Reston, Va., U.S. Geological Survey).

Electric Power Research Institute. 1978. *Stanford Pilot Energy/Economic Model* Report EA-626, vol. 2 (Palo Alto, Calif., May).

Energy Modeling Forum (EMF) 6. 1982. *World Oil Summary Report* (Palo Alto, Calif., Stanford University, February).

Epple, Dennis. 1975. *Petroleum Discoveries and Government Policy: An Econometric Study of Supply* (Boston, Mass., Ballinger Press).

_____, and Lars Peter Hansen. 1981. "An Econometric Framework for Modeling Exhaustible Resource Supply," in James Ramsey, ed., *The Economics of Exploration for Energy Resources* (Greenwich, Conn., JAI Press).

Erickson, E., and R. Spann. 1971. "Supply Response in a Regulated Industry," *The Bell Journal of Economics and Management Science* vol. 2, no. 1, pp. 94–121.

Federal Power Commission. 1973. "Just and Reasonable National Rates for Future Sales of Natural Gas from Wells Commenced or on After January 1, 1973," Docket no. R-389-B, appendix C (Washington, D.C., May 16).

Federal Power Commission. 1977. "National Rates for Jurisdictional Sales of Natural Gas from Wells Commenced on or After January 1, 1977, for the Period January 1, 1977 to December 31, 1978," Docket no. RM77-13, appendix M (Washington, D.C., September 30).

Fisher, Franklin M. 1964. *Supply and Costs in the U.S. Petroleum Industry: Two Econometric Studies* (Baltimore, Md., The Johns Hopkins Press).

Goldfeld, Stephen M., and Richard E. Quandt. 1971. *Nonlinear Methods in Econometrics* (Amsterdam, North Holland Publishing Company).

Hansen, Lars P., and Thomas J. Sargent. 1980. "Formulating and Estimating Dynamic Linear Rational Expectations Models," *Journal of Economic Dynamics and Control* vol. 2, pp. 7–46.

_____. 1981. "Linear Rational Expectations Models for Dynamically Interrelated Variables," in R. E. Lucas, Jr., and T. J. Sargent, eds., *Rational Expectations and Econometric Practice* (Minneapolis, Minn., University of Minnesota Press).

Heal, Geoffrey. 1976. "The Relationship Between Price and Extraction Cost for a Resource with a Backstop Technology," *The Bell Journal of Economics* vol. 7, pp. 371–378.

Khazzoom, J. D. 1971. "The FPC Staff's Econometric Model of Natural Gas Supply in the U.S.," *The Bell Journal of Economics* vol. 2, pp. 51–93.

Kim, Young Y., and Russel G. Thompson. 1978. *An Economic Model—New Oil and Gas Supplies in the Lower 48 States* (Gulf Publishing).

MacAvoy, Paul W., and Robert S. Pindyck. 1973. "Alternative Regulatory Policies for Dealing with the Natural Gas Shortage," *The Bell Journal of Economics and Management Science* vol. 4, no. 2, pp. 454–498.

_____. 1975. *The Economics of the Natural Gas Shortage (1960–1980)* (Amsterdam, North-Holland Publishing Company).

Neri, John A. 1977. "An Evaluation of Two Alternative Supply Models of Natural Gas," *The Bell Journal of Economics* vol. 8, no. 1, pp. 289–302.

Pechman, Joseph. 1977. *Federal Tax Policy*, 3rd ed. (Washington, D.C., Brookings Institution).

Raviv, Artur, and Eitan Zemel. 1977. "Durability of Capital Goods: Taxes and Market Structure," *Econometrica* vol. 45, no. 3, pp. 707–718.

Rozanov, Y. A. 1967. *Stationary Random Processes* (San Francisco, Calif., Holden Day).

Sargent, Thomas J. 1979. *Macroeconomic Theory* (New York, Academic Press).

Solow, Robert M., and Frederic Y. Wan. 1976. "Extraction Cost in the Theory of Exhaustible Resources," *The Bell Journal of Economics* vol. 7, pp. 359–370.

U.S. Department of Energy. *Monthly Energy Review* (Washington, D.C.).

U.S. Department of the Interior, Office of Coal Research. "Prospective Regional Markets for Coal Conversion Plants Products Projected to 1980 and 1985," Research and Development Report, no. 102 (Washington, D.C.).

Index

201